SACRED DUTY

SACRED DUTY

A Soldier's Tour at Arlington National Cemetery

TOM COTTON

WILLIAM MORROW

An Imprint of HarperCollins *Publishers*

Map pages viii–ix: The Old Guard; Page 3: Arlington National Cemetery; Page 13: Sergeant Mary Flynn/National Guard Bureau; Page 34: Mauricio Campino/U.S. Air Force; Page 44: Tom Cotton; Page 49, top: Jim Laufenburg; Page 49, bottom: R.D. Ward/Department of Defense; Page 65: Painting by Alonzo Chappel; Page 81: Tom Cotton; Page 92: The Old Guard; Page 96: The Old Guard; Page 103: Specialist Eric McKeeby/TOG; Page 119, top and bottom: Sergeant George Huley/TOG; Page 122: Sergeant George Huley/TOG; Page 135: Specialist Jared Bradley/TOG; Page 144: Specialist Cody Torkelson/TOG; Page 157: Specialist Jacob Plank/TOG; Page 165: Sergeant George Huley/TOG; Page 166: Rachel Larue/ANC; Page 182: Specialist Lane Hiser/TOG; Page 188: Sergeant George Huley/TOG; Page 191: Sergeant George Huley/TOG; Page 193: Sergeant George Huley/TOG; Page 203: Specialist Gabriel Silva/TOG; Page 208: Benjamin Applebaum/White House; Page 217: The Old Guard; Page 225: The Old Guard; Page 235: Sergeant George Huley/TOG; Page 250: Sergeant George Huley/TOG; Page 255: Sergeant George Huley/TOG; Page 263: TOG; Page 267, top and bottom: Specialist Daniel Yeadon/TOG; Page 277: Captain Zach Kennedy/TOG; Page 282: Specialist Lane Hiser/TOG.

HarperCollins books may be purchased for educational, business, or sales promotional use. For information, please email the Special Markets Department at SPsales@harpercollins.com.

FIRST EDITION

Library of Congress Cataloging-in-Publication Data has been applied for.

ISBN 978-0-06-286315-7

19 20 21 22 23 DIX/LSC 10 9 8 7 6 5 4 3 2 1

To the soldiers of The Old Guard—
past, present, and future

Contents

Arlington National Cemetery

❶Old post Chapel
❷Memorial Chapel

TRANSFERS
❶MC Circle
❷PC Trans
❸Arnold
❹Jessup
❺Coast Guard
❻Clayton
❼Capron
❽JC Trans
❾Old Admin
❿Lincoln
ⒶGrant
ⒷMarshall

FIRING POINTS
❶ Red Springs
❷ Miles Circle
❸ Dewey Circle
❹ Mitchell
❺ Leahy

HITCHING POST
❶ Jackson (JC)
❷ Old Admin
❸ Lincoln
❹ Grant
❺ Patton (PC)
❻ Arnold
❼ Coast Guard
❽ Chapel

Old Guard soldiers carry a laminated copy of this map in their ceremonial caps. Note the legend on the left-hand side: Transfer Points for the transfer of the casket from the hearse to the caisson, Firing Points for the Presidential Salute Battery, and Hitching Posts for the Caisson Platoon's horses.

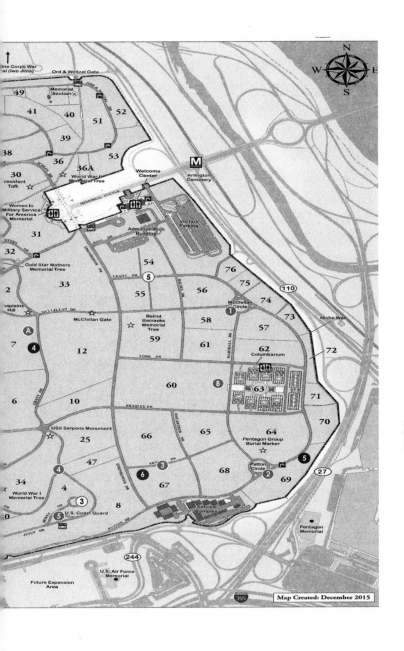

SACRED DUTY

Prologue:
America's Regiment

Every headstone at Arlington tells a story. These are tales of heroes, I thought as I placed the toe of my combat boot against the white marble. I pulled a miniature American flag out of my assault pack and pushed it three inches into the ground at my heel. I stepped aside to inspect it, making sure it met the standard that we had briefed to our troops: "vertical and perpendicular to the headstone." Satisfied, I moved to the next headstone to keep up with my soldiers. Having started this row, I had to complete it. One soldier per row was the rule; otherwise, different boot sizes might disrupt the perfect symmetry of the headstones and flags. I planted flag after flag, as did the soldiers on the rows around me.

Bending over to plant those flags brought me eye-level with the lettering on those marble stones. The stories continued with each one. Distinguished Service Cross. Silver Star. Bronze Star. Purple Heart. America's wars marched by. Iraq. Afghanistan. Vietnam. Korea. World War II. World War I. Some soldiers died in very old age; others still were teenagers. Crosses, Stars of David, Crescents and Stars. Every religion, every race, every age, every region of America is represented in these fields of stone.

I came upon the grave site of a Medal of Honor recipient. I paused, came to attention, and saluted. The Medal of Honor is the nation's highest decoration for battlefield valor. By military custom, all soldiers salute Medal of Honor recipients irrespective of their rank, in life and in death. We had reminded our soldiers of this courtesy; hundreds of grave sites would receive salutes that afternoon. I planted this hero's flag and kept moving.

On some headstones sat a small memento: a rank or unit patch, a military coin, a seashell, sometimes just a penny or even a rock. Each was a sign that someone—maybe family or friends, perhaps even a battle buddy who lived because of his friend's ultimate sacrifice—had visited, and honored, and mourned. For those of us who had been downrange, the sight was equally comforting and jarring—a sign that we would be remembered in death, but also a reminder of just how close some of us had come to resting here ourselves. I left those mementos undisturbed.

After a while, my hand began to hurt from pushing on the pointed, gold tips of the flags. There had been no rain that week, so the ground was hard. I questioned my soldiers how they were moving so fast and seemingly pain-free. They asked if I was using a bottle cap, and I said no. Several shook their heads in disbelief; forgetting a bottle cap was apparently a mistake on par with forgetting one's rifle or night-vision goggles on patrol in Iraq. Those kinds of little tricks and techniques were not briefed in the day's written order, but rather get passed down from seasoned soldiers. These details often make the difference between mission success or failure in the Army, whether in combat or stateside. After some good-natured ribbing, a young private squared me away with a spare cap.

We finished up our last section and got word over the radio to go place flags in the Columbarium, where open-air buildings contained thousands of urns in niches. Walking down Arlington's leafy avenues, we passed Section 60, where soldiers killed in Iraq and Afghanistan were laid to rest if their families chose Arlington as their eternal home. Unlike in the sections we had just completed, several visitors and mourners were present. Some had settled in for a while on blankets or lawn chairs. Others walked

Flags adorn every grave site in Arlington National Cemetery over Memorial Day weekend. Old Guard soldiers place the flags on the Thursday before Memorial Day.

among the headstones. Even from a respectful distance, we could see the sense of loss and grief on their faces.

Once we finished the Columbarium, "mission complete" came over the radio and we began the long walk up Arlington's hills and back to Fort Myer. In just a few hours, we had placed a flag at every grave site in this sacred ground, more than two hundred thousand of them. From President John F. Kennedy to the Unknown Soldiers to the youngest privates from our oldest wars, every hero of Arlington had a few moments that day with a soldier who, in this simple act of remembrance, delivered a powerful message to the dead and the living alike: you are not forgotten.

The Thursday before Memorial Day is known as Flags In at Arlington National Cemetery. The soldiers who place the flags at every grave site in the cemetery belong to the 3rd United States Infantry Regiment, better known as The Old Guard. Since 1948, The Old Guard has served at Arlington as the Army's official ceremonial unit and escort to the president.

I walked through Arlington for Flags In with The Old Guard in 2018. "What better way to show the nation and our fellow soldiers that we care and we never forget," observed Colonel Jason Garkey, the regimental commander. As we walked along streets named for legends like Grant and Pershing, he added, "This mission is really important for The Old Guard, too. It's the only day of the year when the whole regiment operates together. It gives all my soldiers—all my mechanics and medics and cooks—a chance to come perform our mission in the cemetery."

Flags In carries a special meaning for our citizens, too, judging by our conversations that afternoon. Col. Garkey greeted every civilian who approached us. Most were curious about the soldiers they saw walking across the cemetery. As he explained Flags In and The Old Guard, without fail they expressed their fascination and gratitude. In Section 60, we encountered families and friends paying early Memorial Day visits to their loved ones. Col. Garkey thanked them for their sacrifice, and they thanked him for his service and for remembering their fallen heroes. He never mentioned that those were his soldiers or that he had planted flags that day at the graves of his own friends and mentors.

My turn at Flags In came in 2007 during my own tour at Arlington. I had joined The Old Guard a couple of months earlier, after serving a tour in Iraq with the 101st Airborne Division. My path to The Old Guard was unusual—like my journey into the Army itself.

It began the morning of 9/11 in a law-school classroom. In those days before smartphones, we did not learn that America was under attack until class ended, almost an hour after the first airplane hit the World Trade Center. But my life changed in that moment. I knew the life I had anticipated in the law was over. I wanted to serve our country in uniform on the front lines. I finished school and worked for a couple of years to repay my student loans, time I also used to get prepared physically and mentally for the Army. It took my recruiter by surprise when I told him that I wanted to be an infantryman, not a JAG lawyer. To his credit, he signed me up and shipped me out, setting me on the path to Iraq. After more than a year in training, I joined the 101st in Baghdad in 2006, taking over a platoon of Screaming Eagles. We conducted raids, laid in ambushes, dodged roadside bombs and sniper fire, and sorted out the dead in a vicious sectarian war. And at the end of that tour, to my surprise, the Army gave me orders to The Old Guard, even though I had not applied to the all-volunteer regiment.

I knew The Old Guard was a special unit. The regiment has some of the highest eligibility standards in the entire military. Old Guard alumni were among the most squared-away soldiers I knew in the Army. And the mission set—not only conducting daily funerals in Arlington, but also world-famous ceremonies like presidential inaugurations and state funerals—called for the Army's best soldiers, performing at the highest levels. I looked forward to the assignment and I felt honored while serving at Arlington.

But I did not fully appreciate our nation's special reverence for The Old Guard and Arlington until years later, when I entered public life. A political newcomer, I spent the early months of my first campaign introducing myself to Arkansans, telling them about myself and what I hoped to accomplish for them. The most common question I got was not about Iraq or Afghanistan or about iconic Army institutions like Ranger School. No, the most common question, by far, was about my service with The Old Guard. The same holds true today; when I speak around the country to new audiences, questions about The Old Guard outnumber all the others. Likewise, thousands of Arkansans visit me each year in Washington. When I ask them about the highlight of their trip, Arlington tops the list.

Despite its enduring popularity, The Old Guard story is seldom told in full, but rather in passing on Memorial Day weekend or in the many fine books about Arlington. Unlike their comrades in arms in other storied regiments and divisions, Old Guard soldiers remain something of a mystery even though they are on duty at Arlington every day of the year. I want to rectify that by telling the story of the soldiers who dedicate themselves to our sacred duty of honoring those who served and died for our nation. This book is the story of The Old Guard.

The young soldiers of The Old Guard embody the meaning of words such as *patriotism*, *duty*, *honor*, and *respect*. These soldiers are the most prominent public face of our Army, perform the sacred last rites for our fallen heroes, and watch over them into eternity. The Old Guard represents to the public what is best in our military, which itself represents what is best in us as a nation.

These young soldiers are entrusted with our nation's most poignant, sacred rituals: the care and honors for those killed in action overseas. After their units memorialize them downrange, The Old Guard welcomes these fallen warriors home at Dover Air Force Base. And their journey home sometimes ends in Section 60, where The Old Guard lays them to rest among the other heroes of their generation.

The Old Guard has performed these and other critical missions for our nation since 1784. Old Guard soldiers belong to the oldest active-duty infantry regiment in the Army, three years older than the Constitution itself. The Old Guard fought in Mexico alongside Ulysses S. Grant and Robert E. Lee. They faced off against the rebel commander in the Civil War and served at Appomattox Court House when he surrendered to the great Union general. In between, they had camped at Lee's old farm, which started as a memorial to President George Washington but was destined to become the nation's "most sacred shrine." This legacy lives on each day at The Old Guard, and not merely among military-history buffs. I never served in or witnessed another unit so linked to its past and the bravery of its forerunners. That history is a call to arms for today's Old Guard soldiers to uphold the highest standards of what is known as America's Regiment.

We learned about that legacy from our earliest days at Fort Myer, as well as the expectations it placed upon us. Old Guard soldiers dedicate long hours to learning how to march, press uniforms, and assemble medals—all to The Old Guard's unique standards. But more important, we learned why it all matters, how blackening the soles of our shoes or measuring things out to one-sixty-fourth of an inch honors the fallen and their families. Our sacrifices of time, effort, and comfort paid tribute to those we honor, even while paling in comparison to their sacrifices.

Once we entered Arlington National Cemetery, our standard was nothing short of perfection. The Old Guard can conduct more than twenty funerals per day. But for the fallen and their families, each funeral is unique, a once-in-a-lifetime moment. As Old Guard soldiers, we viewed the funerals through their eyes as we trained, prepared our uniforms, and performed the rituals of Arlington. We held ourselves to the standard of perfection in sweltering heat, frigid cold, and driving rain. Every funeral was a no-fail, zero-defect mission, whether we honored a famous general in front of hundreds of mourners or a humble private at an unattended funeral.

We carried the same attitude into ceremonies, our other core mission. Although funerals are The Old Guard's highest-priority mission, the regiment also performs in ceremonies around the capital almost every day. From welcoming foreign leaders at the White House and the Pentagon to honoring retiring soldiers at Fort Myer, The Old Guard represents the discipline and skill of all soldiers. Among its ranks, The Old Guard boasts world-class musicians, the military's most elite color guard, and the Army's premier drill team. They carry the Army story and values to worldwide audiences and the smallest gatherings alike, always with pride and precision.

Among its many specialized troops, one platoon within The Old Guard stands out in the hearts of its countrymen: the Sentinels of the Tomb of the Unknown Soldier. The Tomb is one of the most popular sites in the nation's capital. For eighty-two years, that sacred spot of ground has been under constant, round-the-clock guard. Millions of visitors to Arlington have watched in reverential silence as the Sentinels perform the famous Changing of the Guard. But what they do not see, what they cannot see, is the tireless effort behind that simple ceremony. Though their public performance inspires awe, the Sentinels' devotion to their mission when no one is watching is what truly reflects the nation's love for our war dead.

I am grateful to have served at Arlington, but I am only one of many Old Guard soldiers over more than two centuries. This book tells their story—not mine. I will share some of my experiences. For instance, I will recount how it feels to stand in an aircraft at Dover Air Force Base surrounded by fallen heroes resting under American flags. But I never guarded the Tomb or played a fife or commanded the Drill Team. Thus, I spent many hours over the last year back at Arlington with The Old Guard, observing and learning from today's soldiers. I stayed late nights at the Tomb and I returned to Dover for the first time in a decade. I watched The Old Guard on the South Lawn of the White House and I traveled with them to the National Archives on Independence Day. I met the Caisson Platoon's horses and I inspected an arms room with centuries-old weapons. I observed funerals and ceremonies and I toasted the regiment at an annual ball. This book tells the behind-the-scenes story of America's Regiment as much through its soldiers' eyes and experiences as my own.

Also, I hasten to add, this is not a political book. Presidents, cabinet members, and foreign leaders make appearances, which is inevitable in a book about the official escort to the president. But Arlington National Cemetery and The Old Guard transcend politics. We live in politically divided times, to be sure. Yet the military remains our nation's most respected institution, and the fields of Arlington are one place where we can set aside our differences.

Which itself is something of a historic irony, because our national cemetery was birthed in the most divisive time in our nation's history, when Americans killed each other on such a mass scale that a farm across the river from our capital became the graveyard for those war dead. Perhaps because of those bloody origins, Arlington National Cemetery emerged from the ashes of the Civil War as a place dedicated to healing, reconciliation, and remembrance.

In the end, the story of The Old Guard of Arlington is not only a tale about our war dead and the soldiers who honor them, but also a story about ourselves as a nation. Because what The Old

Guard does inside the gates of Arlington is a living testament to the noble truths and fierce courage that have built and sustained America. We go to great lengths to recover fallen comrades, we honor them in the most precise and exacting ceremonies, we set aside national holidays to remember and celebrate them. We do these things for them, but also for us, the living. Their stories of heroism, of sacrifice, of patriotism remind us of what is best in ourselves, and they teach our children what is best in America.

On the eve of the war that transformed this farm into a national cemetery, President Abraham Lincoln pleaded for unity in his First Inaugural. "Though passion may have strained, it must not break our bonds of affection," he acknowledged, while appealing to the "mystic chords of memory, stretching from every battle-field, and patriot grave, to every living heart and hearth-stone, all over this broad land." In our days, as in his, passions can no doubt strain our bonds of affection, but those mystic chords of memory still stretch from the patriot graves of Arlington across our great land, calling forth yet again "the better angels of our nature."

1

||||

Coming Home

Easy Four-Zero and Easy Seven-One had just landed at Camp
Taji north of Baghdad to refuel and to drop off and pick
up passengers. These two Black Hawk helicopters were moving
troops around Baghdad-area bases on January 20, 2007. As they
took off, Easy Four-Zero had a four-man crew and eight passengers, soldiers with little in common aside from needing a lift
to the airport. Within minutes, Easy Four-Zero began to take
incoming fire from the ground. U.S. Army Specialist David Carnahan, the crew chief aboard Easy Seven-One, looked back to see
a rocket-propelled grenade hit Easy Four-Zero's fuel cell, setting
it afire. Easy Four-Zero crashed hard, the passenger compartment
engulfed in flames.

Easy Seven-One landed immediately, but not fast enough for
Carnahan: he jumped from the helicopter twenty feet off the
ground, armed with only his pistol and a fire extinguisher. Despite coming under fire himself, he and others rushed to rescue the
twelve soldiers from Easy Four-Zero. But all twelve had perished.
Carnahan and his crew defended the crash site as other helicopters
arrived on scene and engaged the enemy forces. "The first thing
that comes to mind when a helicopter goes down is *Black Hawk
Down*, and what they did to the bodies, and we weren't going to
let that happen," Carnahan said. On that day, he earned the Air

Medal for Valor, as did several soldiers, with others earning the Silver Star and the Distinguished Flying Cross.

The Army now had the grim, challenging task of identifying twelve sets of remains from the charred wreckage. Forensic specialists mostly succeeded, allowing for individual burials, including two at Arlington. But some of the commingled remains could not be identified. Thus, a group burial of the unidentified remains was necessary. The funeral would occur in Section 60 of Arlington National Cemetery on October 12, 2007. And Charlie Company of The Old Guard, where I had served as a platoon leader since March, would lead the funeral.

I knew more about this funeral than usual because three deceased soldiers—Captain Mike Taylor, Sergeant Major Tom Warren, and Sergeant First Class Gary Brown—had belonged to the Arkansas National Guard, as did Carnahan. I had read stories about the crash by an embedded reporter with the *Arkansas Democrat-Gazette*. I was seasoned in the cemetery by this point, and I was honored when I learned that we would perform the funeral for Easy Four-Zero.

We approached every funeral with a single standard in mind: perfection. Regardless of whom we laid to rest, we aimed to provide the family and mourners with a final, indelible image of honor for their loved one. They deserved no less, as did our fallen comrade. But this is not to say every funeral was the same; far from it. In fact, no one at The Old Guard could remember a group burial as large as Easy Four-Zero's. We rehearsed the funeral for several days, which itself was unheard of. Although the funeral would follow the normal sequence that we performed several times each day, it also included twelve flag bearers, one for each family. That was my role. We each had a pre-folded flag that we would touch to the casket, one by one, and then present to the next family.

October 12 dawned cool and crisp, with blue skies and plump
clouds rolling over the green fields of Section 60, the famed but
heartbreaking eternal home at Arlington of soldiers killed in the
War on Terror. Dozens of soldiers in ceremonial blue uniforms
milled around Section 60—my fellow flag bearers, escorts, liaisons, and others. Twelve sets of chairs, draped in plush green
covers, formed a horseshoe around the grave site. A large media
contingent gathered, including a crew from *NBC Nightly News*,

*Flag bearers stand at attention during the funeral for Easy Four-Zero. I am
the third man in the second rank.*

which had followed Charlie that week as we prepared for the funeral. We heard the band in the distance, followed by the universal Army cry to get ready: "Square it away!"

As the flag bearers came to attention, the largest funeral procession I would ever see at Arlington came into view: more than ten limousines, five buses, cars stretching back too far to see. Hundreds of mourners gathered around the grave, including the Secretary of the Army, the Vice Chief of Staff of the Army, the Director of the National Guard Bureau, and several state National Guard Adjutants. Black Hawks flew over. The chaplain delivered the eulogy. Charlie's seven-man firing party delivered the crisp three-volley salute. The bugler played Taps. Then, one by one, the flag bearers touched our flags to the casket and presented them to the families.

We marched off as we finished our part and linked up at our buses; Charlie had more funerals to conduct that day, after all. But we shared a sense of pride in the mission we had just accomplished. Easy Four-Zero crashed into Iraq's arid desert, but its heroes now rested in Arlington's tranquil fields.

★　★　★

For all its beauty, Arlington is a working cemetery. The Old Guard and its sister services perform military-honor funerals every weekday aside from holidays. In most cases, the funerals are for veterans of older wars: World War II and Korea in my days, and increasingly Vietnam today. I often stood at the head of a casket at attention with eyes locked forward, listening to a chaplain eulogize a soldier who honorably served our country decades ago and went on to live a life full of love, friendship, and accomplishment, dying peacefully in old age. I tended to view these services as a time not only to mourn their deaths, but also to celebrate their lives.

But Arlington is also a final resting place for soldiers who die in the line of duty, and The Old Guard conducts these funerals, too. Active-duty burials have, thankfully, become less common in recent years, but they happened regularly during my tour at The Old Guard in 2007 and 2008. These funerals carry a deep feeling of sadness, loss, and tragedy. The Old Guard strives to honor the fallen and their families with solemnity, but nothing can reunite loved ones on this side of heaven.

All we, the living, can do is care for the family and properly honor and remember the fallen. And by doing so, we assure our fighting men and women around the world that they, too, will be remembered in death and their families will be cared for. When I joined the Army, I knew what I was getting into; so does every soldier. Yet I also knew that, if I died, my battle buddies would bring me home and the Army would look after my family. That mutual pledge shaped our identity as soldiers and our willingness to fight—and, if necessary, to die—for our country.

Our nation's devotion to our war dead plays out from the moment a soldier falls on the battlefield to the final note of Taps. The soldier's unit works to return the remains and personal effects to the family as quickly as possible, even before conducting their own memorial service. Other military units—not only the Army, not only American—pay their respects as the remains depart the theater en route to Dover Air Force Base in Delaware, where they will be repatriated. At Dover, a dignified transfer occurs planeside, and then the remains and personal effects are prepared for final return to the family. And, if the family chooses, the final resting place at Arlington is Section 60. At every stage, the fallen hero is never alone and the journey is always dignified.

In Theater

While we might wish that war was fought on an abstract, antiseptic battlefield, that is simply not the reality of war. War is waged on the ground, in the mud and the sand, and inflicts violent death—more on the enemy, one hopes, than on one's own troops. The Army therefore prepares its soldiers for this reality of war from the earliest days of their training. Casualty care and evacuation was a central part of my first year of training, from basic training to Ranger School. When we failed to care properly for a "casualty" in an exercise, an instructor might direct us that night to write a letter to the "dead" soldier's family, explaining what happened on the "battlefield."

The same is true collectively for Army units. Infantry brigades, for instance, include a mortuary-affairs expert who teaches the staff and frontline leaders during pre-deployment training. Once "in theater," these leaders get orientation briefings on the mortuary-affairs collection point and its procedures. Thus, if we lost a soldier in combat, we already knew where to transport the remains and what to do. The objectives of this training are to get the remains home as quickly as possible, account for the deceased soldier's personal effects, and help the living to cope with the death of a battle buddy.

I first experienced this solemn process in June 2006, about a month after my arrival in Iraq. My battalion, 2nd Battalion of the 506th Infantry Regiment, was based at Forward Operating Base (FOB) Falcon on the southern edge of Baghdad. FOB Falcon was home to a few thousand troops and, while not luxurious, had basic amenities: electricity, a dining hall, a gym, showers, and decent internet and cell service. We also manned a small observation post, known as OP Red, about four miles to the east, where the city gave way to forested groves near the Tigris River. Unlike FOB Falcon, OP Red was just a house encircled with blast walls, so it had none of those amenities. We used it to support vehicular blocking positions on a main north-south road into the city, which insurgents otherwise could have used to smuggle weapons and bombs into Baghdad. Because we manned these positions around the clock, the platoon responsible for OP Red would spend three or four days in a row there, then rotate back to FOB Falcon for a day to rest and refit—hot chow, showers, email, and phone calls—before returning to OP Red.

Shortly after midnight on June 23, 2006, my platoon—1st Platoon, Baker Company—was on a rotation at OP Red. I was located in the command post, monitoring the platoon radio to stay in touch with our eight vehicular positions and the machine-gun position on the roof. As the night wore on, I heard a faint crash in the distance. Having already experienced up close the boom of a roadside bomb, or improvised explosive device (IED), I suspected one had detonated. A few moments later, my soldiers on the roof called down that they had seen a large explosion in the city. Later that night, we learned that Corporal Ryan Buckley, a twenty-one-year-old gunner from Baker's 2nd Platoon, had died from the blast. We also learned that a platoon from another company would relieve us at OP Red so we could attend the memorial service for Cpl. Buckley.

When we returned to FOB Falcon, the all-too-common routine of responding to a battlefield death had begun. The base was on a communication blackout, meaning private internet service was switched off and personal cell phones were confiscated. We turned in our phones as we parked our Humvees. This blackout was a standard procedure to ensure that Cpl. Buckley's next of kin learned of the death from official channels, not from rumor mills or social media. A casualty-notification officer and chaplain are supposed to arrive at the next of kin's doorstep within twelve hours, though that can be delayed a little to avoid the overnight hours. To be on the safe side, blackouts usually lasted a day or two, which can cause anxiety back home when loved ones are expecting to hear from their soldier. I would later explain to my dad that if he and my mom had not heard from me or a casualty-notification officer in twelve hours, they could be confident I was all right. A Vietnam veteran himself, my dad understood but also said he would not share the morbid logic with my mom; he would just assure her I was okay.

After family notification, the Army's highest priority is the repatriation of a deceased soldier's remains. In those days, given the number of deaths and the volume of flights, the Air Force and Army usually returned the remains to Dover Air Force Base within twenty-four to forty-eight hours. The journey home could start in one of two ways in Baghdad. First, a seriously wounded soldier would be evacuated to the Green Zone's hospital. Because nothing ought to be left to chance when the stakes are so high, my platoon rehearsed the route to the hospital often so we could navigate there without a map or GPS if we took casualties. My patrol briefs also included the emergency signal to bypass Green Zone checkpoints—usually a certain color ChemLight waved in a particular pattern by the lead vehicle's gunner—and race straight to the hospital. If the soldier died at the hospital, he would be moved to a mortuary-affairs collection point, which for my battalion was at the airport west of the city. Alternatively, when a soldier was killed on the battlefield, his remains would go directly to the collection point. The IED blast that took Cpl. Buckley's life that fateful night had killed him instantly, and so his remains went straight to the airport.

In either case, a fellow soldier accompanied the remains to positively identify them to the mortuary-affairs personnel and account for personal effects such as a watch, a wedding ring, or a wallet, all of which stayed with the remains until Dover. From there, fallen soldiers were transported to Kuwait International Airport, the theater mortuary evacuation point, usually by a C-130 cargo airplane. In Kuwait, they would depart for Dover, typically with a refueling stop in Germany. At each stage, from death to the funeral back home, no fallen soldier is alone—another soldier or other service member is always in close proximity.

Back at FOB Falcon, my platoon arrived during an operational stand-down for Baker Company. This stand-down allowed our soldiers, and especially Cpl. Buckley's closest buddies in 2nd Platoon, to begin the grieving process. Other companies in the battalion would cover down on Baker's patrols until the memorial service. We would unfortunately have occasion to repay the favor in the coming months.

In the meantime, Baker's executive officer, Captain Wes Pierce, was inventorying Cpl. Buckley's personal effects, which had to be completed within twelve hours of death. When a soldier is killed, a designated officer has the authority to take control of the deceased soldier's personal effects—uniforms, letters, diaries, books, electronics, and so forth. This process can be very stressful. The inventorying officer, after all, is also mourning the loss of a soldier, but he must complete a zero-defect mission in just twelve hours. And Cpl. Pierce had to search not only Cpl. Buckley's room, but anywhere he might conceivably find personal effects, such as a friend's room or the laundry facility. After documenting all the personal effects and sealing them in footlockers, Cpt. Pierce had to transport them personally to the collection point at the airport and sign over custody to the mortuary-affairs personnel. Cpl. Buckley's personal effects would go to the Joint Personal Effects Depot (JPED) located then at Aberdeen Proving Ground in Maryland. Only once the JPED had returned the personal effects to the family and resolved any discrepancies would an inventorying officer like Cpt. Pierce be released from this difficult duty.

With Cpl. Buckley's remains en route to Dover and his personal effects accounted for, all that remained was the memorial service. Baker Company gathered at the battalion's makeshift chapel, but not only Baker. It seemed like the entire base turned out to pay respects to a young soldier many of them had never met. The sun set on another hot, gritty day in Baghdad as we stood on the rough gravel. In front of us was the famous Battlefield Cross—a pair of boots and an inverted rifle, ID tags hanging from its pistol grip and a helmet resting on its buttstock. A picture of Cpl. Buckley was nearby. The chaplain opened the service with an invocation. Cpl. Buckley's chain of command delivered brief eulogies, including a moving one from Captain Josh Headley, his platoon leader. The service concluded with the symbolic Last Roll Call, when the company's rolls are called until the name of the fallen soldier is reached.

"Corporal Buckley." No reply.

"Corporal Ryan Buckley." No reply.

"Corporal Ryan J. Buckley." No reply.

Cpl. Buckley's name was then symbolically removed from the rolls, a poignant reminder of 2nd Platoon's loss—and our nation's loss. Taps was played as we all saluted, then everyone filed by the Battlefield Cross to say a prayer and our final good-bye.

Sadly, memorial services like Cpl. Buckley's were not rare, nor was his my last. Almost three years later, after my tour with The Old Guard, I participated in a similar service in Afghanistan. This time, because of my experience at Arlington, I helped to plan the memorial service.

I volunteered to join a Provincial Reconstruction Team (PRT) bound for Afghanistan near the end of my Old Guard tour. Army headquarters needed combat-experienced infantry captains to serve as the operations officers for PRTs. Because the PRTs were led and staffed by Air Force or Navy personnel, the infantry captain would be the subject-matter expert on ground combat operations. I would be responsible in particular for a National Guard infantry platoon attached to our PRT as the security force for our engineers, civil-affairs teams, and civilians. The platoon came from 1st Battalion, 178th Infantry of the Illinois National Guard. My team, PRT Laghman, was based in Mehtar Lam, east of Kabul and north of Jalalabad, near the Pakistani border. 1st Battalion's headquarters were co-located with my PRT at FOB Mehtar Lam, giving our province some extra combat power and a connection to the other eleven PRTs scattered across the country.

Our proximity to 1st Battalion also meant PRT Laghman suffered their losses as well, none more grievous than when a large IED killed all four troops in a single Humvee from PRT Nangahar on March 15, 2009. Sergeant Christopher Abeyta, Specialist Robert Weiner, and Private First Class Norman Cain, all from 1st Battalion, and Air Force Staff Sergeant Timothy Bowles perished that day. PRT Nangahar handled the remains and personal effects, and also conducted a memorial service at Jalalabad. The 1st Battalion commander, Lieutenant Colonel Dan Fuhr, and my PRT commander, Air Force Lieutenant Colonel Steve Erickson, agreed that we should also conduct a memorial service at FOB Mehtar Lam given the large number of 1st Battalion troops there, both from our PRT and from the battalion headquarters. While senior sergeants have the primary responsibility in the Army for casualties and ceremonies, I pitched in given my Old Guard experience.

Six days after the terrible loss, FOB Mehtar Lam shut down to honor our fallen comrades. More than two hundred soldiers, airmen, and Afghans gathered under a brilliant sun on the basketball court outside the gym. Four Battlefield Crosses stood in front of the assembled troops. After a eulogy from Lt. Col. Fuhr, the chaplain led a reading of Psalm 23 and "Amazing Grace," then delivered his own message about the meaning of these soldiers' deaths in service of a cause greater than themselves. The symbolic Last Roll Call followed for each of the fallen. Our firing party discharged three rounds and Taps played as we saluted in honored silence.

Our four fallen heroes also received a ramp ceremony at Bagram Airfield, a departure ceremony that was less common during my time in Iraq. The fallen received a solemn, dignified transfer of their remains with an honor guard, but given the high number of deaths—between eight hundred and nine hundred per year from 2004 to 2007 in Iraq—a large ramp ceremony was not always feasible. This changed in Afghanistan because of the lower number of casualties. During the fifteen-month deployment of the 101st Airborne to Afghanistan from April 2008 to June 2009, General Mark Milley, now the Army Chief of Staff and then a deputy commanding general of the 101st, attended almost two hundred ramp ceremonies at Bagram. "They were usually in the middle of the night, very exhausting and emotional," Gen. Milley recalled, "but totally necessary to pay honor to our fallen."

These ramp ceremonies were very large, yet simple and dignified. Anyone at the mammoth airfield wishing to honor the fallen could line the street as the remains passed, often in a tactical vehicle converted for the evening into a battlefield hearse. On the tarmac, units formed many ranks deep at the ramp of the awaiting aircraft. As the vehicles moved into position, the chaplain prayed over the fallen and often read Psalm 23. Honor guards carried the remains to the ramp as the assembled troops saluted, sometimes to the sound of "Amazing Grace" on bagpipes. The ceremony concluded with Taps and one final salute before the troops were dismissed, the ramp closed, and the aircraft began its long flight home.

This is the good-bye that Sgt. Abeyta, Ssg. Bowles, Weiner, and Cain received at Bagram Airfield. The next day, they were welcomed home by Secretary of Defense Bob Gates. In his memoir, *Duty*, Secretary Gates wrote that he took his first trip to Dover Air Force Base that night to observe their dignified transfer. By then in his third year as a wartime secretary, he arranged to be alone with the four. He recalled the scene inside the aircraft:

> I was overwhelmed. I knelt beside each for a moment, placing my hand on the flag covering the case. Tears flooded my eyes. I did not want to leave them, but I finally sensed the chaplain move close behind me, and so I rose, returned to the tarmac, and saluted, as one by one, with extraordinary precision, respect, and care—even tenderness—the honor guard transferred each case to a waiting vehicle.

Dover

Not every fallen hero is greeted by the Secretary of Defense, but all do receive a dignified transfer at Dover Air Force Base. While Dover is the military's largest and busiest freight terminal, the base is most famous as the port of entry for the fallen, whose flag-draped remains create such searing images for our nation. The Dover Port Mortuary opened in 1955 and more than thirty thousand remains have passed through it. Dover airmen take pride in this heritage. Even by the high standards of military bases, Dover sparkled when I returned in July 2018, my first visit there in a decade. Colonel Joel Safranek, the senior commander at Dover, observed to me that "everyone here—airmen, the joint force, even contractors—goes the extra mile, without any extra pay or benefit, to make it look the best they can. We all know that families of the fallen will be here, and we want it to be perfect for them."

A part of that heritage is the dignified transfer of remains. According to Colonel Dawn Lancaster, the commander of Air Force Mortuary Affairs Operations, "there has always been something like a dignified transfer, it's just gone by different names, like honorable carry." As I walked the hallways at Dover, for instance, I saw a photograph of a transfer from 1968. Since the early days of the Iraq War, The Old Guard has performed the dignified transfer of Army soldiers. (Other branches of the military also conduct the dignified transfer for their fallen.)

The Old Guard's first operation order for a dignified transfer is dated March 28, 2003, eight days after American forces crossed into Iraq. Colonel Jim Laufenburg, then the regimental commander and now a senior civilian official at the Military District of Washington, issued the order and the mission was assigned to then-Captain Jason Garkey, who was the commander of Honor Guard Company. Garkey, now a colonel and back at The Old Guard as the regimental commander, preserved the order over all these years and provided me a copy, which bears his handwritten notes. "There was not much advance notice, no long train up," Col. Laufenburg recalled. Col. Garkey added, "I got that order the day prior, and that was it. I think the Army staff, maybe the Chief, wanted an Army team to conduct the dignified transfer, so of course they chose The Old Guard. We're only a couple hours from Dover and this is what we do. I said, 'Roger that, let's move out.' It was a tremendous honor to be chosen."

That first mission established standards that continue today. Most notably, the uniform would be the combat fatigues with white gloves, combat boots, and beret. When I asked Col. Laufenburg and Col. Garkey why they did not choose the ceremonial uniform, they answered that the uniform matches both the fallen soldier and the airmen on the active flight line where the dignified transfer occurs. Another key decision was to conduct the dignified transfer just like the movement of a casket from a hearse to the caisson in a military-honors funeral at Arlington.

As is often the case because of the flight time and time-zone change from Ramstein Air Base in Germany, The Old Guard's first dignified transfer happened in the middle of the night—at 0130 on March 30, 2003, to be exact, as indicated by Col. Garkey's handwritten note on the order. He and his casket team left Fort Myer five hours earlier, arriving with plenty of time for rehearsals before the remains landed in a C-17 cargo airplane. Col. Garkey and a few airmen boarded the aircraft as an advance echelon—the ADVON, in Army terms—to inspect the transfer cases, as the metal containers that hold the remains are known. The ADVON also ensured that the flags on the cases had not shifted or been damaged in flight. Once off the C-17, Col. Garkey rejoined his casket team. With a cool wind blowing across the dark tarmac, they marched up to one case and stood at attention during the chaplain's prayer, then carried it to the awaiting vehicle while the C-17 crew saluted. They repeated the sequence for the second case, Col. Garkey secured both of them inside the vehicle, and the soldiers and airmen saluted as the two fallen heroes were driven away.

When Col. Garkey reflected on The Old Guard's first dignified transfer, he stressed the impact it had on him as a young captain and his team. On the ride back to Fort Myer, "there was a lot of reflection. No one on the bus had been in combat." While they had performed funerals in Arlington, he recalled, "there's a big difference between handling remains in ceremonial blues in Arlington weeks or months later and carrying them off a C-17 at Dover a few hours later. It's just so immediate." That freshness of the loss is one reason why, Col. Garkey said, "even though you knew no one was watching, in typical Old Guard fashion, we had to get it perfect—those were our fallen brothers."

Col. Garkey performed the next several dignified transfers as well. Within a few weeks, the Army added a general officer to the mission team, demonstrating its high priority for the Army. The Military District of Washington's 12th Aviation Battalion also began to support the mission with a Black Hawk helicopter. Otherwise, the dignified transfer changed little from Col. Garkey's time to when I arrived at The Old Guard in March 2007—aside from the sorrowful increase in the number of missions as the Iraq War ground on.

Because it takes several weeks for new officers to be certified for funerals and ceremonies, the dignified transfer was my first true Old Guard mission, which in retrospect seems appropriate. Nothing drives home the significance of what The Old Guard does more than a "Dover mission," as the dignified transfer was known inside the regiment by my arrival there.

Sadly, the missions were so frequent that the regiment needed a monthly duty roster for junior officers; most lieutenants and captains pulled three or four duty days per month. My name first appeared on the April 2007 roster. That was near the height of the Iraq Surge, when we had Dover missions virtually every day. I always assumed that I would be going to Dover on my duty days. For the next several months, unfortunately, I was not proven wrong.

The Old Guard got about thirty-six to forty-eight hours' advance notice for Dover missions. When a mission fell on my duty day, I connected with the casket team and its leader. Unlike officers, with our daily shifts, the casket team was on duty for a full week. We checked the weather forecast since inclement conditions would ground the 12th Aviation's helicopters, forcing us to take a van to Dover. Ground transport added many hours to the mission, but like funerals in the cemetery, a dignified transfer was a no-fail mission. When the remains landed, The Old Guard would be there one way or another.

I received no advance training for my first Dover mission, partly because the dignified transfer is a simple sequence, but mostly because it happened so often that everyone else was an expert. The casket team and I linked up at Fort Myer about three hours before the mission. We did a quick uniform inspection and departed for the helicopter landing zone, usually either Fort Mc-Nair in southwest Washington or Fort Belvoir, south of Washington on I-95 in Virginia. There, we met the general officer, which the Army assigned from another duty roster of generals serving in the capital region. The flight was quiet and reflective—books and iPods, common during noncombat flights, were prohibited on Dover missions.

Upon landing, we went into the passenger terminal, where the USO provided snacks and drinks and the lead Air Force officer conducted a talk-through rehearsal with magnetized schematics on a whiteboard. To my surprise, the remains were arriving on a Boeing 747, not an Air Force cargo aircraft. In fact, that was the standard practice, and I never conducted a Dover mission on anything besides a civilian cargo aircraft. The reasons were simple. Military aircraft were heavily committed in Iraq and Afghanistan, while the military contracted extensively with civilian cargo companies to move troops and matériel in and out of the theater. Thus, the fastest way to get the fallen home in those days was usually a contracted flight.

Though feeling more comfortable, I still pulled the Air Force officer aside and told him this was my first dignified transfer. He reassured me that The Old Guard officer's role was straightforward: lead the ADVON onto the aircraft, inspect and position the cases, and then wait for the casket team and official party to enter the aircraft. I would remain in the aircraft for the transfer itself, which was a change in the officer role since Col. Garkey led the first Dover mission. In those four years, the casket team had gone from eight to six men, which better suited the size of the transfer cases. The casket-team leader could therefore march behind the team and secure the cases in the transfer vehicle, instead of being part of the carry team. The officer, in turn, could stay in the aircraft during the transfer on the ground.

Within a few minutes, we got the word that customs officers had cleared the aircraft and the ADVON could board. I departed the terminal with the Air Force chaplain and three airmen. We walked across the tarmac and climbed the front stairs of the 747. As I entered the cargo hold, I realized why customs had to check the aircraft first. It was full of heavy cargo: engines, weapons, equipment boxes—pretty much anything used in combat. I squeezed past the cargo until I reached an empty space in the middle, right by the side cargo door. That is when I first saw the three silver cases draped with American flags. I paused at the striking sight, but I moved ahead with the tasks at hand, not wanting to betray emotion in front of the young airmen.

The first task was to inspect the flags. On this mission, one flag needed to be straightened, but none had to be replaced. Next, we began to position the cases for the casket team. Because of the aircraft's height, we used a K loader, a vertical lift under a large flat cargo platform, to lower the cases to the ground. Our job was to carry two cases to the far edge, then place the final case halfway on the K loader and halfway in the cargo hold. The three airmen and I positioned ourselves at the corners of the first case and prepared to lift on my command.

"Ready, down." We squatted and secured the handles of the

case. Once I saw that the airmen had a good grip, I continued. "Ready, up." I was not prepared for how heavy the case was— easily four hundred pounds, maybe more. We strained to carry the case to the edge of the K loader. I learned later that much of the weight was ice that was packed and repacked around the re- mains at each stop on the journey. Also, some fallen soldiers were still in their body armor when rushed off the battlefield on the journey home; the armor could add another seventy-five pounds.

We returned to the cargo hold and repeated the process for the second case, which was a little lighter, but not much. Finally, we prepared to position the third case in the cargo door. Upon my command, we picked up what turned out to be a very light case. I later learned that lightweight cases were also common. These contained the partial or dissociated remains of an IED victim, a painful reminder of the enemy's most deadly weapon.

With the remains in place, an airman called the passenger terminal for the casket team and the official party, which usu- ally included the Army general and his aide, the Air Force base commander, and the Air Force officer-in-charge of the dignified transfer. They boarded the aircraft a few minutes later. The casket team gathered around the last transfer case, while the official party stood to one side of the door and the ADVON stood to the other. The chaplain prayed over the fallen heroes and then the casket team carried the final case onto the K loader before exiting the 747, followed by the official party and the chaplain. I remained in the door with the rest of the ADVON while an operator lowered the K loader to the ground.

On the ground, the official party stood to the side, about half- way between the K loader and the transfer vehicle, a box truck parked opposite the K loader. The six-man casket team positioned itself at the edge of the K loader, three men on either side of the first transfer case. The team leader stood in the middle, walking backward as he pulled the case off the K loader, with the team taking the handles and assisting as the case reached them. Once the case was fully off the K loader, we saluted while the remains were being carried, just as it happens at Arlington. The casket team moved the other two cases in a similar fashion, then stepped back from the vehicle and saluted. A young airman, known as the door marshal, secured the vehicle's back doors and then stepped to the left, the driver's cue to start the engine. As the taillights came on, we all saluted one last time as the vehicle drove off. The casket team then marched off the tarmac, followed by the official party and finally the ADVON.

With the dignified transfer complete, the casket team, the Air Force officer-in-charge, and I gathered outside the terminal for an after-action review. We all agreed the transfer went well as the whine of the Black Hawk's engine told us it was time to leave. We loaded the helicopter and took off, with the lights of Dover fading into the dark farmland of Delaware and Maryland. As I looked out, I realized the last time I had flown on a Black Hawk was on an exuberant flight from FOB Falcon to the Baghdad airport as Baker Company began our trip home the previous November. My feelings on this trip could not have been more different.

Over the next sixteen months, I would make that trip more than thirty times. I conducted Dover missions at all times of day and under all conditions. On a hot, muggy summer afternoon, we had to transfer nineteen cases, raising and lowering the K loader several times to complete the mission, which took more than two hours. I was soaked in sweat and exhausted from carrying the cases onto the K loader, and my casket team was even worse for wear on the hot tarmac. Yet they carried the nineteenth case with the exact same precision and care as they had the first case. On another mission, with a winter storm moving in, we drove to Dover two days early to avoid grounded helicopters and impassable roads. On the icy drive back to Fort Myer, no one complained about the time and effort spent to welcome home a single fallen comrade.

By the time of that winter mission, though, the frequency of Dover missions had declined because the Iraq Surge had succeeded. My third month at The Old Guard, May 2007, was the third bloodiest for American troops in Iraq, behind only April and November 2004, when the First and Second Battles of Fallujah were fought. By contrast, my last month at The Old Guard, July 2008, had the fewest casualties of any month since the start of the war. Thus, no longer did I assume that I would have a Dover mission on my duty days; on the contrary, I was surprised when I did.

But a mission did come down on my final duty day. On the flight, I reflected on how many times I had made the trip and how many fallen comrades I had welcomed back. I knew this was my last Dover mission. As I inspected the flags on the two cases, I noticed that a cargo strap had left a small black smudge on one of the flags. We replaced it, and I told the airman that I wanted to keep the damaged flag. After the mission, he handed it to me and I had the casket team fold it into a tight triangle. I have kept that flag close ever since; today, it sits in a shadow box in my Senate office. I do not know the name of the soldier whose transfer case it adorned. The cases do not have external identifying information, only an internal pouch for paperwork. Thus, I view my flag as a memorial for every soldier whose remains I carried, and for all the soldiers who laid down their lives in the wars we fought.

After I had left The Old Guard and deployed to Afghanistan, major changes came to the dignified transfer. First, on the recommendation of Secretary Gates in early 2009, President Barack Obama opened the transfer to the families of the fallen and the media.

"The Air Force outdid itself in implementing this decision," in Secretary Gates's words, building in less than a year a Campus for the Families of the Fallen, complete with an inn, pavilion, garden, and waiting space akin to a funeral parlor. The family's presence has altered The Old Guard's timeline for Dover missions. The soldiers now arrive earlier so the Air Force officer-in-charge can brief the Army general and other distinguished visitors in the official party about the family before the party meets them to offer condolences. While the planeside sequence remains largely the same, the transfer lasts a little longer to accommodate the family's arrival at and departure from the tarmac.

Second, as American forces were withdrawn from Iraq and substantially drawn down in Afghanistan, fewer troops downrange has translated, thankfully, into fewer dignified transfers. Dover has conducted two to five transfers per month for the last five years, versus the daily missions during my time. Col. Lancaster thus can train her mortuary-affairs personnel to perform the ADVON's preparatory duties, which removes The Old Guard officer from that role.

Third, the slower pace of missions allows senior military and civilian leaders to attend the dignified transfer. Gen. Milley attends every Dover mission unless he is traveling, in which case General Jim McConville, the Vice Chief of Staff, attends in his place. As Gen. McConville put it, "Dover is the number-one priority for the Chief and me. We will drop anything to be there." Sergeant Major of the Army Dan Dailey does the same: "If I'm in Washington, I go to every dignified transfer of remains. I will cancel everything on the schedule to get to Dover." Secretary of the Army Mark Esper also attends regularly. President Obama and President Donald Trump, as well as Vice President Joe Biden and Vice President Mike Pence, have also traveled to Dover.

Finally, with fewer missions, The Old Guard team usually can infer the identity of the fallen soldier for whom they conduct the dignified transfer, even though the cases remain unmarked on the outside. An example is the Dover mission on June 12, 2018. It was no secret that Staff Sergeant Alex Conrad of 1st Battalion, 3rd Special Forces Group was killed four days earlier in Somalia, and no other soldier had died overseas in the meantime. Thus, Major General John Deedrick, the Special Forces commanding general who had traveled from Fort Bragg, briefed The Old Guard team about Ssg. Conrad and how he died. Sgt. Maj. Dailey also tries to tell The Old Guard team about the fallen. He does not, however, rehearse the transfer with them. "I'm never worried about them, because they are so precise, so perfect in what they do," he explained, "and they know more than anyone you can't give back that solemn moment to the family. So I just thank them."

A few days after the dignified transfer for Ssg. Conrad, I discussed the mission with some of The Old Guard soldiers. Captain Dave Heikkila was the officer-in-charge, conducting his second and final Dover mission before moving to Fort Benning. (To contrast how much things had changed since the height of the Iraq War, I conducted three Dover missions in my first month.) With his Old Guard tour concluding, he acknowledged, "toward the end now it's gotten emotional again as I've been able to reflect on everything I've done." He was the sentry posted with the transfer case on the K loader, about which he said, "I was really grateful to be given that opportunity to pay my respects in such a way."

Sergeant First Class Isaac LaBelle was conducting his first Dover mission. A veteran of multiple tours, he has lost several friends and soldiers in combat—some of whom are buried in Arlington. He said that participating in a dignified transfer, just like service at Arlington, has "definitely given me closure" about their deaths and the honors rendered to them. Sfc. LaBelle hoped the dignified transfer would provide some measure of comfort to the

An Old Guard casket team performs the dignified transfer of remains on June 12, 2018, for Staff Sergeant Alex Conrad. Sergeant Brian Harrison, the team leader, is on the left front of the transfer case.

Conrad family: "Knowing that if I could get closure here, and if I can help a family member get closure, then I'm a success at what I do here." Sergeant Brian Harrison, the casket-team leader on his third Dover mission, agreed: "When you see the family around you, you know exactly what you're doing for that family."

But for the family, the loss "is still so fresh," as Sgt. Harrison put it, and the dignified transfer is just the beginning. Col. Lancaster has participated in dozens of dignified transfers, and she believes "this is the hardest moment for the families. Not the knock on the door or the funeral, but when they see that transfer case. That makes it real." That reality, according to Sgt. Maj. Dailey, is why "it's very positive that the family can be there. It's not immediate closure, for sure, but it starts a process for them."

After the dignified transfer, as the family returns to the Campus for the Families of the Fallen and The Old Guard flies back to Washington, that healing process passes into the hands of Air Force Mortuary Affairs Operations. In their complex at the end of the runway, uniformed personnel and civilians prepare the remains for return to the family and final burial. I did not know what happened at this stage when I served at The Old Guard, and what stood out the most during my behind-the-scenes tour there in July 2018 was the care and dedication of the men and women responsible for this most solemn mission. They display the tenderness and reverence that we would all want for loved ones, which is not surprising since the fallen comrades are their second family.

Many of these personnel are not mortuary-affairs specialists and are only temporarily stationed at Dover. Mobilized reservists, or what the Air Force calls "deployers," from other bases are a large part of the workforce. The reason, according to Col. Lancaster, is partly the emotional toll of the work, but also "the twenty-four-hour-a-day, seven-day-a-week, unpredictable nature of the mission. It's like a deployment that way." Yet many troops volunteer for multiple tours in the mortuary, and some civilians are veterans who moved back to Dover to work in mortuary affairs. When I asked them why they came back, they invariably cited the honor of serving our fallen heroes and their families.

The first stage is the Medical Examiner and the Personal Effects Section. The medical examiners confirm the identity of the remains through fingerprint, dental, and DNA records. They also conduct an autopsy, the results of which are analyzed to improve body armor and battlefield techniques, a final service rendered by the fallen to better protect the living. Meanwhile, the "transfer effects" that came with the remains are accounted for. Some will go home with the remains. Staff Sergeant Fred Heston explained, "We'll send the obvious things home—wedding rings, religious items. Sometimes the family will pass on a specific request for something we might not otherwise send." Other effects go to the new JPED, which opened next door in 2011, and await the "theater effects" to arrive from the inventorying officer a few days later.

Col. Lancaster's team next prepares the remains and a uniform for burial. Whenever possible, the remains are restored for viewing at the funeral. "Families always want to view their loved one," explained Chris Schulz, a civilian mortician with thirteen years at Dover, "so we do everything we can to get them ready." Col. Lancaster added, "These guys are miracle workers. They'll describe what they've done, but I can't even see it." In the Uniform Section, Air Force Staff Sergeant Michelle Johnson and Army Staff Sergeant Luis Diaz assemble a final, custom-made uniform. They work in a large room full of uniforms from all five services and hundreds of commonly used insignia. Ssg. Diaz stressed that "we have to be fast and we have to be perfect."

At the Dress and Restoration Section, young airmen put on the fallen hero's final uniform for the last time. I met four deployed airmen in this section. A few months earlier, they worked in food service or fitness centers, and they would soon return to such jobs. But Staff Sergeant Ron Holmes said, "This is the best job I've ever had, being able to honor these heroes and give closure to the family." He told me that he would "definitely" volunteer for another tour at Dover, and the others all agreed.

The final stop is Departures, where the remains are placed into a casket. Uniforms are straightened, lint is rolled off, loose threads are clipped—no detail is too small before the airmen close the casket lid at Dover for the final time. And when it comes time for the escort officer to leave with the casket, the mortuary-affairs team conducts a private "reverse dignified transfer of remains." Whether the remains are loaded into a charter aircraft for a distant flight or a hearse for a short drive, an Air Force honor guard carries the casket while others are present to salute their fallen comrade one final time.

Section 60

After fallen heroes depart Dover Air Force Base, they are escorted to their final resting place. One destination is home to more than any other: Section 60 of Arlington National Cemetery. Section 60 is where those killed in Iraq, Afghanistan, and other theaters of the War on Terror are laid to rest. Unlike other sections in the cemetery, a steady flow of moms and dads, husbands and wives, sons and daughters, and friends and battle buddies visit their loved ones in Section 60, which is why it is sometimes called "the saddest acre in America."

Section 60 is in the southeast part of Arlington, the newest and most active burial area of the cemetery. This area became part of Arlington in the 1970s. In the early twentieth century, it belonged to the Department of Agriculture's experimental farm. The War Department took it over in 1940 and converted part of the farm into military offices and barracks known first as Arlington Cantonment and later as Fort Myer South Post. (Another portion became the Pentagon.) South Post included what is now Sections 54 to 76, essentially the area south of Memorial Drive and east of Eisenhower Drive, then the boundary of the cemetery and now its main north-south road. As older parts of the cemetery filled up in the 1960s, the Army demolished the buildings on South Post and transferred the land to the cemetery.

Despite its nickname, Section 60 is actually about fourteen acres in size, one of the largest in the cemetery. Four streets frame the rectangular section: Eisenhower Drive on the west, York Drive on the north (named for Sergeant Alvin York, among the most decorated soldiers of World War I), Marshall Drive on the east (named for General George Marshall), and Bradley Drive on the south (named for General Omar Bradley). Burials began in Section 60 soon after it opened, with some graves near Eisenhower Drive dating back to the late 1970s. As one moves east, row after row contains the graves of World War I veterans and, eventually, World War II veterans.

But two graves stand out a little more than halfway across the northern side of Section 60, near where Halsey Drive runs into York Drive. A headstone marks the grave of Staff Sergeant Brian Craig, the first soldier killed in Afghanistan to be buried in Section 60. (A few Afghanistan veterans who died earlier are buried in other sections, and a grave for a seven-person flight crew who crashed and died a few months earlier in Pakistan is located on the southern side of Section 60.) Ssg. Craig was one of four soldiers killed in an explosion while disarming Taliban rockets on April 15, 2002. He also occupies the grave adjacent to his own, with the commingled remains of the other three soldiers. His grave only foretells the losses to come, since the rest of his row reverts to graves for veterans of earlier wars.

All that changes in the next row, though. Captain Russell Rippetoe of the 75th Ranger Regiment was killed by a suicide bomber near the Haditha Dam in Iraq on April 3, 2003. The Old Guard laid him to rest in Section 60 one week later. Cpt. Rippetoe was the first soldier killed in Iraq to be buried at Arlington, but his fallen comrades joined rapidly: the row is full of those killed in the early days of the Iraq War. Section 60 had now become the eternal home for Americans killed in the global War on Terror.

At the outset of the Iraq War, Arlington officials decided to bury those fallen heroes together in a single section. They selected Section 60 for a few reasons, according to Joe Mercer, a twenty-five-year veteran of the cemetery and before that an Old Guard soldier. First, the large section offered thousands of available grave sites. Second, the proximity to three different starting points for funerals—Patton Circle, McClellan Circle, and McClellan Gate—would provide flexibility for future funeral planning. Third, funeral processions could reach the section from either York or Bradley Drive, both well suited for what was expected to be large crowds.

Unfortunately, this logic proved to be sound. Over the four years from the start of the Iraq War to my arrival at The Old Guard, this patch of Section 60 grew by another seven rows, more than three hundred fallen heroes. And during my sixteen-month tour, The Old Guard laid to rest more than one hundred soldiers killed in Iraq or Afghanistan. As with the dignified transfer at Dover, the pace of these funerals reflected the intensity of fighting overseas. We performed eleven active-duty funerals in August 2007 alone, for example, but only two in June 2008.

Bravo and Charlie Companies conducted most funerals during my tour, so Charlie performed about half of these active-duty funerals. Our commander, Captain Dave Beard, usually served as the officer-in-charge and the Escort Platoon leader, Lieutenant Erich Feige, usually marched his own platoon as the escort commander. Thus, I did not participate in many active-duty funerals. But on occasion—probably half a dozen times, due to leave, illness, or other things—I was the escort commander. And while The Old Guard sequence for an active-duty funeral did not differ from other military-honor funerals I had performed, everything else did.

What I recall most about active-duty funerals is the size and emotions of the family and other guests. For most funerals, five to ten people attended; twenty-five was an unusually large group. In many cases, after all, loved ones had to travel long distances and a funeral service had usually occurred in their hometown. Further, given the wait time for a funeral and the older age of the deceased, the family was mostly composed at the graveside. I presented dozens of flags to elderly widows and adult children; very seldom did the next of kin lose composure or do something besides thank me or return my salute. Their loss, though painful, was usually not unexpected, and it had sunk in over several weeks or months.

This was not the case with active-duty funerals. The processions for these funerals were very large, sometimes more than one hundred people. At the transfer point, where remains are moved from the hearse to the caisson, it could take the cemetery representative a full five minutes to get everyone out of their cars and into position to observe. And it took as long to move the family and guests from York or Bradley Drive to the grave itself. Once the graveside service began, I had a clear view of the family— usually parents and a young widow, often young kids as well. Even though I stood fifty yards away or more, I could still see the anguish of losing a loved one just a few days earlier on their faces. Most cried, some uncontrollably. They held tight to each other. The next of kin usually broke down when presented with the flag.

The immediate aftermath of these active-duty funerals was also different from others. There was no small talk—there was no talk at all, unless it was mission-related for the next funeral. I reflected on my time in Iraq and those we had lost, as well as the pain of their Gold Star Families. I suspect the other officers and sergeants on the bus were doing the same, with the junior soldiers perhaps looking ahead to a time when they would go downrange. Those thoughts would fade as we prepared for the next funeral. But we passed Section 60 in the bus almost every day on the way to funerals, watching as the grass turned to dirt made by fresh graves. The memory of our fallen comrades was never far from my mind.

I had left The Old Guard for Afghanistan by the time the Iraq War began to draw down and Afghanistan began to heat up. But I still return to Section 60 from time to time, sometimes with my wife and young boys, to recall my days on that sacred ground, to pay my respects to its heroes, and to teach the next generation about the heroes of Arlington and the price of freedom. I can trace the history of my generation's two wars on those walks among the headstones. By 2009, Afghanistan veterans begin to overtake Iraq veterans, while veterans from earlier wars who survived combat start to rejoin the Iraq and Afghanistan veterans.

"Section 60 is not exclusive to KIAs," Mercer explained. "It's an active burial section and used to suit the logistical challenges of the cemetery." Veterans from earlier wars continued to be buried on the south side of Section 60 during my tour at The Old Guard. And as the pace of active-duty burials slowed, these older veterans took their place on the north side among their children and grandchildren.

In the rows with graves from 2010 to 2012, the intensity of the fighting in Afghanistan becomes evident with another spike in active-duty burials. After 2013, though, Section 60 returns to its origins and resembles the other working sections of the cemetery. Active-duty burials still occur—especially for the special-operations forces upon whom the nation calls so frequently—but World War II, Korea, and Vietnam headstones predominate.

Like many regular visitors to Section 60, I visit one grave in particular: that of Lieutenant Colonel Mark Stratton, the commander of PRT Panjshir. Mark knew my commander, Lt. Col. Erickson, so we met and worked together during our pre-deployment training at Fort Bragg. We were not close friends—our rank necessarily imposed a certain formality—but we were friendly comrades. It was hard not to get along well with Mark, who was a cheerful and motivated leader. Mark perished in an IED blast on May 26, 2009. I try to visit his grave every year on the anniversary of his death, and any other day when I visit Section 60. Through these visits, I came to meet his widow, Jennifer, and their three children, Delaney, Jake, and A.J., learning more about Mark from them, and also sharing some of my experiences with him at Fort Bragg.

But I also like to walk among all the other rows and graves. Section 60 is unusual not only for the number of visitors, but also for the things they leave behind. Stones, rocks, coins, and other mementos sit on headstones, signifying a recent visit. Flowers and balloons commemorate birthdays and anniversaries. Photographs of the fallen with loved ones are common, as are pictures of kids, growing up and making new memories to share with their absent mom or dad. I always like to stop and look at these items, which tell stories of loss and pain, but also love and life. They add a human element to the marble headstones, a reminder of the lives lived by these heroes. When items have fallen or gotten dirty, I pick them up and clean them as best I can so the next visitors can also learn from them—or so the family, if they visit, will know that strangers care for their loved ones and will look after them when the family cannot.

As I walk around Section 60, I recognize many names of the fallen from my time in the Army and at The Old Guard. Ross

McGinnis was a nineteen-year-old private first class with the 1st Infantry Division on the north side of Baghdad when I was deployed with the 101st Airborne on the south side. Two weeks after I returned home, he was a machine-gunner in a Humvee when an insurgent threw a grenade into the hatch. Rather than jump out, as every instinct must have screamed, McGinnis fell on the grenade. He died instantly, but his four battle buddies lived—and he earned the Medal of Honor posthumously. Two days later, Marine Major Megan McClung died in an IED blast in Anbar Province. She was the first female Marine officer killed in Iraq. Just a few steps away rests her fellow Marine, Major Doug Zembiec, known as "The Lion of Fallujah" for his heroism in the First Battle of Fallujah. He was killed in May 2007 by small-arms fire while leading a raid with the Iraqi troops he had trained. I had joined The Old Guard a couple of months earlier, and I remember learning at the time about Maj. Zembiec's life from the media coverage of his funeral.

I also learn new stories on my walks in Section 60. Staff Sergeant Adam Dickmyer and I overlapped at The Old Guard, though we did not know each other then. I first met him in Section 60 a few years back when I noticed the unusual headstone above his grave. The stone bore a silver replica of the Tomb Badge he earned as a Sentinel of the Tomb of the Unknown Soldier. He later deployed with the 101st Airborne to Afghanistan, where he was killed in 2010. One reason I wanted to write this book was to share his story and others like it.

Stories like that of Corporal Ben Kopp. When I read a headstone, I sometimes think about where I was when the soldier was killed, especially if I was in the Army at the time. When I first came upon Cpl. Kopp's grave, I noticed that the young Ranger had died just a few days after I had left Afghanistan. Curious, I looked up his story. He was shot while I was still in country,

On a family visit to Arlington, I showed my son, Gabriel, the headstone of Staff Sergeant Adam Dickmyer, a former Sentinel of the Tomb of the Unknown Soldier, who died in Afghanistan. The silver replica of the Tomb Badge is visible at the grass line.

fell into a coma, and died at Walter Reed hospital outside Washington. But Cpl. Kopp lives today because he had volunteered to be an organ donor. His organs saved four lives, and his bones and tissues benefited dozens more. His heart was a match with Judy Meikle, and she lived because of his sacrifice. Judy visits his grave on occasion, and she and his mother, Jill Stephenson, have become friends through the experience.

When I think about Section 60, these are some of the heroes on my mind. Section 60 is not a mere resting place for the dead, but also a testament to the lives they lived and the sacrifices they made. The steady stream of family and friends, the school field trips, the spontaneous conversation and friendships, the things they leave behind—all these things keep their spirit alive. I understand why some people call this bucolic patch of land the saddest acre in America, but I prefer to think of Section 60 as the noblest acre in America.

The nobility of Section 60 runs deep in the soil of Arlington and in the soul of our nation. Over the years, I have noticed something about Arlington. Although a sign welcomes visitors to "our nation's most sacred shrine," no rules are posted. Yet visitors somehow understand a proper code of conduct. Adults speak in hushed tones. Children stay on their best behavior. Joggers and cyclists circle the cemetery but do not enter. Strangers treat each other with kindness.

The same holds true for The Old Guard. We had a different code of conduct in Arlington, widely known but mostly unwritten. No exercise, except for large-unit runs. No cadence calls when running. No combat fatigues, only Army dress uniforms. Old Guard soldiers follow these rules scrupulously; I cannot recall a single infraction during all my time in the cemetery.

Arlington elicits instinctive reverence from citizen and soldier alike because this land is more than a cemetery. Arlington truly is sacred ground for our nation. For more than a century and a half, our nation's fallen heroes have journeyed from the battlefield to Arlington much as did Ross McGinnis and Ben Kopp in our time. And before that, Arlington was our nation's first memorial to George Washington. On the eve of a dreaded civil war, this land passed to the stewardship of Robert E. Lee, then among the nation's finest military officers, but soon the commander of rebel forces. His choice turned Arlington into an encampment, then a graveyard, and finally our national cemetery.

The Old Guard's own history is intertwined with the tragic history of this land. War came to Arlington in the early days of the Civil War and on 9/11—and in both cases, The Old Guard was present for duty. In between and ever since, our nation has buried its war dead in this soil. And while The Old Guard has borne this solemn responsibility for the last seven decades, it has dedicated even more years to the nation's defense on the battlefield, a heritage that still echoes across the plains and hills of Arlington today.

2

||||

America's First Defenders

September 11, 2001, began like any day for The Old Guard. Colonel Jim Laufenburg, the regimental commander, started the morning doing outreach at a local school. Though new to the role, Col. Laufenburg had served previously with The Old Guard. After hearing that a second airplane had hit the World Trade Center, "I guess just something dawned on me. I said, 'I better get back to Fort Myer, because something's happening,' " he recalled. "At the same time, I grabbed my son out of class, threw him in my car, and we drove back to Fort Myer."

Back at the cemetery, the first funerals had already begun, as always, at 0900. Sergeant First Class James Jones's caisson team had completed its part in the funeral and begun to prepare for its next funeral. As the riders and their horses waited, though, they saw an airplane flying almost due east, not along the normal north and south routes into and out of Reagan National Airport. He remembered that one of his riders said, " 'Hey, look at that plane.' All of us looked over and saw the plane. We see lots of planes flying above Fort Myer. But this one was out of place."

What they saw was American Airlines Flight 77 immediately before it slammed into the western face of the Pentagon at 0937. The impact site was barely two hundred yards across Washington Boulevard from the southeastern corner of the cemetery.

Col. Laufenburg did not see the impact on his drive back to Fort Myer, where he also lived, but he said, "I started hearing sirens, then more sirens. And they were coming from all different directions. Then I kind of gazed up and saw smoke rising off to the horizon, off the Pentagon."

When Col. Laufenburg reached the regimental headquarters, he told his deputy commander, "Bring in the regiment. Let's lock them down. Have them go into contingency ops, get their tactical gear." Across the river at Fort McNair, home of the Military District of Washington, The Old Guard's higher headquarters, Major General James Jackson saw the smoke rising from the Pentagon and rushed to the scene. He called Col. Laufenburg with simple guidance: "Send your medical assets down to the Pentagon." The Old Guard's Medical Platoon, with its military ambulances on modified Humvees, were the regiment's first soldiers to arrive at the Pentagon, and thus some of the first uniformed personnel on a battlefield of the new war.

Back at Fort Myer, the threat of more attacks locked down the base. Aside from soldiers conducting funerals, the regiment secured the base and prepared for the unexpected. Perimeter gates were shut and armed guards were posted at key facilities. It was an all-hands-on-deck operation. Even the Fife and Drum Corps, which usually performs in the 1779 Continental Musician uniform, stored its fifes and drums that day, put on combat fatigues, and drew Kevlar helmets and gas masks to guard the regimental headquarters. Specialist Lauren Panfili, a new flutist, understated matters when she said, "The day that they issue gas masks to the Fife and Drum Corps is not a good sign."

But everyone had to pitch in at the "chaotic" crash site—the word used by both Gen. Jackson and Col. Laufenburg. Fires raged, the walking wounded received aid from volunteers, and first responders rushed in. In need of "a coherent structure, orga-

Old Guard soldiers in Tyvek suits and gas masks fold a flag discovered at the Pentagon in the aftermath of 9/11.

Secretary of Defense Donald Rumsfeld thanks Old Guard soldiers on September 12, 2001 for rushing to the Pentagon after the attack on 9/11. The Old Guard remained at the Pentagon for the following month.

nization, manpower," Gen. Jackson recalled, "the obvious thing was The Old Guard. I get young, physically fit troops, I get a chain of command, and I get a commander who I know I can grab right away and make it happen." By late afternoon, Col. Laufenburg had three companies on site for crowd control and to support civilian first responders. Another company went on patrol in the cemetery to help the Park Police remove visitors who were watching the events unfold across the street. While there, these soldiers also discovered the airplane parts that the crash had blasted into the cemetery.

For the next month, The Old Guard never left the Pentagon. Col. Laufenburg estimated that, in addition to funeral duties in the cemetery and security for Fort Myer, he kept three to four hundred soldiers on site at all times, twenty-four hours a day. Far from an anomaly, though, this deployment to the first front line of the War on Terror continued an Old Guard tradition stretching back more than two centuries. Soon enough, The Old Guard would return solely to funerals and ceremonies. But for now, they walked in their ancestors' footsteps.

★   ★   ★

Most Americans who visit Arlington National Cemetery do not know about The Old Guard's long and distinguished history on the battlefield, or that it remains an infantry regiment with the training standards of other active-duty infantry units. They do not see soldiers loading combat gear for the drive to training ranges at Fort A. P. Hill, ninety miles to the south. They observe instead the Changing of the Guard at the Tomb of the Unknown Soldier, watch the horse-drawn caisson roll along Arlington's avenues, or catch a glimpse of soldiers marching in a funeral. These funerals and ceremonies are indeed The Old Guard's primary missions, as they have been since 1948.

Yet the regiment's lineage runs back three times longer in

American history; indeed, The Old Guard is older than our Constitution. For more than a century and a half, The Old Guard fought our nation's battles from the frontier to the Civil War, from Mexico to the Philippines. The Old Guard is literally The *Old* Guard, the oldest active-duty infantry regiment in the Army. Old Guard soldiers live this history every day. Their uniforms bear distinctive insignia, such as the eighteenth-century buff strap, to commemorate the regiment's origins—and some soldiers wear a colonial uniform for ceremonies. The soldiers march with bayonets fixed, a privilege reserved only to The Old Guard, to honor the regiment's bravery in the Mexican War. And the regimental colors bear fifty-five campaign streamers to celebrate The Old Guard's history of battlefield valor. While these echoes of the past may not be apparent to outsiders, Old Guard soldiers cannot help but soak in their rich history and hold themselves to the exacting standards of their forerunners.

The professionalism, the precision, and the striving toward perfection for which The Old Guard is so well known have their roots not only in the history and solemnity of Arlington, but also in the regiment's own distinguished history. That story begins with The Old Guard's colonial roots and its early defense of our young republic.

Origins

I am sometimes asked why The Old Guard is the oldest active-duty infantry regiment in the Army. Why do more regiments not trace their lineage to the colonial era? The answer lies chiefly in the founding generation's skepticism of standing armies.

The founders believed, from history and their own experience, that large, standing armies threatened the liberties of their own people. They faulted standing armies in part for the fall of the Roman Republic and the wars that convulsed Europe in the seventeenth and eighteenth centuries. Moreover, American colonial militiamen fought the French and Indian War from 1754 to 1763 alongside British redcoats, whom they often found undisciplined.

The lingering effects of that war, the North American theater of the Seven Years' War, also soured the founders on standing armies. With Great Britain deep in war debts, Parliament imposed a series of unpopular taxes on the colonies. The Americans widely resisted the taxes and adopted the famous rallying cry "no taxation without representation." More unpopular still were laws requiring colonists to shelter and feed the British redcoats in public inns and similar houses. Such provocations festered and multiplied until the colonists finally declared independence from Great Britain. And listed among the particular grievances against King George III in the Declaration of Independence was keeping "in times of peace, Standing Armies without the Consent of our legislatures" and "for quartering large bodies of armed troops among us."

Thus, the Continental Congress essentially disbanded the Continental Army after the British defeat in the Battle of Yorktown in 1781—the kind of rash military drawdown after a conflict that happens all too often across our history. The Army shrank from sixty infantry battalions at Yorktown to fewer than one hundred troops by 1784. As often happens, though, Congress realized that it had cut too deeply and created a single regiment of infantry to provide the new nation a small cadre of professional soldiers.

And thus was The Old Guard born on June 3, 1784, as the First American Regiment. To this day, The Old Guard crest includes both the year 1784 and the revolutionary motto *Noli Me Tangere*—"touch me not" or "don't tread on me"—to commemorate its heritage. In a world of loosely organized, sporadically trained state militias, the First American Regiment was the lone regiment of professional soldiers, or "regulars" as they were often called. This distinction between the "regulars" and the volunteer militias would influence The Old Guard's identity and its missions all the way through World War II.

The First American Regiment spent its early years on the frontier of the Northwest Territory, the lands stretching from present-day Ohio to Minnesota. After the war, Great Britain had ceded the territory to America and committed to withdrawing its troops. But the British maintained garrisons there to support an insurgency among Indian tribes who did not recognize American sovereignty. As attacks on travelers and settlers grew, President George Washington ordered a military campaign against the tribes in 1790. The First American Regiment saw its initial combat in what became known as the Northwest Indian War, commencing more than a century of battles between the regiment and Indians on America's frontier.

These early campaigns were bloody disasters. General Josiah Harmar, the regiment's first commander, attached about three hundred of his soldiers to a larger group of ill-trained state militiamen. In October 1790, this force started out from Fort Washington (in modern-day Cincinnati) with the objective of pacifying Indian resistance near modern-day Fort Wayne in northeast Indiana. But the numerically superior Indian forces repeatedly overwhelmed Harmar's soldiers, forcing them to retreat to Fort Washington after just two weeks. Known as Harmar's Defeat, these battles inflicted the regiment's first casualties and were the worst American defeat by Indian tribes at the time.

But Major General Arthur St. Clair seized that sorry title the following year. He essentially refought Harmar's campaign without addressing the same training and logistical deficiencies.

Two-thirds of the American troops were killed—more than six hundred men—and most of the rest wounded in November 1791 near modern-day Fort Recovery, on the Ohio-Indiana border. St. Clair's Defeat remains the worst defeat of the American military by Indians—worse even than the Battle of Little Big Horn.

Reaction to the St. Clair fiasco was far-reaching. Congress conducted its first oversight investigation of an executive-branch failure. Though a routine practice in which I participate today, it was not yet an established part of our system of checks and balances. I doubt, however, that many witnesses before Congress would celebrate this part of The Old Guard's legacy. Next, Washington augmented the infantry with cavalry and artillery and Congress redesignated the Army as the Legion of the United States, styled after the Roman Republic's military. Also, Congress authorized longer periods of enlistment and higher pay, always good for recruitment. Finally, Washington gave command to Major General Anthony Wayne, who had led infantry regiments for him during the Revolutionary War. His audacious tactics and colorful personality had earned him the nickname "Mad Anthony."

Despite his nom de guerre, Wayne was anything but mad. In methodical fashion, he imposed strict discipline and order on his new army in 1792 and 1793, while various envoys met with the Indian federation to discuss a negotiated peace. As is often the case, it is not clear whether diplomacy failed and led to war, or diplomacy succeeded by buying time for the military preparations for war.

In any event, Wayne's legion—including the First American Regiment—defeated the Indian federation as decisively as the Indians had defeated Harmar and St. Clair. They entered Indian territory in late 1793, building Fort Recovery near the site of St. Clair's Defeat and settling in for the winter. In August 1794, Wayne and his legion prevailed in the Battle of Fallen Timbers, near present-day Toledo and named for the tornado-felled trees used unsuccessfully by the Indian tribes as defensive obstacles against Wayne's forces. The engagement ended the Northwest Indian War and drove the British into Canada for good.

Fallen Timbers marked the first military triumph of today's Old Guard, and the regiment commemorates the campaign every day. On their left shoulder, Old Guard soldiers wear a black-and-tan "buff strap," which mimics the shoulder straps on the rucksacks carried by Wayne's troops. The buff strap, earned by passing the uniform and marching tests required to conduct funerals in Arlington, visibly distinguishes Old Guard troops from all other soldiers. Further, the oldest streamer on The Old Guard's regimental colors dates back to this campaign. Finally, The Old Guard's 1st Battalion today goes by the nickname "One Legion," an homage to the brief period when the Army was known as the Legion, which Congress abandoned after Wayne's death in 1796.

The First American Regiment spent much of the next fifteen years manning forts in the Northwest Territory. In those years, the French Revolution and the Napoleonic Wars convulsed Europe and sometimes spilled over into the New World. Congress swung between improvident demobilization, as happened again after the Northwest Indian War, and hasty buildups, as when the French Republic threatened American neutrality at sea. But naval hostilities declined after Napoleon seized power in 1799, and Thomas Jefferson won the presidency the next year with a continued aversion to standing armies. By 1802, only the First and Second Regiments remained under arms. As ever, though, military weakness invites foreign aggression and the threat of war returned, this time with Great Britain harassing American shipping at sea. This tension escalated into the War of 1812, and Congress again rushed to grow the Army by forty-six regiments from 1808 to 1814. Not surprisingly, these regiments varied widely in size and skill. Many had little more training and experience than a volunteer state militia. By contrast, the First American Regiment remained the professional bedrock of the Army in the northern theater of the war.

The regiment's two largest and most consequential battles occurred near Niagara Falls in July 1814 to establish control over Lake Ontario and Lake Erie. With Napoleon's abdication, American leaders wanted a decisive victory before Britain's European units could reinforce their North American ranks. On July 5, the regiment participated in the Battle of Chippewa, just south of the falls. Chippewa was a decisive American victory and pushed the British to the southern shore of Lake Ontario, threatening the entire Niagara Peninsula.

But the British reinforcements moved across Lake Ontario from York (modern-day Toronto) and prepared to counterattack. On July 25, British troops came upon exposed American forces on Lundy's Lane, a path just west of the falls. One of the most brutal battles of the entire war followed. Artillery and rifle fire gave way to bayonet charges, with American troops gutting British artillerymen and seizing their cannons. Both sides gained and lost the initiative throughout the day, and by midnight the First American Regiment was engaged in bloody hand-to-hand combat. With all the troops exhausted and depleted, the British withdrew north to Lake Ontario and the Americans south to Lake Erie.

These battles, though indecisive in the moment, established two strategic points as the war wound to its conclusion. American regulars had demonstrated that they could fight their British counterparts at least to a draw. At the same time, now numerically superior British forces on the peninsula could prevent the Americans from invading Canada and achieving a decisive strategic victory there. Perhaps not coincidentally, peace negotiations began a few days later and concluded by year's end.

The War of 1812 netted the First American Regiment three more campaign streamers—Canada, Chippewa, and Lundy's Lane—and a valuable patron. The regiment had fought along-side Winfield Scott, then a brigadier general at the young age of twenty-eight. Scott would become the longest-serving general in American history and lead the regiment in the Mexican War, after which he gave the regiment the nickname it has borne ever since.

The war also led indirectly to the regiment's formal name. I am sometimes asked of The Old Guard, "If it's the oldest regiment in the Army, why is it the 3rd Infantry and not the 1st Infantry?" The answer lies in Congress's foolish pattern of troop drawdowns and the Army's sometimes inscrutable bureaucratic logic. Congress slashed the Army by two-thirds, providing for eight infantry regiments. The First American Regiment was combined with four others to form the 3rd Infantry. Rather than preserve the regiment's numerical designation given its distinguished history, the Army numbered the new regiments based on the seniority of their commanders. This consolidated regiment had the third-most senior commander; hence it was designated the 3rd U.S. Infantry. Somewhat arbitrary, perhaps, but that is where the designation comes from and why the Army recognizes the 3rd Infantry—not the 1st or the 2nd—as its oldest active regiment.

The newly christened 3rd Infantry spent the next twenty-five years as a frontier force. As the nation's frontier moved westward, so did the 3rd Infantry. From Detroit in the aftermath of the War of 1812, the 3rd Infantry moved to Fort Howard (modern-day Green Bay), then to Jefferson Barracks outside St. Louis, and next to Fort Jesup in western Louisiana. The only detour came in 1840, when the regiment deployed to central Florida for the

Second Seminole War. The 3rd Infantry was scattered around small outposts to protect civilians from Indian raids, a kind of proto-counterinsurgency campaign that foreshadowed the regiment's future in the Philippines.

After the Seminole War, the 3rd Infantry returned to Jefferson Barracks, where it developed a reputation as the Army's most disciplined, well-trained regiment. As war clouds gathered with Mexico, the Army began to assemble forces under the command of General Zachary Taylor. With its reputation for professionalism and its recent combat experience in Florida, the 3rd Infantry joined Taylor's command at Fort Jesup as part of the "Army of Observation of Texas." When Taylor received orders to move to Corpus Christi in 1845, he renamed his forces the "Army of Occupation." The name change portended the coming invasion.

As the year closed, this deployment had placed American forces on the disputed border with Mexico, and the United States had annexed Texas, which Mexico viewed as a breakaway province. By early 1846, war seemed inevitable. The ensuing conflict would cement the 3rd Infantry's reputation for battlefield valor and create traditions that echo today on the parade fields of Fort Myer and the rolling hills of Arlington.

The Mexican War

The Mexican War was controversial from the beginning. On President James Polk's orders, Taylor moved into disputed territory on the Rio Grande. Mexican forces soon attacked a small American patrol. Ulysses S. Grant, then a lieutenant in Taylor's army, later wrote in his *Personal Memoirs* that the operation was designed to provoke a Mexican attack and thus provide Polk and Congress with the grounds for a declaration of war. A young first-term congressman, Abraham Lincoln, introduced the so-called Spot Resolutions, demanding that Polk identify the "spot" of American soil on which the attack occurred. But these political debates mattered little to the soldiers of the 3rd Infantry and the other regulars on the front lines. Over the next sixteen months, they fought in the war's two major campaigns, consistently shouldering the most dangerous missions because of their skill and experience.

The first campaign, Taylor's march on Monterrey, was already under way when Congress declared war on May 13. The Mexicans barely knew what hit them. They had laid siege to the Americans' small fort near modern-day Brownsville, Texas, but Taylor had taken most of his forces to the coast to secure his supply lines. The Mexican Army raced to intercept Taylor before he could return to the fort. The Battle of Palo Alto ensued on May 8.

Taylor's army was outnumbered almost three-to-one, but the Mexicans could not match the better trained, armed, and led Americans on open terrain. Taylor maneuvered the 3rd Infantry to his right flank, where along with the 5th Infantry they repelled a Mexican assault, counterattacked, and forced the enemy to retreat. Taylor's subsequent account credited superior artillery, with American guns outranging the antiquated Mexican cannons—an early example of the technological superiority that would become central to the American way of war. Still, it was the 3rd and 5th Infantries that screened for the artillery, allowing the guns to fire for effect without reprisal. This is why, I must observe as an old infantryman, the infantry is known as the "queen of battle"—versatile and agile—and the artillery as the "king of battle"—powerful but ponderous and thus vulnerable.

A bigger rout lay ahead the next day at the Battle of Resaca de la Palma. Mexican forces had fallen back across a dry riverbed hoping the terrain would impede the American attack. But they had no such luck. Taylor again put the 3rd Infantry on the right flank, this time with the 4th Infantry. While they had to break up into small units to traverse the heavy forest and thick underbrush of the riverbed, they ultimately turned the Mexican line, seized their artillery, and scattered the Mexican Army in a disorganized retreat across the Rio Grande.

Taylor paused at the Rio Grande to regroup and prepare for the march to Monterrey in July 1846. The movement took two months and proved almost as dangerous as the fighting. The 3rd Infantry and the rest of Taylor's troops fought extreme thirst, dysentery, scorpions, red ants, tarantulas, and fevers as they slogged across two hundred miles and up 1,700 feet through blazing summer heat and dense chaparrals. When Taylor's weary forces arrived at the northern outskirts of Monterrey, the tactical picture was unfavorable. The Americans were again outnumbered. The Mexicans had also prepared the battlefield well, digging in fighting positions on the high ground. The mountains protected them to the south, and a large open plain to the north offered clear fields of fire and no cover for an advancing army.

The Battle of Monterrey lasted for three days and witnessed the most intense, protracted combat of the Mexican War—and the 3rd Infantry faced some of the worst fighting. Taylor planned a double envelopment of the city from the east and west. The 3rd Infantry was tasked to the eastern flanking force, which planned only a diversionary attack to distract the Mexicans while the western force seized the high ground on that side of the city. On September 21, Taylor launched the coordinated operation, but it bogged down because the terrain made communication nearly impossible. The western forces, supported by artillery, seized one of two key fortified hills outside the city with few casualties. Unfortunately, for the 3rd Infantry and the other eastern forces, the fighting did not go so well.

What began as a diversion devolved into a frontal assault across five hundred yards of open terrain with no cover or concealment against dug-in artillery on the high ground—an infantryman's nightmare. The 3rd and the 1st Infantries reached the city's edge with limited casualties by maintaining proper intervals and thus limiting the damage one shell could inflict, a basic infantry tactic that my soldiers and I still practiced in Iraq. But the volunteer forces fighting with them approached too closely and took heavy casualties. Inside the city, but isolated and inexperienced in urban combat, the 3rd Infantry and other eastern forces suffered heavy casualties. Mexican snipers targeted the American soldiers with impunity. Intersections brought heavy volleys of grapeshot, a kind of shotgun shell for artillery. With casualties exceeding half their forces, the Americans retreated to a fortification on the city's eastern edge.

On day two of the battle, the western forces seized the other fortified hill on the city's western edge, allowing the 3rd Infantry and the other eastern forces to regroup and prepare for more street-to-street fighting. They received valuable coaching from Texas volunteers serving alongside them. The Texans had fought the Mexican Army in towns and cities during their own revolution a decade earlier. This battlefield instruction in basic breaching and house-clearing techniques—akin to the way we fought in Iraq in the twenty-first century—proved vital because the Mexican commanders had withdrawn their troops overnight to the city's central plaza, forcing the Americans to fight all the way there.

And that is exactly what happened as September 23 dawned. The American troops began a pincer movement toward the plaza, clearing houses as they went. The vise tightened on the Mexicans all day until Taylor halted the advance and ordered a mortar to fire into the plaza every twenty minutes. He hoped to compel a surrender without further loss of American or civilian life. The tactic worked, and the Mexicans raised the white flag as midnight approached. Monterrey had fallen, but at a very high price. In his *Personal Memoirs*, Grant recounted the valor and sacrifices of the 3rd Infantry:

> All advances into the city were thus attended with much danger. While moving along streets which did not lead to the plaza, our men were protected from the fire, and from the view, of the enemy except at the crossings; but at these a volley of musketry and a discharge of grape-shot were invariably encountered. The 3d and 4th regiments of infantry made an advance nearly to the plaza in this way and with heavy loss. The loss of the 3d infantry in commissioned officers was especially severe. There were only five companies of the regiment and not over twelve officers present, and five of these officers were killed.

Taylor and the Mexican commanders came to terms: the Mexicans surrendered Monterrey and Taylor accepted a two-month armistice during which he would not advance beyond the city. In truth, Taylor needed the respite because the march up and the battle had nearly broken his force. But the armistice displeased Polk, who had hoped a decisive victory at Monterrey would induce the Mexicans to seek peace. Instead, he transferred many of Taylor's forces to General Winfield Scott, whom he directed to launch the war's second major campaign against Mexico City.

A modern coda to the Battle of Monterrey demonstrates our nation's commitment to our fallen war dead and the 3rd Infantry's role in honoring them. Most soldiers killed in the battle were buried there, the military custom of the time. In 2011, human remains were discovered during construction work around Monterrey. Researchers concluded that the remains likely belonged to Tennessee militiamen who fought with the 3rd Infantry on the eastern flank. No different than with contemporary deaths in Afghanistan or Iraq, the remains were flown to Dover Air Force Base. On September 28, 2016, 170 years after their death, these fallen soldiers came home, with the dignified transfer performed by their old comrades in arms, the 3rd Infantry. This story was reported widely across military-news outlets, a reminder to our troops today that the living will never forget the dead, and will always strive to bring our fallen back home.

For the living, though, there remained a war to win. The 3rd Infantry and other regulars marched over three hundred miles to the coast, where they integrated new soldiers and linked up with Scott for the campaign against Mexico City. Thirty-three years after the Battle of Lundy's Lane, Scott and the 3rd Infantry would fight together again on the other end of the continent. Their bold campaign of audacious offensive maneuvers compelled the Mexicans to negotiate peace, while also adding to the 3rd Infantry's already storied history.

Scott's army set sail for Veracruz, which invading armies going back to Hernando Cortés and his conquistadors had used as a foothold to march on the capital city. The Mexican army therefore had fortified the port, deterring a direct attack. Instead, Scott planned the nation's first major amphibious landing about three miles south of Veracruz. The landing of troops, weapons, horses, and supplies on March 9, 1847, was largely uncontested. Within a week, the 3rd Infantry and other forces dug in siege lines around the city. On March 22, Scott bombarded the Mexican forces with mortars and even larger naval guns in the port. After a few days, the Mexicans surrendered and withdrew from the city. In just three weeks, the fortress port had fallen. And with a highway running from Veracruz to Mexico City, Scott seemingly had a clear avenue of approach to the capital city.

Alarmed at the prospect, famed Mexican General Antonio López de Santa Anna marched twelve thousand men east along the highway to stop Scott. Around the village of Cerro Gordo, about fifty miles northwest of Veracruz, the Mexicans placed their artillery on steep hills on both sides of the highway, which ran through a canyon below and was surrounded by dense forests. As Scott approached with 8,500 men, the tactical situation could not have been more favorable for the Mexicans: a numerically superior force occupying heavily armed high ground with the enemy channeled into a narrow pass below.

But the Mexicans made two grave mistakes at Cerro Gordo. First, they fired prematurely at American scouts on April 12, thus revealing their positions. Second, Santa Anna believed the surrounding forest and ravines were impassable—but he was wrong. In an early display of his legendary audacity, then–Captain Robert E. Lee—who would play a central role in the fates of both Arlington National Cemetery and The Old Guard—scouted the terrain and reported to Scott that a bold flanking maneuver could succeed.

With Lee leading the way, the 3rd and 7th Infantries and the 1st Artillery conducted the flank. And bold it was. They hacked a path through the forest, using ropes to lower artillery guns into the ravines and then to haul them up the other side. By April 17, they had positioned their artillery on a nearby hill. They initiated the assault at daylight the next morning with artillery pounding the Mexicans. The 3rd Infantry led a bayonet charge up the hill, killing or capturing the enemy forces, then turning the Mexican artillery on other Mexican positions. The attack was conducted flawlessly, as Scott recounted in his report on the battle:

The style of execution, which I had the pleasure to witness, was most brilliant and decisive. The brigade ascended the long and difficult slope of Cerro Gordo, without shelter, and under tremendous fire of artillery and musketry, with the utmost steadiness, reached the breastworks, drove the enemy

U.S. Army soldiers rout Mexican forces at the Battle of Cerro Gordo on April 18, 1847. To commemorate its decisive bayonet charge at Cerro Gordo, The Old Guard is the only unit in the Army authorized to march with bayonets fixed to their rifles.

from them, planted the colors of the First Artillery, Third and Seventh Infantry—the enemy's flag still flying—and, after some minutes of sharp firing, finished the conquest with the bayonet. It is a most pleasing duty to say that the highest praise is due to . . . their gallant officers and men, for this brilliant service, independent of the great results which followed.

Scott's other forces flanked the remaining Mexican positions. Facing encirclement, Santa Anna's troops broke and fled into the mountains. The Battle of Cerro Gordo was over: the Mexicans suffered more than a thousand casualties and lost three times that as prisoners, despite outnumbering the Americans.

Cerro Gordo was the last battle on the march to Mexico City because Santa Anna retreated to defend the capital, but Scott's army stalled nonetheless. Several thousand volunteer troops quit when their terms of enlistment expired, putting his numbers below six thousand. Waiting for reinforcements, Scott probably appreciated regulars like the 3rd Infantry, populated with professional soldiers who stuck it out in the middle of a fight. After more than three months of delay, he began the steep ascent to Mexico City with ten thousand troops. By August 10, Scott was within twenty miles of the capital, but stymied by heavy fortifications and much larger enemy forces.

Scott conceived his boldest operation yet: his army bypassed the entire city and its defenses, attacking from the west instead. Lee, intrepid as ever, scouted a path through and around marshes and a large rocky lava bed, which Santa Anna again wrongly thought was impassable. On August 20, the Americans surprised the Mexicans, attacking their rear outside the village of Contreras, southwest of the capital. The Battle of Contreras lasted only seventeen minutes, but Scott's forces killed seven hundred Mexicans and captured eight hundred.

Within a few hours, Santa Anna and his forces regrouped at Churubusco, a small village on the way to Mexico City. They occupied a thick, stone-walled convent and a fortified bridgehead. The Mexicans ferociously defended for hours one of the last strongholds between the Americans and the capital. But Scott's forces eventually seized the bridgehead, and the 3rd Infantry conducted the decisive assault on the convent just as the Mexicans began to surrender. Scott wrote about the battle, "The white flags, however, were not exhibited until the moment when the Third Infantry . . . had cleared the way by fire and bayonet and had entered." Scott knew the Battle of Churubusco had ended when he saw "hung out from the balcony the colors of the gallant Third."

With casualties mounting, Santa Anna proposed negotiations after the Battles of Contreras and Churubusco. Scott reciprocated with an armistice. Within two weeks, though, Scott concluded that Santa Anna was only playing for time—always a risk with a wounded but not yet defeated enemy. He prepared for a final assault, even though Santa Anna had nearly twice as many troops and the advantage of high ground and the city's defenses. On September 8, the fighting renewed at the Battle of Molino del Rey, the rare battle involving neither Lee nor the 3rd Infantry; both remained in reserve. Before the Americans now lay Chapultepec, a castle on a large hill then just outside the city.

The Battle of Chapultepec was the last major battle in the Mexican War. The castle, then in use as a military academy, was lightly manned but heavily fortified. Scott's artillery softened the castle's defenses on September 12 and his infantry assaulted it the next day. The 3rd Infantry took up the right flank and ended the battle—and effectively the war—with a final bayonet charge up the hill. Scott pressed his advantage toward Mexico City, taking two gates by nightfall despite continued heavy resistance. At daybreak, however, the Americans realized that Mexican forces had fled the city overnight. The capital was theirs, and the war was over.

All that was left was to enter the city. In recognition of their valor, their sacrifice, and their heritage—and perhaps his fond memories dating back thirty-three years to the Battle of Lundy's Lane—Scott granted the 3rd Infantry the honor of leading the march into the city plaza. As they passed the reviewing stand, Scott instructed his staff, "Gentlemen, take your hats off to the Old Guard of the Army." And since that day, the 3rd Infantry Regiment has been known as The Old Guard.

And their nickname is not the only tradition carried forward by The Old Guard from the Mexican War. The regimental colors display eight campaign streamers from the war. In honor of its famous bayonet charge at Cerro Gordo, the 3rd Infantry is authorized to march with bayonets fixed to their rifles. The practice, unique in the Army, was first approved in 1922. In ceremonies today, Old Guard troops fix bayonets to the beat of a drum while the announcer tells the story of their forerunners' bravery in 1847.

After Mexico City, the regiment returned to its frontier roots in Texas, Kansas, and New Mexico. The Old Guard spent the turbulent 1850s building forts, protecting settlers, and skirmishing with Indians. By 1860, the regiment was based in Texas when Abraham Lincoln was elected president and the Civil War loomed.

The Civil War and Arlington

As 1861 dawned, The Old Guard found itself deep inside what had become enemy territory. Needing to escape, the regiment's dispersed companies marched separately toward the gulf coast. Some companies, warned of threats in San Antonio, marched defiantly down its main highway in full dress uniform with the band playing—not The Old Guard's last parade, to be sure, but perhaps its most audacious. Although the retreat was hasty and decentralized, and some companies were temporarily detained by Confederates, every Old Guard soldier reunited with the regiment, a testament to their professionalism and patriotism. Ultimately, The Old Guard arrived at a Virginia farm that had become a makeshift staging ground for Union forces—Arlington.

But Arlington was no ordinary farm. Already, it occupied a central place in the hearts of Americans as "Washington's Treasury," an unofficial memorial to the father of our country. Washington's adopted son—Jacky Custis, Martha Washington's son by her deceased first husband—had acquired the land in 1778 so he could raise his family near Mount Vernon, where he had grown up just a few miles down the Potomac River. Washington advised Jacky on the purchase even while still at Valley Forge that winter. But our country's final triumph in the Revolutionary War also shattered the family's dreams: Jacky accompanied Washington to the Battle of Yorktown in 1781 and died from a fever he contracted there.

Jacky's farm now passed to his six-month-old son and the great general's namesake: George Washington Parke Custis, known as Wash. Washington and Martha adopted the infant and raised him at Mount Vernon as well. Wash worshipped the only father he ever knew, lived through the first presidency with him, and then returned to Mount Vernon with his parents. After Washington died in 1799 and Martha in 1802, Wash's reverence turned into a lifelong mission to commemorate his adoptive father. Wash had just turned twenty-one and taken control of his estate, moving up the road to the farm he named Mount Washington.

The name, though, was only the beginning. He acquired from his sisters and others as many relics and heirlooms from Mount Vernon and Washington as he could. He also constructed a Greek

Revival mansion on the heights of Mount Washington, not merely as a home, but as a shrine to his namesake. The construction took sixteen years, but once complete the mansion with its vast columns appeared magnificent for miles into the new capital city, as it remains today from the Lincoln Memorial and Memorial Bridge. Although Wash renamed the farm Arlington after an ancestral Custis estate, his home nevertheless served as a kind of public memorial to Washington, with a steady flow of visitors and well-wishers.

Arlington welcomed a new resident in 1831 when then-Lieutenant Robert E. Lee married Wash's only surviving child, Mary. Lee himself came from a distinguished family with its own direct ties to Washington. His father was Washington's trusted cavalry commander in the Revolutionary War and had eulogized Washington at his funeral with the famous line "first in war, first in peace, first in the hearts of his countrymen." For thirty years, Lee and Mary made a life together at Arlington. They raised seven children in Arlington House, the home to which they returned between his assignments and for most Christmases and winters. Lee also spent two years turning around Arlington's woeful finances after Wash died in 1857. In early 1861, like The Old Guard, Lee was stationed on the Texas frontier when his old commander from the Mexican War and by then general-in-chief of the Army, Winfield Scott, recalled him to the nation's capital.

Scott had long esteemed Lee as "the very best soldier that I ever saw in the field" and intended to offer him command of the Union Army. Moreover, Lincoln and his political advisors believed that Lee's fame and his influence in Virginia might undercut support for secession in that critical state. Thus, on April 18, 1861, Lee reached the pinnacle of his career—offered command of an army on the verge of a great war, an opportunity to rival Washington himself in the Revolutionary War. But Lee declined on the spot. Though he opposed secession, his loyalty always ran to Virginia over the nation. A disappointed Scott scolded, "Lee, you have made the greatest mistake of your life, but I feared it would be so."

The Virginia convention voted to secede the next day, forcing the decision upon Lee. He paced around Arlington House's garden and on its grand porch, with the Capitol visible in the distance. After dark, he paced his bedroom, as Mary and the family listened and waited downstairs. The pacing stopped when he sat to write a one-sentence letter of resignation and a longer letter to Scott. "Save in the defense of my native State," he concluded, "I never desire to again draw my sword."

Lee had sealed Arlington's fate. Word of his resignation spread quickly. Confederate leaders summoned him to Richmond. He departed Arlington on April 22—never to return.

The Union occupation of Arlington was only a matter of time. Anyone who has stood at Arlington House and looked across the Potomac to the National Mall—even more so, on Whipple Field at Fort Myer—can see that it occupies the commanding heights above Washington. Confederate artillery could range much of the capital from Arlington. While Mary hesitated to leave her lifelong home, Lee importuned her to flee as well. She eventually acceded to his wishes, leaving behind much of the "Washington Treasury," locked away in the attic and cellar. On May 15, Mary departed her home, handing the keys—and symbolic authority for Arlington House—to Selina Gray, a trusted slave who managed the house.

The United States Army occupied Arlington on May 24, 1861—and it has held the ground ever since.

At first, the Army respected the old shrine to General Washington, whose legacy its officers carried in their hearts. Scott ordered the occupying forces to prevent harm to Arlington House. Brigadier General Irvin McDowell, the Union commander and an old associate of Lee, wrote with such assurances to Mary within a week. McDowell even pitched a tent on the lawn, rather than reside in her home. He also assisted Gray in protecting the "Washington Treasury." When she later protested that his troops had pilfered the relics, he crated and moved the rest to the Patent Office for safekeeping. Some damage occurred, of course, as soldiers trampled the fields, dug latrines, foraged for lumber, and so forth, but the Union troops—including The Old Guard—minimized their impact as they staged at Arlington in the early days of the war.

While at Arlington, The Old Guard combined with other regular infantry units under the command of Major George Sykes, who had fought alongside them in the Mexican War. These soldiers called themselves and became known as "Sykes' Regulars," a contrast to the state-based regiments that predominated in the Union Army. Over the next two years The Old Guard would fight with its fellow regulars in the major battles in the Eastern theater, all the way through Gettysburg. Union commanders often held them in reserve while starting the fight with the state-based regiments. Thus, the regulars could be a decisive force in a battle—or, less gloriously, cover a Union retreat.

In their first mission together, the regulars prevented the disastrous Union defeat at the Battle of Bull Run on July 21 from turning into a catastrophe. Union forces seized the initiative at first, but the Confederates counterattacked. The inexperienced Union troops broke and fled in an uncontrolled retreat. When Confederate troops threatened to cut off the fleeing army, the regulars held their ground and provided covering fire to protect the Union retreat. Many Union forces staggered the twenty-five miles back to Arlington after the battle, while Sykes commended his regulars for setting "an example of constancy and discipline worthy of older and more experienced soldiers." Likewise, McDowell praised the regulars to Lincoln during a review of troops a few days later as "the men who saved your army at Bull Run."

The Battle of Bull Run was the bloodiest day in American history to that point, but merely a foretaste of the slaughter to come. The shocking result and the poor performance of the Union Army undermined public confidence that the war would end quickly and easily. For nearly a year, the war was largely silent in the East. Both sides focused on recruiting, training, and equipping their armies. As these new soldiers trained, Old Guard troops served on military police duty around the capital.

At Arlington, meanwhile, Bull Run ended the Union's gentility toward Lee's home. The defeat exposed the capital to a Confederate attack that, though it never came, transformed Arlington. Forts, trenches, embankments, and roads all sprung up. The soldiers felled Arlington's virgin timber for these fortifications, and for stables, lodging, and firewood as winter approached.

The defeat also cost Arlington its chief protectors in the Union Army. McDowell was replaced and Scott resigned a few months later. At the same time, Brigadier General Montgomery Meigs had become the Quartermaster General. In early 1862, Edwin Stanton became the Secretary of War. Many Union officers had served with the Confederate generals in Mexico or on the frontier and they often sympathized with their Southern counterparts. Not Meigs and Stanton. They detested the Confederates, viewing secession as simple treason. And they particularly loathed Lee as a traitor. Together, they plotted in the years ahead to prevent Lee from ever returning to Arlington.

———

The fighting renewed in 1862, with The Old Guard participating in the failed Peninsula Campaign of Major General
George McClellan, the new Union commander. The offensive
against Richmond started with the army moving by ship to Fort
Monroe—incidentally, built by a young Lee on his first assignment after marrying Mary. From there, McClellan's forces encountered light resistance on the march up to the outskirts of
Richmond. But the Battle of Seven Pines on May 31 and June 1
halted McClellan's momentum. As important, the Confederate
commanding general was wounded at Seven Pines and replaced
by Lee, who launched a series of counterattacks against the cau-
tious McClellan. From June 25 to July 1, the Seven Days Battles compelled McClellan to retreat from Richmond. The Old
Guard, until then held largely in reserve, stopped Confederate
advances at the Battle of Gaines' Mill on June 27 and the Battle
of Malvern Hill on July 1, holding the line once again to enable
a Union retreat.

With the threat to Richmond neutralized, Lee marched north
to attack the Union forces in northern Virginia. The regulars
followed not far behind. They arrived as reinforcements for the
third and final day of the Second Battle of Bull Run. The Old
Guard joined an assault on the Confederate lines late on August 30, which failed in the face of a massive counterattack. The
regiment and other regulars fell back and covered another Union
withdrawal from almost exactly the same ground they had held
a year earlier. McDowell, again retreating from the battlefield at
Bull Run under the cover of The Old Guard, called out as he
passed, "God bless the regulars!"

Lee now had the strategic initiative and invaded Union territory for the first time. He needed food and supplies, and he
also believed the invasion could influence the midterm election,
which might lead to a negotiated peace. But McClellan surprised

Lee with his rapid pursuit. They clashed in the Battle of Antietam on September 17, the bloodiest day of the war, with more than twenty-two thousand casualties.

McClellan halted Lee's invasion but again failed to press his advantage. He kept The Old Guard and other regulars in reserve all day, even declining their request to join the fight. Had McClellan gone for the jugular, the regulars might have cut off Lee's only path for retreat across the Potomac and destroyed his army. Instead, Lee escaped across the river—The Old Guard chased him until driven back by Confederate artillery—and regrouped his forces. Tired of McClellan's caution, Lincoln removed him from command a few weeks later.

But the new commander, Major General Ambrose Burnside, led his army into a senseless bloodbath at the Battle of Fredericksburg. Like McClellan, he decided to march on Richmond instead of attacking Lee's army, which Lincoln preferred. He approached Fredericksburg by mid-November, but waited three weeks for pontoon boats to cross the Rappahannock River. Lee thus had time to prepare his defenses, waiting until Burnside's army crossed the river and attacked on December 13. After a morning of inconclusive fighting south of the city, Burnside ordered frontal assaults repeatedly against Confederate artillery and infantry on the high ground west of the city. The Union forces were predictably slaughtered; in fact, the battle prompted Lee's famous observation, "It is well that war is so terrible, or we should grow too fond of it." Again held in reserve, the regulars crossed the river in the late afternoon to establish a defensive line against a potential Confederate counterattack. Through the night and the next day, The Old Guard covered yet another inglorious retreat of Union forces.

By early 1863, both armies had hunkered down for the winter outside Fredericksburg. On the Union side, Major General Joseph Hooker had replaced Burnside. Lee's forces, though they had fought well over the last year, now suffered supply shortages and were outnumbered by more than two-to-one. Lee was running out of time and this coming year of battle would prove fateful for him, and The Old Guard as well.

The fighting season in the East started with the Battle of Chancellorsville in early May. The battle is sometimes called Lee's "greatest victory" or "perfect battle." Hooker had planned a massive flanking maneuver to get behind and envelop Lee's army. When the battle began, the regulars, including The Old Guard, finally took the lead and fought very well against Lee's forces. But Hooker hesitated, ordering them to fall back to defensive positions. Lee exploited Hooker's indecision with the same audacity he had displayed at Cerro Gordo and Contreras in the Mexican War, dividing his outnumbered forces to conduct bold flanking attacks three times in four days. On each occasion, the Confederates drove back the Union Army until it finally retreated across the river.

After the Union's humiliating defeat at Chancellorsville, Lee again seized the strategic initiative. He covertly slipped away from Fredericksburg, marching through the Shenandoah Valley into the North for a second time. By late June, Lee's army had reached southern Pennsylvania. Hooker gave chase until Lincoln replaced him with General George Meade, who received the president's consistent but oft-neglected instructions: locate and destroy Lee's army. Realizing that Union forces were closing in on him, Lee consolidated his widely dispersed army a few miles northwest of a small town called Gettysburg. Meade's army approached from the south and east, cutting off a possible retreat. The commander-in-chief would get the decisive confrontation he had long desired: the Battle of Gettysburg.

The epic battle, the bloodiest of the Civil War, lasted from

July 1 to July 3. The Old Guard was absent on the first day. Like many regiments on both sides, it was still marching to the battlefield. As they marched, the numerically superior Confederate troops eventually broke the Union lines and forced the Union troops to retreat south of Gettysburg.

Overnight, Meade and the rest of his army arrived and established a defensive line—the famous "Fish Hook"—that would define the rest of the battle. The Union defenses ran along the high ground of Cemetery Ridge from the two Round Top hills on the south to Culp's Hill on the northeast. In response, Lee planned to attack the Union's two flanks, first near the Round Tops and then near Culp's Hill, while keeping the Union center engaged to prevent Meade from reinforcing his flanks.

The Old Guard started July 2 assigned to the center, but an ill-advised decision by Major General Daniel Sickles fatefully shifted the regiment's mission that day. Without Meade's approval, Sickles moved his corps off Cemetery Ridge to what he considered more advantageous terrain to the west. But Sickles had created a weakened salient that Lee attacked aggressively. Momentum shifted throughout the afternoon, as the Confederates threatened to take Cemetery Ridge, only to be repelled by Union forces such as Colonel Joshua Chamberlain's 20th Maine Regiment and its famous bayonet charge at Little Round Top.

Meade rushed reinforcements to his southern flank, including The Old Guard. Along with other regulars, the regiment fought late in the day in the Wheatfield, which earned the nickname "Bloody Wheatfield" due to the ferocity of the combat. The Old Guard took heavy casualties—more than one-quarter of its troops—but bought precious time for more Union forces to reinforce the Fish Hook before the regiment fell back to Little Round Top. A volunteer soldier, observing from that high ground, later wrote, "For two years, the regulars taught us how to fight like soldiers. At the Wheatfield at Gettysburg, they taught us how to die like soldiers."

Despite more Confederate attacks on the opposite flank near Culp's Hill, as the sun set on July 2, the Union lines on the Fish Hook had held, setting up the final day of battle. The Old Guard remained in the vicinity of Little Round Top on July 3, but did not see significant action. The regiment's weary soldiers listened as the Union forces turned back another attack around Culp's Hill in the morning. And The Old Guard watched that afternoon as their brothers-in-arms defeated Pickett's Charge, the famous and final assault by Lee. The Battle of Gettysburg was over, as was Lee's second invasion of the North.

And while the war was far from over, major combat was over for The Old Guard. Two years of brutal fighting from First Bull Run to its small but valiant part at Gettysburg had inflicted heavy casualties on the regiment. The Old Guard had fewer than two hundred men remaining, and these losses were not easy to replace for a regular, or federal, infantry regiment. Much of the Union Army was raised through state governments—hence names like the 20th Maine. When a state-based regiment took high casualties, the state usually created a whole new regiment, which absorbed the surviving remnants of its older regiment. But this practice did not work for regular regiments like The Old Guard— the 3rd *United States* Infantry—especially after Gettysburg.

Federal troops were needed in New York because of draft riots, however, and The Old Guard deployed there shortly after Gettysburg. A new military-draft law—the nation's first, and one that allowed the rich to buy their way out of the draft—sparked the riots, which remain the worst civil disorder in American history and form the backdrop of the movie *Gangs of New York*. When the rioters overwhelmed the police, Lincoln deployed several regiments to restore order, including The Old Guard. Though it did not arrive until August, after the riots had stopped, The Old Guard patrolled the tense streets for three weeks. And while this was the first time The Old Guard deployed to gain control over civil unrest, it would not be the last.

The regiment briefly rejoined Meade's command, now back in Virginia, but after the horrors of Chancellorsville and Gettysburg that summer, neither side's army had much fight left in it. Both commanders also sent multiple corps to their fellow commanders in the Western theater. While they probed each other's lines, there were no more significant battles in 1863 in the East before both armies went to winter quarters.

The Old Guard did not remain for the winter, returning instead to New York, where it garrisoned Forts Richmond, Hamilton, and Columbus on the harbor. The Old Guard stayed in New York for most of 1864, a contingency force against more civil disorder. Thus, the regiment missed the horrific combat that year in which Ulysses S. Grant, now a general who had taken command of all Union armies, gradually ground down Lee's army. That gruesome year of combat also fostered the conditions that led to the creation of our national cemetery.

Throughout 1862 and 1863, Stanton and Meigs had continued to transform Arlington to foreclose Lee's return, especially after the second rout at Bull Run. About one thousand yards west of Arlington House, Fort Whipple was constructed as part of the Arlington Line, an interlocking series of fortifications to protect the capital from attack. (After the war, the Army retained Fort Whipple and later renamed it Fort Myer, the future home of The Old Guard.) The Army also built huge stables and constructed a hospital on the high ground. And Stanton directed the construction of a Freedmen's Village for the benefit of slaves freed by the Emancipation Proclamation. Few missed the symbolism of such a village on the land of the Confederate commander.

But Stanton and Meigs's masterstroke against Lee rested on the war's awful reality: death on a vast, unimaginable scale. The Civil War remains our bloodiest war by far—rivaling the aggregate deaths from all our other wars combined. Battlefields like Gettysburg, Chancellorsville, Shiloh, and Antietam saw more Americans die than have perished in the entire Iraq or Afghanistan Wars.

As Quartermaster General, Meigs bore responsibility for the burial of the Union's war dead. With the capital's cemeteries reaching capacity and Grant's brutal Overland Campaign just beginning, Meigs's department selected Arlington as a new cemetery. On May 13, 1864, Private William Christman became the first soldier buried at Arlington, in the northeast corner, with more to follow in the coming days.

Yet Meigs did not merely want to create a cemetery—he wished to punish Lee and forever prevent his return. On June 15, he wrote to Stanton for approval to establish a national cemetery around Arlington House and suggested "that the bodies recently interred be removed to the National Cemetery." Stanton, whose hatred of Lee rivaled Meigs's, ratified the proposal that very same day.

Meigs struggled at first to execute his plan. "It was my intention to have begun the interments near the mansion," Meigs later wrote, "but opposition on the part of officers stationed at Arlington" interfered with the plan as they turned away the burial crews. They did not want to live among the dead any more than Lee would have. Meigs ultimately took matters in his own hands, personally overseeing the interment of twenty-six soldiers on the edge of Mary Lee's garden. He also evicted the recalcitrant officers and assigned chaplains to Arlington House instead.

———

Private William Christman was the first soldier interred at Arlington on May 13, 1864. One hundred fifty-five years later, visitors still place rocks and mementos on his headstone to mark their visit and honor his memory.

As the war reached its conclusion, The Old Guard returned to Washington in October and then joined Grant's headquarters in February 1865. Therefore, the regiment witnessed at Appomattox Court House the surrender of their old scout from Cerro Gordo and Contreras. With Lee vanquished, the Civil War finally ended. The Old Guard had suffered more than 250 casualties, equal to its average strength during the war. For its service during the Civil War, The Old Guard added twelve more streamers to its regimental colors.

All that remained was the grand review in Washington of the Union Army. In recognition of its history and contributions during the war, The Old Guard led the infantry column during the parade. After this celebration of the soldiers who saved the Union, the state regiments demobilized and returned to their homes. For the professional soldiers of the regular infantry regiments, however, there was no homecoming. Before year's end, The Old Guard had returned to frontier duty.

Yet, the story of Arlington National Cemetery's creation did not end with the Civil War. Meigs executed one final blow against Lee's potential return to Arlington. He ordered the transfer of more than two thousand unknown remains to Arlington, where they were reinterred in a large pit, twenty feet deep and round, right next to Mary Lee's garden. The Civil War Unknown Monument sits above the sealed pit, designed by Meigs himself and easily visible from Arlington House. The mastermind of our national cemetery keeps eternal watch over its first tomb for unknown soldiers from his grave site in Section 1—just a short walk down Meigs Drive.

Meigs and Stanton went to such lengths to block Lee's return to Arlington partly because they worried about the government's legal claim to the land. Their concerns explain Meigs's efforts "to more firmly secure the grounds known as the National Cemetery, to the Government by rendering it undesirable as a future residence or homestead," as one aide described the plan. If the government's claim failed as a legal matter, they wanted to undermine Lee's claim as a practical and political matter. The postwar dispute over Arlington not only confirmed their fears, but also vindicated their strategy, ending with a poignant moment of reconciliation for a still-divided nation.

They had good reason to doubt the government's claim to Arlington. Congress had imposed a wartime tax on rebel lands and landowners had to pay the tax in person—hardly possible for the Lees. They instead sent Lee's cousin, whom the tax commissioners turned away. When the government put the property up for sale in January 1864, it was the sole bidder—perhaps because shrewd businessmen recognized the cloud on the title.

After the war, the Lees explored the possibility of reclaiming Arlington, but failed. Lee understood the political sensitivity of the former rebel commander attempting to evict Union war dead from the new cemetery. He discreetly consulted with lawyers, but took no further action before his death in 1870. Mary had no such reserve. Within two months of Lee's death, a friendly senator introduced legislation on her behalf to explore the possibility of disinterring more than sixteen thousand remains so she could return to Arlington. Republican senators, many of whom had fought for the Union, virulently denounced the proposal to benefit "the family of the traitor" and "a traitor's widow" and voted it down, fifty-four to four. Mary would not regain her family home before she died in 1873.

It was left to the Lees' oldest son, who inherited Arlington, to carry on the family's claim. A Confederate soldier himself, his full name nevertheless reflected the nation's deep roots at Arlington: George Washington Custis Lee. Custis, as he was known, filed another petition with Congress, seeking only just compensation for the land, not any disinterments. But it went nowhere, so he turned to the courts. In 1877, he sued to evict as trespassers the cemetery's superintendent, Fort Whipple's commanding officer, and hundreds of freedmen. For five years, the Lees and the government clashed once again, this time through legal briefs and courtroom hearings. Finally, in *United States v. Lee*, the Supreme Court held that the tax sale had denied the Lees due process of law and upheld Custis's claim. After more than two decades, the controversy was finally settled. The Lee family once again owned Arlington.

Fortunately for the government, the nation, and the souls at rest in Arlington, Custis was magnanimous in victory. He did not attempt to evict anyone, living or dead, offering instead to negotiate a fair price, as he had first proposed to Congress. Within a few months, Custis deeded the land back to the government in return for $150,000.

And the Secretary of War who accepted the deed was Robert Todd Lincoln, the son of President Lincoln. Just eighteen years after their fathers had fought a terrible war against each other, the firstborn sons of the great president and his famed rebel antagonist acted in concert to establish America's national cemetery. With this final act of reconciliation, Arlington's dead could now rest in peace for eternity.

The Frontier Era—at Home and Abroad

Throughout these years of political and legal wrangling, The Old Guard had returned to its frontier origins. The regiment's first stop was St. Louis, where it nursed itself back to health after the brutal war, integrating six hundred new recruits to the ranks.

Over the next fifty years, The Old Guard marched forward as America stretched its frontiers across the West and ultimately around the world.

The first stop was Kansas and Indian Territory (modern-day Oklahoma), where for a decade the regiment's dispersed companies defended forts and fought Indians and outlaws. Though small and often lost to history, these skirmishes produced genuine heroism: in 1868, two Old Guard soldiers earned the Medal of Honor. Sergeant James Fegan earned the medal by repulsing, as the citation put it, "a party of desperadoes" who attacked his supply convoy in Kansas. Six months later, Corporal Leander Herron was delivering mail between Kansas forts when he and another soldier came to the aid of four soldiers under attack by fifty Indians. The other courier rode away to get reinforcements while Herron fought alongside the four wounded men through the night. The reinforcements arrived the next morning and all five men survived. Herron received the Medal of Honor fifty-one years later, just in time to serve as an official mourner for the burial of the Unknown Soldier at Arlington in 1921.

In the late 1870s, after a tour in Mississippi and Louisiana to enforce new civil-rights laws during Reconstruction, The Old Guard again headed to the frontier, this time to the Montana Territory. The Battle of Little Big Horn—more famously known as Custer's Last Stand—had occurred in 1876, with the destruction of George Custer's 7th Cavalry. The Army deployed more regulars to the territory to preserve order. Over the next decade, The Old Guard constructed a series of new forts to protect settlers throughout the territory.

By 1888, the regiment moved to Fort Snelling, just south of Minneapolis and St. Paul. The Old Guard now had its first base near a large city and its first long-term home—relatively speaking, since the regiment would spend about thirty of the next fifty years at Fort Snelling. Because of these ties between The Old Guard and Fort Snelling, locals called the regiment "Minnesota's Own" and accounted for many of its recruits in this era. During their first decade at Fort Snelling, The Old Guard continued to skirmish with Indian tribes in the Dakotas and northern Minnesota, while also training local militia, providing humanitarian relief after forest fires, and even participating in the 1893 World's Columbian Exhibition in Chicago. Fort Snelling was also The Old Guard's home station during its deployment, in 1898, to the nation's next conflict.

The Spanish–American War had its roots in the Cubans' struggle for independence from Spain, which President William McKinley tried to mediate, to no avail. He then dispatched the U.S.S. *Maine* in January 1898 to Havana Harbor, where it sank on February 15. The Navy concluded that the *Maine* had struck a mine, a finding that remains controversial to this day. Nevertheless, amid a public outcry Congress soon declared war against Spain. The lopsided war would end barely after it began.

The Old Guard departed Fort Snelling in April and sailed from Tampa in June with other regular army regiments for Santiago Bay in southeastern Cuba, home of the Spanish fleet. They disembarked about ten miles east of fortified Santiago under chaotic but unopposed conditions—reminiscent of the regiment's landing outside Veracruz a half century earlier. Within a few days, the American expeditionary forces had reached San Juan Heights, a little over one mile east of Santiago.

The Spanish forces proved no match for the Americans. The Old Guard missed the famous Battle of San Juan Hill on July 1, instead protecting the northern flank of San Juan by neutralizing a Spanish stronghold in the Battle of El Caney. By the next day, the American forces began to dig siege lines around Santiago, with The Old Guard on the left flank. The Spanish fleet tried to escape Santiago Bay on July 3, but could not avoid the American naval blockade. At that point, it was only a matter of time until Spanish leaders capitulated. The Americans occupied Santiago on July 17.

But the American expeditionary forces departed Cuba as quickly as they had deployed, to escape further casualties from the brutal Cuban heat and yellow fever. Following a brief medical quarantine on Long Island to screen for communicable diseases, The Old Guard returned home to Fort Snelling in September amid much celebration from the local community.

The Spanish–American War, despite its short duration, still reverberates in our world today. The Old Guard's regimental colors carry the Santiago campaign streamer. In Arlington, Old Guard soldiers pass the mast of the U.S.S. *Maine* every morning as they drive by a memorial to the ship's crew. And the United States gained new overseas possessions, which would expand America's global power and influence in the coming century.

But before The Old Guard could turn its attention to the twentieth century, it had one final battle to fight from the nineteenth century. Shortly after The Old Guard returned home, federal agents requested assistance in a dispute between local authorities and the Chippewa Indians near Leech Lake in northern Minnesota. The Old Guard deployed a small company, which engaged the Indians in a fierce firefight on a peninsula called Sugar Point. Seven soldiers died and ten were wounded. In the carnage, the company's medic repeatedly exposed himself to enemy fire as he tended to the wounded men. For his bravery, Private Oscar Burkard became the third Old Guard soldier to earn the Medal of Honor. And the Battle of Sugar Point was the last battle in more than a century of war between the Army and Indian tribes.

———

After fighting that final battle of the past, The Old Guard looked to its future—and America's—with its first deployment outside the Americas. Like the Cubans, the Filipinos had struggled for independence from Spain. When the Spanish–American War transferred sovereignty for the Philippines from Spain to the United States rather than grant independence to the island nation, the Philippine Army simply continued its fight, only now against the Americans. Over two deployments in the next decade, The Old Guard helped to end the insurrection and learned lessons still relevant today.

While The Old Guard set sail in February 1899 for the Philippines, the Americans there strengthened their hold on Manila in the middle of Luzon, the largest island in the archipelago. From that stronghold, the primary objective was securing the railroad running from Manila to Dagupan, on the island's northwest coast. The only railroad in the country, it was a vital supply line for the Filipinos. If American forces wanted to defeat the insurgents, they needed control of the railroad.

The Old Guard went straight to the front lines upon arrival, fighting in two of the early campaigns to take control of the railroad. The Malolos campaign succeeded in taking the insurgent capital just north of Manila Bay in late March 1899. But the campaign did not destroy the enemy army, partly because the mountainous terrain and jungles impeded large flanking maneuvers, the Americans' preferred style of attack. In the San Isidro campaign, therefore, American forces launched frontal assaults on the overmatched Filipinos. For six weeks in April and May, The Old Guard pushed northward to the secondary insurgent capital, San Isidro, until threats to their supply lines impeded their advance.

Such considerations marked the regiment's time in country. The Filipinos had learned the hard way that they could not stand and fight against the American forces. Thus, they dispersed throughout Luzon, disrupting the railroad, ambushing American troops, and hiding among a friendly population—all classic techniques of insurgent warfare. In response, American forces established small outposts across the island to secure their lines of communication and win over the civilian population, much as The Old Guard had done in Florida during the Seminole War and across the frontier for the previous century.

If all that sounds like Iraq and Afghanistan in the twenty-first century, that should not be surprising. The Army learned some of its first counterinsurgency lessons in the Philippines. Those lessons were largely forgotten, however, which is why I and other young officers in the early years of the Iraq War read about the Philippine Insurrection in obscure professional journals and hot-off-the-press books about counterinsurgency warfare. Until the Army made counterinsurgency the main effort in Iraq during the Surge of 2007, the lessons of history guided us as we led our soldiers in an old style of combat, which seemed new only to those unaware of that history.

Just as in Iraq, of course, this is not to say The Old Guard did not again see real combat in the Philippines. For instance, Captain James McRae earned the Silver Star in early 1900 while clearing the area around the railroad of insurgents. Such small offensive operations, often conducted at the platoon or even squad level, continued throughout 1900. While few missions made the history books, each built momentum for the counterinsurgency campaign. And there are no "small" or "minor" battles for those who fight them—to soldiers on the front lines, every firefight is their Gettysburg, their D-Day. By early 1901, the cumulative effect turned the civilian population against the insurgents and in favor of the Americans. The Old Guard faced its last hostile fire in April 1901 and returned home in March 1902.

But the regiment was not finished with the Philippines and the consequences of the Spanish–American War. The Old Guard moved around Kentucky, Ohio, Alaska, and Washington for seven years, developing new forts and connecting them with roads, cables, and telegraph lines. Then, in 1909, the regiment deployed for a second tour in the Philippines, this time to the large southern island of Mindanao and the Sulu Archipelago between Mindanao and Borneo. On this deployment, The Old Guard served under General John "Black Jack" Pershing, beginning the regiment's long association with the great general. The Old Guard and Pershing would cross paths many times, until the regiment laid him to rest in Arlington nearly forty years later.

For the last decade, American forces in the southern Philippines had faced a low-intensity, intermittent insurgency by the Moros, the Muslim peoples who had lived there for centuries. Today is not much different: Islamic radicalism remains a threat in this region and both al Qaeda and the Islamic State have operated there. The Old Guard thus encountered America's most recent enemy a century early.

On this second tour, The Old Guard built on the counterinsurgency lessons of its Luzon deployment. In one example, Moro pirates harassed shipping around the Dutch East Indies (modern-day Indonesia), imperiling American relations with the Dutch. Pershing took two Old Guard companies to Jolo, a small island in the extreme southwest of the Philippines known as an insurgent hotbed. Under his command, Old Guard soldiers captured the pirates, earning the gratitude of the Dutch Governor General. On another occasion, Pershing ordered the Moro rebels to disarm in late 1911, again facing resistance on Jolo. Pershing returned to the island with three Old Guard companies for a short and decisive campaign against insurgent camps. For three years in all, The Old Guard contributed to a measure of order in the region, while also building lessons for the future. And when the regiment returned stateside, it carried another five campaign streamers earned in the Philippines.

The World Wars

The Old Guard was destined to play supporting roles in the coming world wars. The Army remained very small in peacetime, as it had since the Revolutionary War. Thus, both world wars required millions of new recruits, trained specifically for those wars. As the only troops in active service as war approached, the old regulars often conducted that training or performed essential early missions. While these missions happened away from the front lines and out of the limelight, they were nonetheless critical to the overall war effort.

In World War I, The Old Guard deployed to the southern border to counter threats arising from the Mexican Revolution. In 1914, American troops had occupied Veracruz for seven months to stop abuses of Americans ashore and illicit weapons shipments. Two years later, Pancho Villa, a leading revolutionary, attacked a border town in New Mexico, which led to both The Old Guard's deployment and an expedition into Mexico in a failed attempt to capture Villa. And in 1917, the German government proposed an alliance with Mexico in the secret Zimmermann Telegram, promising to assist Mexico in recovering territories lost during the Mexican–American War. The Old Guard, like many regular Army units, therefore guarded the border throughout the war, again serving under Pershing.

Serving with The Old Guard was also a young officer named Matthew Ridgway, arguably the regiment's most famous veteran. Later in his career, he commanded paratroopers in Sicily and Normandy during World War II, turned the tide of the Korean War, replaced Dwight Eisenhower as Supreme Allied Commander in Europe, and finished his career as Chief of Staff of the Army. And in 1993, his old regiment laid Ridgway to rest in Section 7 of Arlington.

After World War I, The Old Guard finally returned to Fort Snelling. Following a brief detour to Ohio to assist with training and demobilization, the regiment lacked funds in the shrinking Army budget for transportation and thus conducted a legendary foot march of nearly one thousand miles back to their old home. The Old Guard then remained at Fort Snelling for two decades, again integrating into the Twin Cities community with parades and ceremonies. In a foreshadowing of its future, the regiment

Old Guard soldiers conduct machine-gun training at Fort Snelling for students in the Citizen Military Training Camp.

resurrected its colonial-era uniforms to celebrate its heritage. In 1922, the Army first approved the two distinctive customs still authorized for The Old Guard today: the buff strap to commemorate the regiment's service under "Mad Anthony" Wayne in the Northwest Indian Wars and the privilege of marching with bayonets fixed to celebrate their forerunners' bravery at Cerro Gordo.

This garrison era of calm and stability ended with World War II—and, for The Old Guard, almost a year before the bombing of Pearl Harbor. In 1940, President Franklin D. Roosevelt and British Prime Minister Winston Churchill reached the Destroyers for Bases Agreement, which transferred old American destroyers to Great Britain in return for American basing rights in Canada and the Caribbean. The agreement, a precursor to the Lend-Lease Act of 1941, allowed Roosevelt to support the British war effort while also preventing British colonies in the Western Hemisphere from falling into enemy hands if Germany conquered Great Britain, a real possibility as the Battle of Britain still raged. Newfoundland, in the extreme northeast of Canada, was a critical port for trans-Atlantic shipping and thus in need of defense. In early 1941, The Old Guard deployed to a new base just outside St. John's, chosen in part because of its experience at Fort Snelling in cold-weather operations. Once the Lend-Lease Act became law a few months later, Newfoundland also became a critical staging base for sending aircraft and ships to the European theater.

By 1943, the threat of German invasion had receded and American units fighting overseas needed frequent reinforcements. Many Old Guard troops deployed as replacements to get those units back to fighting strength, while the regiment itself moved stateside to assist in training new recruits at bases in North Carolina and Georgia. By late 1944, the regiment deployed to Europe as a result of the Battle of the Bulge. The surprise German offensive had destroyed entire regiments, so the Army sent whole regiments as replacements. The Old Guard helped to reconstitute the 106th Infantry Division. After brief engagements with holdout German forces in the Atlantic Wall along France's western coast, The Old Guard and the 106th moved to western Germany to oversee prisoner-of-war camps. In early 1946, they moved farther east to join the Allied occupation force in divided Berlin.

It was there, in Berlin, that Army bureaucrats accomplished what no enemy had achieved on the battlefield against The Old Guard for 162 years. Caught up in yet another wave of rapid, even haphazard, postwar demobilizations, The Old Guard was inactivated and its colors were cased and returned to the United States on November 20, 1946. But this would not last for long.

A New Beginning

Sixteen months later, the *Washington Post* ran a cryptic headline over a short story: "Top Men Sought for Military District Outfit." The story noted that applicants must be "at least 5 feet 9 inches in height and weigh at least 145 pounds but not over 200 pounds." In the days ahead, the *Post* revealed that "Washington's new palace guard" would be The Old Guard, which the Army had reactivated. Eighty-seven years since its first visit to Lee's farm, The Old Guard had a new home: among the heroes of Arlington.

In those years, Arlington had become the nation's sacred shrine for mourning and remembrance of all who served. At first a Civil War cemetery for Union war dead, Arlington over time had opened its gates to the veterans of past and future wars—and to Confederate veterans, in another gesture of national unity. The Tomb of the Unknown Soldier, dedicated in 1921, became a site for pilgrimage by the humblest citizens and foreign heads of state alike. The Memorial Bridge, which opened in 1932, symbolically linked Lee's old home with the Lincoln Memorial. And now, America's oldest regiment settled into the high ground of Fort Myer, the northwestern corner of Jacky Custis's land, from which it would stand sentry over our fallen heroes.

In the early days at its new home, two memorable events foreshadowed The Old Guard's new responsibilities for ceremonies and memorial affairs. First, The Old Guard rushed to reactivate for Army Day ceremonies on April 6, 1948. The Old Guard stood up, filled its ranks, and rehearsed in just five weeks—an extreme version of the last-minute, high-profile missions it gets today. After its activation ceremony on the East Plaza of the Capitol, The Old Guard had the honor of returning the "Flag of Liberation," which had flown over the Capitol on Pearl Harbor Day and was subsequently raised over the Axis capitals of Rome, Berlin, and Tokyo. The Old Guard presented the flag to the Speaker of the House and the President Pro Tempore of the Senate. From there, the regiment led the Army Day parade down Constitution Avenue—much as it had in 1865. They marched, as always, with bayonets fixed in honor of the Battle of Cerro Gordo. More than 150,000 people watched as the "Famed Third Marches Again," as the headline read the next day in the *Post*.

Then, three months later, the death of General Pershing highlighted The Old Guard's memorial-affairs mission. Since leading The Old Guard in Jolo and on the Mexican border, Pershing had earned immense fame for commanding the American Expeditionary Forces in Europe during World War I. He was promoted to General of the Armies, a rank he still shares with only George Washington. President Harry Truman, who had served under Pershing in Europe, ordered a state funeral and a period of national mourning. Pershing lay in state at the Capitol Rotunda before a funeral service at Arlington. Three hundred thousand mourners witnessed the funeral procession, which included more

After its reactivation ceremony on the East Plaza of the Capitol on April 6, 1948, The Old Guard presents the "Flag of Liberation" to the Speaker of the House and the President Pro Tempore of the Senate. The flag had flown over the Capitol on Pearl Harbor Day and was subsequently flown over Rome, Berlin, and Tokyo.

than a dozen generals who had served under him and matured into the heroes of World War II. Men like Dwight Eisenhower and Omar Bradley marched through the muggy heat and an afternoon downpour to honor the great general. And with Pershing every step was The Old Guard. The regiment stood vigil in the Rotunda and marched the four miles from the Capitol to

Arlington, where they conducted a brief ceremony at the Tomb of the Unknown Soldier before the service inside the Memorial Amphitheater.

The *Washington Post* called Pershing's funeral "the most impressive funeral procession Washington has seen since the Unknown Soldier was buried in 1921," in which Pershing himself had marched. Yet the day ended in humble fashion. Pershing had declined a special place of honor, asking for a standard headstone and a grave site he had chosen among his fellow World War I veterans. The Old Guard laid their old commander to rest in Section 34—or as it is known today, Pershing Hill—closing out a chapter from its past as it started a new one for its future.

The Old Guard has grown since these early days at Arlington, just as the cemetery itself has grown, but its missions have remained essentially the same. The regiment therefore did not fight the nation's wars for the rest of the century. Veterans of those wars joined The Old Guard, as I did, and Old Guard soldiers later fought in them, but the regiment itself did not deploy away from Arlington. Although the Army designated two of the many battalions created to fight in Vietnam as the 2nd and 4th Battalions of the 3rd Infantry, neither battalion served at Arlington and both were deactivated shortly after returning from Vietnam. Nonetheless, The Old Guard honors their service by flying their campaign streamers on the regimental colors. And the regimental headquarters is named in honor of Corporal Michael Folland, who served in Vietnam with 2nd Battalion and earned the Medal of Honor posthumously for jumping on a grenade to save his fellow soldiers.

Yet all was not quiet for The Old Guard in this era. The funeral of President John F. Kennedy ignited public interest in Arlington. For months, visitors lined up to see the Kennedy grave site and pay their respects. Likewise, more eligible veterans began to request burial in the cemetery. This increased demand is one reason why the old river-bottom farmland, which had remained an experimental government farm for years and then become the South Post of Fort Myer, finally joined Arlington's hills as part of the cemetery. And more burials, of course, meant more missions for The Old Guard.

The regiment also answered the call after the assassination of Dr. Martin Luther King Jr. on April 4, 1968, when riots broke out in more than one hundred cities, including Washington. The rioters and looters overwhelmed the local police, compelling President Lyndon Johnson to call out more than twelve thousand federal troops. For four days, "the Capital's crack ceremonial unit," as the *New York Times* called it, hung up its ceremonial uniforms and put on its tactical gear. Old Guard soldiers protected the White House from riots just two blocks away on 14th Street, assisted other troops arriving at Andrews Air Force Base, and ultimately restored order.

The riots disrupted life in the nation's capital, but one thing was not disrupted: military funerals at Arlington. Even as hundreds of Old Guard soldiers shuttled daily across the Potomac River, others remained at Fort Myer to conduct funerals. Then, as now, memorial affairs was a no-fail mission for The Old Guard. The regiment will work around, reschedule, or cancel its other activities to ensure that every funeral in the cemetery is performed on time and to standard. Even as smoke filled the air across the river during the riots, our nation's veterans received the honors in death that they had earned in life.

9/11 and The Old Guard

The Old Guard maintains the funeral-first standard to this day. Even on 9/11, as Col. Jim Laufenburg rushed his troops to the

Pentagon, the regiment still performed funerals as scheduled in Arlington. But everything else changed for The Old Guard on that day and in the following month while its soldiers worked around the clock at the crash site.

The Old Guard performed three basic missions during its month at the Pentagon. First, it conducted what Col. Laufenburg called "internal security." The site needed to be secured not only from the outside, but also on the inside from Pentagon personnel. Many survivors wanted to get personal effects and papers from their offices. But the Pentagon was still a crime scene and still dangerous. Old Guard soldiers were therefore posted in the hallways just beyond the crash site. Col. Laufenburg observed that as a general rule the higher the rank, the more the survivor wanted back into his old office. He grinned when recalling that the regiment "had specialists and privates telling colonels and generals that they couldn't go to their office. I was proud of those guys."

Second, Old Guard soldiers assisted in the search-and-recovery operations for remains inside the Pentagon. This work was the most physically demanding and thus had to be assigned to infantrymen. Gen. James Jackson recalled that it was still hot that September and the soldiers had to wear sterile Tyvek suits, gloves, and boots to protect against biohazards, asbestos, and other pollutants. "We needed able-bodied people because there was no other way to do this," he explained, "it had to be manpower." The Old Guard provided that manpower, freeing up the military's mortuary-affairs personnel to focus on their very rare, specialized skills.

Old Guard leaders from that period recalled the backbreaking nature of the work, but also the high morale of their troops. According to First Sergeant Steven Stokes of Charlie Company, carrying out the remains in water, over rubble, and through a jungle of wires "was very, very physically demanding" and required "human chains" of soldiers to pass the remains out of the wreckage. But he stressed that the main limiting factor was not his soldiers' stamina or motivation but the limited number of sterile suits and respirators. He even had a soldier return from being absent without leave, knowing that he faced a court-martial, yet the soldier "worked like a dog." Captain William Besterman, the Alpha Company commander, offered his soldiers a chance to opt out if anyone could not handle the mission. No one quit. Afterward, he said, "I'm very proud of the way the soldiers in this company worked together down there, and it was a difficult job. It wasn't really pleasant, especially in the middle of the night."

This kind of work takes a toll on a soldier, and not only the soldier. Col. Laufenburg recalled the strain on his soldiers' families, and one stress in particular:

> It was about a week into us rotating down there and dealing with body parts and body bags and the blood and guts and all that stuff like that. And through the wives' channel, I had a complaint surface to my level. And the complaint was, "Can't you do something when my husband comes off of a shift? He smells like death." What we ended up doing was cutting a contract with one of the local dry-cleaning places. We said, "Before you go home, you will bag up all your uniforms, you'll take it to the local dry cleaner who will have it laundered for you and you will take a shower." I guess those are things when you're in command, you don't necessarily think of.

The Old Guard's final mission was debris removal and sorting, which was more emotionally draining than it sounds. After removing identifiable human remains from the crash site, Old Guard soldiers and others moved debris in bulk to the Pentagon's north parking lot. Then the soldiers had to "walk through the debris looking for personal effects and remains," as Col. Laufenburg explained, aided by cadaver dogs. And they had to look for all the little things that make a life worth living. Captain Lance Green, the Honor Guard Company commander, recalled that "there were so many coffee cups, personalized coffee cups in there. Stuffed animals, framed pictures, planners, personal planners, name plates for desks, stuff like that. That was probably the worst thing." These personal effects were collected and sent to a building on Fort Myer for families to search for reminders of their lost loved ones.

After a month on duty at the Pentagon, The Old Guard participated in a ceremony to retire the giant flag that had hung from the roof and returned to its normal schedule of funerals and ceremonies. When asked about The Old Guard's performance, Gen. Jackson replied, "I was not surprised. The Old Guard performed like they perform everywhere else. They came down and they saw a real-world mission, and they went to it. It's what you would expect from them." Once again, America's history and The Old Guard's history intersected at a turning point. 1st Sgt. Stokes probably spoke for the entire regiment when he said, "I'm glad I was there to help. It was definitely a huge part of American history, and makes you feel good that you could go down there and help."

Although The Old Guard returned to Fort Myer as their fellow soldiers deployed to Afghanistan, the regiment has not spent the War on Terror only at Arlington. By the summer of 2003, the growing insurgency in Iraq and the war in Afghanistan were straining the Army. The pattern of rash downsizing that dated back to the Revolutionary War—and contributed to the creation of The Old Guard—had recurred after the Cold War, again leaving the Army with too few soldiers. The Army therefore stretched its forces in unconventional ways. As a result, for the first time in its modern history, The Old Guard deployed its troops overseas, a testament to the regiment's heritage and its continued readiness to perform any mission when the nation calls.

Over the coming seven years, a company from The Old Guard deployed in support of the War on Terror on three separate occasions. The first two deployments were to Camp Lemonnier in Djibouti, a tiny but strategically located country on the Horn of Africa. Bravo Company deployed from December 2003 to July 2004 and Delta Company from March 2007 to June 2008. Old Guard soldiers provided security for Camp Lemonnier and for civil-affairs and other humanitarian missions in Djibouti and nearby countries. They also trained the local security forces and conducted their own training, learning skills like rappelling and desert survival. In the third deployment, Charlie Company went to Camp Taji just north of Baghdad from August 2009 to August 2010. Charlie had responsibility for the prison on the sprawling base, much like the regiment's occupation duty in the aftermath of World War II.

These deployments took the companies out of Arlington for more than just their time overseas. Sergeant First Class Stan Villiers was my platoon sergeant before I deployed to Afghanistan in 2008, and he remained in that role for Charlie's Iraq deployment. He recalled that "we spent at least two months, probably more, training up on unit-level infantry tasks and basic detainee operations." On the back side, when the companies returned to Fort Myer, the soldiers had to recertify on individual and collective tasks before they could return to funerals and ceremonies. Fortunately, one thing Charlie did not have to do was start from scratch on their ceremonial uniforms. "We had hung them up neatly in the press room and locked it down for the whole deployment,"

*Soldiers from Bravo Company conduct a live-fire training exercise during
their deployment to Djibouti.*

Sfc. Villiers explained. "They were in pretty good shape when we
got back, just required some touch-up."

Meanwhile, back at Arlington, these deployments put stress
on The Old Guard's other companies. My tour at Arlington

coincided almost exactly with Delta's deployment, so I lived through the impact. Without Delta, only Bravo and Charlie were routinely available for funerals; the other companies occasionally performed funerals, but their priority mission was ceremonies. And because daily funerals often require more than one full company, we struggled to complete missions or tasks besides funerals and ceremonies. For instance, our tactical proficiency slipped because of the difficulty of getting to Fort A. P. Hill for training exercises.

Of course, these stresses could not compare to the stress faced by Delta Company overseas and away from their families for fifteen months, much less what soldiers faced in combat in Iraq and Afghanistan. When the consecutive weeks in the cemetery piled up, I sometimes reminded my soldiers of what other soldiers deployed overseas faced every day. Not that it was really necessary. For most soldiers, keeping faith with our battle buddies, carrying more than one's share of the load, helping out a buddy in need—these are the things that motivate soldiers to keep going when the going gets tough. No one wants to let down the soldier on his left and right.

The Old Guard has another reminder of its purpose in front of its soldiers every day. At each funeral, a family is about to say good-bye to a fellow soldier. Just as every soldier wants to do right by his battle buddies, Old Guard soldiers want to give those soldiers' families a moment of perfection to remember.

And finally, The Old Guard's own illustrious heritage inspires its soldiers every day. All those campaign streamers atop the regimental colors, from Fallen Timbers to Iraq, flutter as a reminder that The Old Guard's history of battlefield valor predates even the storied divisions of the world wars. Every soldier, from the most junior private to the regimental commander, wears the buff strap in honor of the regiment's colonial roots. Old Guard soldiers march with bayonets fixed to commemorate the gallant charge up the hills of Cerro Gordo. And all this happens on the sacred ground of old Arlington, with its deep ties to George Washington, Robert E. Lee, and the Civil War.

To my knowledge, no other unit in our military has such constant reminders of its heritage, of the traditions and standards its soldiers are expected to uphold. Not many Old Guard soldiers understand these things when they report to Fort Myer and start their training; they mostly know about the regiment's modern ceremonial mission. But none can fail to learn of its storied past, and all soon feel the pride that comes with serving in The Old Guard of the Army.

3

"Honor, Values, and Tradition"

I stared at the treetops swaying in the breeze on the far side of Summerall Field, the main parade ground on Fort Myer. "I must be getting close to the end," I thought. I had been standing motionless for what seemed like hours. I was conducting a standing-proficiency test, which required me to stand at attention, completely still, for seventy-five minutes.

It was a beautiful morning in May 2007, a day toward which I had worked since reporting to Fort Myer two months earlier. Every Old Guard soldier must pass a battery of tests to be certified to perform funerals in Arlington National Cemetery and to march in ceremonies. The standing-proficiency test was the first and least understood outside The Old Guard. "How hard can it be to just stand there?" was a question I heard more than once.

"Just standing there" is harder than it sounds. Blood flow to the brain slows down when one stands in a single position for even a few minutes. Passing out is a real possibility. And among the worst sins at The Old Guard is falling out of a funeral or ceremony, doubly so for officers standing alone in front of their troops. Thus, the standing-proficiency test is a rite of passage at The Old Guard, and the officer's seventy-five-minute trial is one of the longest.

Not that I worried much about the physical demands of a long stand. I started running marathons before I joined the Army, which prepared me well for its most demanding physical rigors. I went into Ranger School at the peak of marathon training, I ran a race right before I deployed to Iraq, and I had completed the Boston Marathon just a few weeks before this standing-proficiency test. Though never the biggest or strongest soldier, I excelled in tests of stamina and mental toughness.

And mental toughness was necessary to maintain ceremonial composure for seventy-five minutes. Ceremonial composure, a watchword at The Old Guard, is the ability to stand ramrod still, no matter the circumstances. A common reason to fail a standing-proficiency test is moving to get the blood flowing. The slightest shift of the feet or flexing of the knees can end the test. Ceremonial composure also extends to external distractions. Sweat roll into your eye? Fly land on your nose? Car alarm go off? So much as a flinch is a break in ceremonial composure, end of test. My grader still lurked somewhere behind me, watching.

As I stood there, staring at those swaying treetops, I reflected on what brought me to this strange moment. 9/11 was almost six years past. I had joined the Army because of those attacks, and I had already been to Baghdad and back. Now it was the height of the Surge in Iraq, with more than one hundred troops killed in action this month, some being laid to rest just beyond those trees in Arlington. I wanted to honor their ultimate sacrifice for our nation, and these tests were all that stood between me and the cemetery.

"I can stand here for as long as it takes," I thought to myself, without moving a muscle.

★ ★ ★

The Old Guard is a unique unit in the Army, with unique practices and customs. I had not heard of a standing-proficiency test until I arrived at The Old Guard, nor am I aware of other units requiring one. No other Army unit besides The Old Guard wears colonial-era uniforms—or "wigs and tights," as we called them. The Old Guard has the Army's only full-time equine unit. I could give more examples, but perhaps the best comes from The Old Guard's table of organization and equipment. Every Army unit has a table, which lays out its allotment of personnel, weapons, and equipment, plus the number of such units in the higher head-quarters. Colonel Joe Buche, the regimental commander in my day, enjoys pointing out that The Old Guard's table states "one per United States Army."

Because of its special status, The Old Guard gets outstanding soldiers. One of the Army's few all-volunteer units, the regiment has some of the Army's highest physical, mental, and moral stan-dards. Officers and sergeants must apply and must have demon-strated superior performance in their previous assignment. New privates must satisfy the same exacting standards. A consistent theme among Old Guard leaders, who have all served in the Army outside the regiment, is the intelligence, maturity, and discipline of their soldiers. My soldiers were certainly top-notch, up there with my platoon from the 101st Airborne.

The Old Guard is unique in another, ironic way given the cali-ber of its soldiers: not a single soldier is trained to execute its core missions when they arrive at Fort Myer. The Old Guard's uni-forms are unique and uniquely varied. The regiment's marching style is distinct and unlike anything else in the Army. No matter the rank, every new soldier must spend weeks in training and pass several tests before becoming a full-fledged member of the Army's oldest active-duty infantry regiment.

Along the way, Old Guard soldiers learn more than how to press a uniform or march at a ceremony—they learn why these things matter. "It's a difficult thing for a young private to under-stand," Colonel Jason Garkey, the regimental commander, said of The Old Guard's mission. New soldiers sometimes think The Old Guard performs the same funeral or ceremony over and over again. But in reality, he said, "we do a series of firsts here. The family only gets one funeral. The family only gets one retirement ceremony." Old Guard soldiers "uphold the honor, values, and tradition of those who came before me," in the words of the regimental creed, as a tribute to our nation's fallen, its warriors, their families, and our common heritage of freedom for which they sacrificed.

Joining The Old Guard

The Old Guard's eligibility standards exceed the Army's basic criteria because of the sensitivity and prominence of its missions. The Army leadership wants to showcase strong and disciplined soldiers to the public, and the families of the fallen deserve our very best. Further, Old Guard soldiers often operate at high-profile locations in small teams on decentralized missions without senior leaders, which requires mature, responsible soldiers. The Old Guard is therefore one of the rare Army units composed only of applicants and volunteers.

Aspiring Old Guard soldiers must satisfy physical and character requirements. Male soldiers must be between five-ten and six-four (or five-eight and six-two for women) and meet Army weight standards. The height standards can be waived—I am six-five—but usually only upward, and weight standards are not waived. Soldiers also must have high scores on the Army's physical-fitness test and no physical restrictions. The Old Guard requires a score on the Army's general-intelligence test otherwise reserved for rare Army specialties like a cyber-operations specialist or Special Forces recruit. And soldiers cannot have civil or military convictions, drug or alcohol problems, or financial issues. Put these things together and The Old Guard has some of the Army's most capable, squared-away soldiers.

Officers and sergeants must submit a detailed application that goes even further. The packet includes a full-length photograph, letters of recommendation, a personal statement, and one's last three performance evaluations. The recommendations carry special weight if they come from The Old Guard's strong and devoted alumni network. When a battalion commander or a sergeant major with Old Guard experience puts his reputation on the line for a lieutenant or junior sergeant, the regiment's leadership takes notice.

In fact, Old Guard soldiers and alumni are some of its best recruiters. Captain Rob Schaar, the commander of Honor Guard Company, applied with the encouragement of his battalion commander, who had served as a guard for the Tomb of the Unknown Soldier two decades earlier. Two of his best soldiers were Old Guard alumni, Cpt. Schaar said, so he knew that the regiment produced high-quality troops. His executive officer, Captain Travis Roland, has a similar story. After performing in local funerals for veterans near Fort Hood, a fellow officer and a sergeant major suggested he apply to The Old Guard. In my day, First Sergeant Javy Montanez, my first sergeant in Charlie Company, had been a team leader with the 101st Airborne for my platoon sergeant, Sergeant First Class Jody Penrod, and later recruited him to The Old Guard.

The Old Guard also breeds a lot of "repeat offenders," joked Col. Garkey. He should know: with three separate tours, he has spent almost a quarter of his Army career at Fort Myer. My old commander, Col. Buche, had served an earlier three-year tour with the regiment, when he was the officer-in-charge for President Richard Nixon's funeral. From my days, by-then First Sergeant Penrod returned for another tour with The Old Guard, as did Lieutenant Colonel Jody Shouse, whom I had known as Major Shouse during my tour, to serve as the commander for 1st Battalion.

But not every officer follows these paths to The Old Guard—I sure did not. As my tour in Iraq with the 101st Airborne wound down in 2006, I knew that I would hand over my platoon to a new lieutenant and likely get a staff job at Fort Campbell—or be a "PowerPoint Ranger," as we sometimes called staff officers. But I had joined the Army to lead troops, not to sit at a desk, so I was considering options for more troop-leading time. The Old Guard was one, 75th Ranger Regiment was another, Special Forces was a third. I had made no decisions, however, when I received an email from Infantry Branch Headquarters in October that said "your application to The Old Guard has been accepted." That was curious, since I had not submitted an application.

That night—morning at Fort Myer—I walked across our dusty base to the call trailer, where I reached the regimental adjutant, Captain John Nemo. He explained that The Old Guard was short on officers because of deployments to Iraq and they had "hand-selected" six lieutenants, all returning from Iraq in the coming weeks. Being "hand-selected" in the Army is usually a sign of superior performance. Alas, Cpt. Nemo burst my momentary bubble of pride when he elaborated that he had screened for the normal requirements—height, weight, physical fitness, character, Ranger-qualified, Airborne-qualified, and (in those days) combat experience—and then just picked the six tallest. Cpt. Nemo told me to give it some thought and let him know if I wished to decline the orders, which he could probably rescind. The Old Guard is a demanding place, he added, and it needed motivated officers who wanted to be there.

I spent a couple of conflicted days thinking about the assignment. I knew an Old Guard tour would foreclose the Ranger

Regiment and Special Forces as options. But I had no guarantees that either would work out; my timeline might not be correct and I would need my chain of command's support. A few hours researching The Old Guard confirmed my favorable impressions from observing the Changing of the Guard at the Tomb of the Unknown Soldier. A good friend from Officer Candidate School, J. R. "Ace" Acquistipace, had served at The Old Guard as a young private and had always spoken well of the regiment. After talking with some other Army friends, I emailed Cpt. Nemo that I would accept the assignment. I was now bound for America's Regiment.

While my path to The Old Guard was unusual, all officers and sergeants followed a very different path from most of the regiment's soldiers, who come straight from basic training. As with any infantry regiment, these young privates constitute most of The Old Guard's manpower. They arrive at Fort Benning for basic training and advanced infantry training unsure of their next duty assignment. The most promising—and the tallest—new privates have an opportunity, however, to control their fate by volunteering for The Old Guard. The regiment deploys a sergeant to Fort Benning to recruit soldiers who meet The Old Guard's standards, most of whom know nothing about it. Yet by expressing interest in The Old Guard, they share a common bond with the regiment's most senior officers and grizzled sergeants: they volunteered to honor our nation's finest at Arlington National Cemetery.

Learning The Old Guard ROPs

All incoming Old Guard soldiers share another trait: not a single soldier, from the youngest private to the new regimental commander, is qualified to execute the regiment's mission. The Old

Guard's mission is so different from anything else in the Army that new soldiers must spend weeks in training before they can perform in a funeral or ceremony.

The regiment's distinctive buff strap is the reward for completing this initial training. The black-and-tan strap resembles the shoulder straps of the rucksacks carried by the First American Regiment's soldiers in their first combat victory, the Battle of Fallen Timbers in 1794. Old Guard soldiers wear the buff strap around their left shoulder to commemorate this early chapter in their long history—and to set themselves apart. Still today, I look for buff-strap-wearing soldiers when I attend events at Arlington or Fort Myer and need information; I assume they will be squared away.

For new privates and junior sergeants—the ranks of sergeant and staff sergeant—this training occurs through the Regimental Orientation Program. Known as ROP (pronounced "rope"), the initials could also stand for "rite of passage." ROP not only teaches new soldiers how to prepare a uniform and march to The Old Guard standard, but also why they do it. The regiment's zero-defect mentality honors our nation's heroes: there are no do-overs in Arlington.

ROP is an isolation-training program that shields soldiers from other duties, but they already belong to a company, which "provides a sponsor as well as a chain of command to augment ROP instruction," Col. Garkey explained. That was the case in Charlie. 1st Sgt. Montanez used to yell down the hallway at platoon sergeants and squad leaders to get their "ROP-ees" ready for the weekly Friday test. He rode them hard because Charlie needed those soldiers trained and on the marks in the cemetery or on the parade field.

ROP lasts for four weeks, but in the Army's inimitable style, the first week is known as Week Zero, as if to drive home how little one has accomplished. (My first week at basic training was also known as Week Zero.) Week Zero is full of administrative tasks common to any new post. Week One turns to uniform preparation and maintenance. Weeks Two and Three cover the standing and marching manual of arms with the ceremonial M14 rifle, teaching soldiers the basics about The Old Guard's distinctive style of drill and ceremony. Each week ends with a test on the week's material and a standing-proficiency test.

Although Week Zero is an administrative week, it previews The Old Guard's special status in the Army. ROP students visit the Central Issue Facility, or CIF as it is known across the Army. Soldiers usually draw tactical gear from CIF when reporting to a new unit—helmet, body armor, rucksack, and so forth—and return it all when leaving. The experience is common and routine; for instance, I drew from and cleared CIF six times during my service. While soldiers draw tactical gear from Fort Myer's CIF, the main focus is on ceremonial uniforms and equipment.

The volume of ceremonial uniforms surprises every new soldier, as it did me. Two dark blue wool blouses (the Army's name for a suit coat), two light blue wool trousers, two short-sleeved white dress shirts, five pairs of white cotton gloves, a ceremonial belt, a ceremonial cap, a black necktie, black socks, suspenders—and those are just for indoor and fair-weather events. For inclement and cold weather, soldiers also receive a raincoat, a rain cap cover, an overcoat, a white scarf, a trooper cap, black dress gloves, and cold-weather boots. Finally, soldiers are issued two pairs of black Corfam shoes, with steel plates on the soles. These plates create the distinctive "clicking" sound of Old Guard soldiers marching through Arlington.

A team of CIF tailors, armed with sticks, measuring tapes, and pins, measure all these uniform items to fit each soldier, many of whom have never owned a suit but now have professional tailors buzzing around them. Blouses are tapered from the chest to the waist. Trousers fit snugly in the seat and the waist. Even the rain-coats are tailored to the soldier's body. "I was struck by how expert and professional they were," observed Captain Larry Harris, the commander of my old company, Charlie. "If you get something tailored in the civilian world, it takes forever and might not be perfect. These guys knock it out perfectly in a matter of hours and the train never stops rolling with new soldiers coming in."

Another stop is the Ceremonial Equipment Branch, a unique office in the entire Army. Old Guard soldiers call it "the Flag Shop" because it stores flags for all fifty-six states and territories and every nation on earth. The Flag Shop also has crowd-control stanchions, leather chairs, red carpet, and anything else needed for a major ceremony. My default answer to soldiers with ceremonial needs was, "Call the Flag Shop." For ROP soldiers, the Flag Shop provides ribbons and medals, special-skills badges, unit citations, and any other insignia, all in anodized metal for the best appearance. Simply put, CIF provides the uniforms and the Flag Shop provides the stuff that goes on the uniforms.

The ROP leader, Staff Sergeant Thomas Dodson, holds one of the most critical jobs in the regiment, teaching reverence for The Old Guard's missions and the techniques to execute them. He exudes the maturity imparted by his two combat deployments and his age—having enlisted at thirty-five and now in his forties, he is among the oldest soldiers in The Old Guard. "I enjoy teaching people," he said. "I'll handpick each instructor for training weeks to make sure that it is somebody extremely good at their job, professional, and who can get the point across," he added.

Ssg. Dodson and his cadre start from scratch and patiently build a common foundation among all students. While The Old

Guard gets promising soldiers, he joked that "many of these soldiers come out of basic not knowing how to do a load of laundry," but they need to leave ROP ready to prepare immaculate uniforms every day. Yet he and other ROP instructors are not drill sergeants. Though direct and authoritative, they seldom yell or scream. They explain the regiment's standards, equip students with tools to succeed, and then hold them to those exacting standards. Ssg. Dodson stressed that the cadre "make sure that they're upholding the standards of The Old Guard, because this is, like everybody says, the face of the Army."

During Week One, soldiers learn not only the uniform standards, but also why they matter. At first, new soldiers may see only needless formality; soon enough, they understand the purpose behind the smallest details. Take the ceremonial belt. Soldiers must cut it very tight—"If you can breathe, it's not tight enough," Ssg. Dodson quipped—and must reinforce the buckle with heavy wire to withstand the resulting tension. A tight belt accentuates the soldier's V-shaped torso and supports the weight of a scabbard, while a loose belt sags and projects a sloppy appearance. Yet the tension on the tight belt risks a catastrophic failure during a funeral—the buckle breaking and the belt falling off—that would mar the family's memories. What drives this degree of attention to detail is not stuffy formality, but the honor due to our nation's heroes.

Week One begins with the belt and smaller items and works up to the uniform itself. Soldiers therefore gather around small desks in a cramped classroom, aided by instructional posters and the regiment's seventy-nine-page pocket-sized uniform manual. They "build up" the ceremonial cap with the same heavy wire and fit stiff cardboard in its top to prevent "doming," or the appearance of the head pushing against the cap's fabric. They get a laminated map of Arlington National Cemetery, which Old

Guard soldiers must keep in their caps at all times to know their whereabouts and to aid visitors in the cemetery.

The medals rack gets special attention. Unlike ribbon racks, which are commercially available, medals racks are hard to find, so Old Guard soldiers use the materials from the Flag Shop and the local hardware store to construct their own. The preferred materials are lightweight balsa wood for the rack and a "Beware of Dog" or "No Parking" sign for the ribbon backing. "Balsa wood builds separation between the rows so they don't rest on top of each other," Cpt. Harris said. "The metal sign provides the rigid backing for the ribbon," which hangs from the rack and supports the medal itself. A good rack can take several hours and multiple tries for a novice. Outside ROP, skilled soldiers earn a nice profit by building racks for other soldiers.

Week One also introduces students to the industrial-quality press machines, which have two ironing-board-size panels, one stationary and one movable, that lock together. Each company has several machines in the barracks. Students also learn how to use garment steamers to remove pressed-in lines from pockets, seams, and liners, as well as other wrinkles. The trousers' creases must be crisp—no "railroad tracking," as dual lines are known—and must run all the way to the belt line to ensure the blouse covers them. Soldiers will spend hours in the press room mastering these techniques and then maintaining their uniform after long days in the cemetery.

The ceremonial blouse takes the most effort. First, soldiers cut off the buttons, which allows for a flat press across the front. They place the anodized buttons from the Flag Shop on the blouse using heavy diaper pins, which further accentuates the torso's taper. Next, they remove "fuzz," or the wool's nap, with cigarette lighters and masking tape. Then they press the sleeves flat along the natural crease formed by aligning the bottom seam. Finally and most challenging, soldiers press pleats into the back of the blouse, along the side seams. These pleats gather any loose fabric to present a crisp, tight appearance when soldiers "blouse up," or put the ceremonial belt on over the blouse.

The final step for the blouse is pinning on the medals, badges, and other insignia. A single blouse can have more than ten measurements, which I never tried to memorize, but instead hung a diagram on the wall next to where I pinned my blouse. A small metal tailor's ruler, about the size of a nail file, is a key piece of equipment for pinning a blouse. Most of my soldiers wrongly called this tailor's ruler a "micrometer," which is a kind of caliper, but I suppose that name reflects the spirit of a ruler calibrated down to the sixty-fourth of an inch.

Week One culminates on Friday morning with a uniform test and forty-five-minute standing test. Soldiers report with their sponsors, sporting a fresh haircut—no visible hair below the cap line—and the blue polyester dress uniform issued at basic training since they are usually waiting for their tailored items. Several soldiers usually fail the first test, but barring major deficiencies, soldiers and their sponsors have a chance to fix the uniform and retest later that day. Those who pass have taken their first step toward adding another item to their uniform, the buff strap.

While Week One teaches ROP students to look like an Old Guard soldier, Weeks Two and Three teach them how to march like one. Week Two focuses on stationary movements with the M14 rifle and Week Three on marching with the rifle; combined, these weeks prepare soldiers to march in a funeral or ceremony. In some cases, they will do so immediately. Charlie's manpower was stretched so thin throughout my tour that 1st Sgt. Montanez often put a soldier on the marks on Monday who had graduated

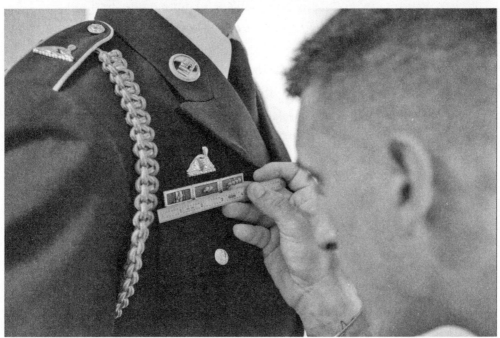

Regimental Orientation Program instructors conduct uniform inspections of Old Guard soldiers.

ROP on Friday. ROP therefore must turn out competent, trained marchers ready to perform.

ROP instructors must teach new skills and break old habits. "They don't teach you all these movements in basic training," Ssg. Dodson explained; "they're giving you just the basic movement, like parade rest with a rifle." ROP introduces new concepts, such as ceremonial at-ease, the most comfortable position for long speeches during a ceremony. But other instruction must reteach movements in The Old Guard style. "We do the movements a little bit differently here," he continued. "Because it's ceremonial, there's more flair to them."

New soldiers also have to learn how to handle and march with the M14 rifle. The M14 was originally developed in the 1950s to replace several different rifles. While accurate and powerful in semiautomatic mode, it was less reliable in burst mode. In the early years of the Vietnam War, the Department of Defense replaced it with the M16. Although M14 variants remain in use today as a sniper rifle—my squads' designated marksmen in Iraq carried an M14—few soldiers have handled the rifle with smooth wooden ceremonial stocks. Further, the soldiers must learn how to control the weapon while wearing white gloves. "When you don't have gloves, you've got some traction on your hands," Ssg. Dodson observed. "When you've got a pair of cotton gloves, not so much traction. So, it's a little bit more difficult."

In addition, individual mastery is not enough—soldiers must learn to synchronize their movements with those of their fellow soldiers. With white gloves against dark navy blouses, mistimed movements stand out like a sore thumb. The Old Guard's distinctive style of voice commands, moreover, complicates the soldiers' efforts to synchronize their movements. Though the words are the same as those used by the regular Army, the inflection and cadence is different, somewhat akin to English spoken in Arkansas and in Scotland. Some soldiers come to prefer The Old Guard's bugle calls and drumbeats as commands. Moreover, the ears can pick up mistakes that the eyes miss when M14s pop in the soldiers' hands or against the ground. Specialist Matthew Gibbs, a ROP marching instructor, emphasized the point often: "One sound right here, folks. *One sound!*"

Marching is therefore more challenging than uniform preparation, especially for less coordinated soldiers, and students fail the marching tests (especially standing manual at the end of Week Two) at higher rates. A failed test requires a repeated week of training. Not that ROP instructors want to fail students. On the contrary, they have worked in line companies and understand the need to get qualified soldiers on the marks. They insist upon The Old Guard's high standards, though, and they have the backing of the regimental commander and sergeant major. "I don't want garbage going out of the orientation program," Ssg. Dodson explained, "because that's when it starts getting reflected back on The Old Guard."

The training schedule and environment sets soldiers up for success. In both weeks, the sixteen stationary movements and the twenty marching movements are taught early. This front-loaded schedule leaves the rest of the week for repetition, practice, and coaching. And the ROP training day ends by 1530, leaving plenty of time for extra practice with one's sponsor back at the company. The classes also occur in a room lined with full-length mirrors, enabling soldiers to watch themselves as they drill, while Ssg. Dodson and his cadre walk among the rows of students, both issuing commands and correcting mistakes. During Week Three, ROP moves outside for marching exercises and a series of long practice marches, before dedicating all Thursday to one-on-one instruction, remedial coaching, and test preparation.

Test day for both marching weeks resembles the Week One

Colonel Jason Garkey awards the buff strap to soldiers after the successful completion of the Regimental Orientation Program.

test. The day starts with another uniform inspection. Then soldiers begin their standing-proficiency test, sixty minutes for Week Two and seventy-five minutes for Week Three, with twenty-five minutes at attention during each test. While it may seem unfair to stress the students with a long stand before the marching test, this sequence reflects the Army's train-as-you-fight mentality. Soldiers may stand for up to an hour during speeches and awards in a ceremony. Yet they are expected to come to attention and execute the rest of the ceremony to standard, even when their arms and legs are on pins and needles. The students therefore must show they can execute the manual of arms after a long stand.

For those who pass the Week Three test, only one activity remains: the ROP graduation and Buff Strap Ceremony. On Monday morning, the newly certified soldiers form up for a brief ceremony with the regimental commander and sergeant major— but not before one final haircut and uniform inspection by the ROP cadre. In what is likely their first encounter with the regiment's senior leaders, the commander welcomes them to the ranks of Old Guard soldiers and puts the buff strap around each graduating student's left shoulder. These soldiers now belong officially to The Old Guard of the Army, the regiment that fought at Fallen Timbers in 1794 and pulled bodies from the Pentagon on 9/11.

Earning My Buff Strap

Unlike its junior soldiers, The Old Guard's new officers and senior sergeants—the ranks of sergeant first class, master sergeant, and sergeant major—do not have organized training. "I bring them on as leaders immediately," Col. Garkey explained, adding that platoon leaders, platoon sergeants, and more senior leaders must perform "their day job" while also training on the side to pass seven distinct tests. Col. Garkey did not exempt himself; he trained and tested again when he became regimental commander despite his two previous tours.

Instead of a dedicated training program, senior leaders rely on their units to coach and prepare them. My training experience was without question a team effort, led by Captain Doug Coutts and Sfc. Penrod. Cpt. Coutts was a fellow platoon leader and my sponsor. Sfc. Penrod was my platoon sergeant and, like any good platoon sergeant, he intended to see his lieutenant succeed.

Our first stop was CIF. Cpt. Coutts ensured I received the correct officer's uniforms, which vary slightly from enlisted ones, and Sfc. Penrod cajoled the staff to provide brand-new items, not recycled ones. They also guaranteed that I receive a properly sized saber, which Old Guard officers carry instead of an M14. As with most things at The Old Guard, the standard for saber length is precise: the saber's tip must reach "a point adjacent to the lowest portion of the external ear opening and extend no further than the midpoint of the external ear opening." Because I was one of the regiment's tallest officers, it took a while to find the right one.

Now I had to learn how to use my new saber. I worked around Charlie's funeral schedule, training while my soldiers were in the cemetery. Cpt. Coutts, who had arrived just a few weeks before me, had not yet passed all the tests, but he had passed the standing and marching manual, so he worked with me in the parking lot out back. What would have been quite a scene at most Army bases—me in combat fatigues with a black ceremonial training belt, dress shoes, and a saber, and Cpt. Coutts clapping to imitate a drumbeat while I marched—was just another day at Fort Myer.

When Cpt. Coutts was busy, Sfc. Penrod would come out to help, though I suspect he secretly wanted some quality control. With Cpt. Coutts only a few weeks ahead of me in training, he probably feared a blind-leading-the-blind aspect to the officers training together. By contrast, Sfc. Penrod had spent the last two years at Charlie. Although senior sergeants carry a sword, which is straight and designed for thrusting, whereas an officer's saber is curved and designed for slashing—an homage to nineteenth-century warfare, when officers were often mounted—the techniques and standards for both are the same. Together, the three of us went through the sixteen standing tasks and twenty marching tasks, over and over again.

Like everyone, I struggled at first with "tip control," one of the hardest skills to master in saber training. When the saber points down and forward alongside the right leg, two errors are common. First, the tip should be six inches off the ground; anything else is "tip high" or "tip low." Second, the tip should not "flare" to the left or right. Because an officer must maintain ceremonial composure at all times, I could not look down to check my tip, but instead had to rely only on muscle memory—and corrections. With every command, Cpt. Coutts or Sfc. Penrod might call out "tip low" or "flare out" before evaluating the rest of the movement. I also developed another way to build the muscle memory. On weekends, I took my saber and gloves home, where I had cut a six-inch block from a two-by-four. I positioned the block on the ground where my saber would touch its midpoint so I could feel the proper height and direction without looking.

Sfc. Penrod was also my main instructor for the voice test, partly because this sixteen-part test had twice tripped up Cpt. Coutts. Several of the commands were new to me and all had the unusual cadence and inflection that threw off ROP students. Voice commands either came naturally to the officer or not. Even after training and passing the test, some officers always struggled with it. Fortunately, the commands came easily to me, even though I cannot sing at all. (If I sing around my son today, he cries, "No sing, Daddy, no!")

But the most important part of the voice test was not natural or easy: condolences to the next of kin. I cited condolences whenever a soldier complained about some exacting standard: "You know when I stand in front of a widow and present the flag? Can you imagine how terrible it would be to choke? Unimaginable, right? Well, you should have that same feeling about everything." The testing standards for condolences reflected that gravity. Officers had to perform the other voice commands correctly two out of three times each and could pass the voice test with an overall score of thirteen out of sixteen. But condolences were a "zero-mistake" test: I had to recite the condolences perfectly the first time or I failed the entire voice test. I rehearsed condolences in my head hundreds of times before the test—while running, showering, waiting in traffic, and pretty much anywhere else with time on my hands—and I kept doing it for my whole tour at The Old Guard.

I was getting the hang of the saber manual, marching, and voice commands, but I was conflicted about my uniform preparation. From my earliest days in training, I learned that officers lead from the front and do their own work. I always—*always*—cleaned my own rifle and carried my own gear. But new lieutenants are also told to trust and rely on their sergeants, advice my father also gave me. As a platoon leader in the 101st Airborne the previous year in Baghdad, I had learned a lot from my platoon sergeant and squad leaders. Though I had more Army experience now, I still knew nothing about how to prepare an Old Guard uniform. Nevertheless, when my tailored blouses and trousers arrived from CIF, my first instinct was to prepare them myself. But Sfc. Penrod insisted that I would only embarrass myself, him, and Charlie if I did that—and he recruited my fellow officers to his side.

We compromised by making my uniform preparation a team effort. Sfc. Penrod assigned two of our top performers, Sergeant Matthew Perry and Specialist Stephen Anthony, to press my blouse and trousers, but I observed them to learn how to do daily uniform maintenance. As they pinned two-inch pleats into the back of my blouse on the press machine, I accepted the wisdom of my platoon sergeant's counsel. Pin too loose and the pleat pops out; pin too tight and the press machine leaves pinholes. I did both and they did neither, but they taught me the right way and also offered a few more pointers on the sleeves and trousers.

Sfc. Penrod and I worked together on the smaller uniform items in our office. We built up my ceremonial cap and cut down my ceremonial belt—making it extra snug for the test. My saber and scabbard received extra coats of polish. I also prepared my shoes, which require the inverse amount of work as do normal dress shoes. The uppers were made of glossy Corfam, so just a little Windex made them sparkle. In The Old Guard, though, even the bottoms of the soles must be darkened, to avoid the appearance of "flashing" with light-colored soles when marching away from the family at a funeral. Over several days, I applied dozens of coats of edge dressing to the leather soles and steel plates. The only thing that neither Sfc. Penrod nor I attempted to prepare was my medals rack, which he assigned—for the fair-market rate—to Sergeant Robert Schmeidler, one of Charlie's master rack-builders.

As my uniform came together, we turned to the three remaining tests, which cover ceremonial sequences specific to officers. Two tests were simple because they merely applied skills from the standing and marching manual. The first tested the NCO–Officer Exchange, which occurs after sergeants have marched the formation onto the parade field and the officers take charge of their units. The second tested the dressing sequence, in which the officers march in unison to the ends of their platoons and "dress," or align, the soldiers in each rank. These two tests really just evaluated one's ability to memorize specific step counts and movements, not a hard skill. The final test, though, was the dreaded "chute."

The chute is the nickname for the pass-in-review at the end of many Old Guard ceremonies. The units march past the reviewing stand as the dignitaries observe them—hence, the name "pass-in-review." For soldiers, the chute is easy; while marching, they simply snap their heads toward the reviewing stand on the officer's command of "eyes, right." But officers must execute several difficult actions while marching. To start with, I had to time my steps to issue the command of "ready, eyes, right" at a specific line on the ground—without looking down. At the same time, I had to execute my own saber salute, while marching and snapping my head to the right. Then came the hardest part of all: I had to march "through the chute" with my saber tip staying the standard six inches off the ground. With a normal arm swing, however, the saber naturally swings in an arc. Thus, I had to pop my wrist back and forth while swinging my arm. We called it "vacuuming the floor": push forward, pull back. Finally, at the end of the chute, I had to command "ready, front" to return to the normal marching style—again at a line I could not see.

The chute is the hardest test for Old Guard officers. Cpt. Coutts was not yet fully certified because he had failed it twice. We worked through it in stages. First, I marched—without a saber—through chalk lines in the parking lot to nail the timing of the voice commands. Then we added the saber to work on the marching salute. Finally, I "vacuumed the floor" down the length of asphalt—more than a football field—even though the chute itself is only forty feet long. As I put all the steps together, I felt better but still not fully confident.

But sooner or later, I needed to take the tests—and for our commander, Captain Dave Beard, it needed to be sooner, so I could start performing in funerals. The Old Guard back then had only one officer to administer the test, Captain Gary Kaldahl, the subject-matter expert on ceremonies and memorial affairs from the headquarters staff. We booked a morning in mid-May on Cpt. Kaldahl's busy schedule, about two months after I reported to Fort Myer and three weeks after receiving my tailored uniforms. The afternoon before the test, Sfc. Penrod and I assembled my blouse, measuring all the medals, badges, and other insignia on the hanger and on my body. Satisfied, we hung it up and secured a strip of microfiber between the rows of medals to prevent scuffing.

Test Day got off on the right foot: clear skies, light breeze, low humidity, and mild temperatures. While most of Charlie exercised, Cpt. Coutts, Sfc. Penrod, and I prepared for my test. I went to the barbershop and got the back and sides of my head scalped close. I shaved twice, and Sfc. Penrod inspected my face and neck. But then I stayed off my feet, ate breakfast, and relaxed; a clear, confident mind and a rested body, not stressful cramming, has always been my approach to big moments like this one.

About thirty minutes out, we suited up with the same focused intensity of our combat patrols in Baghdad. I put on my trousers, shirt, and tie, but not my blouse, instead wearing my black windbreaker. Sfc. Penrod carried my blouse on a hanger to preserve its condition. I also wore my rubber-soled Corfam shoes; Cpt. Coutts carried my ceremonial steels, one in each hand. I carried my belt in one hand, saber in the other. A few junior soldiers followed, carrying all the gear needed for last-minute maintenance: cigarette lighters, nail clippers, masking tape, microfiber cloths, edge dressing, Windex, and more. Cpt. Beard followed along, for moral support and gallows humor.

The scene on the elevated, redbrick reviewing stand at Summerall Field resembled what I assume the back stage of a fashion show looks like. The soldiers laid down a towel and placed my shoes on it. I stepped into them, then they tied the laces and tucked them away—one of one hundred testable uniform items. I donned my blouse, which Sfc. Penrod buttoned for me to avoid wrinkles in my sleeves. They next bloused me up, buckling my belt while holding the back pleats in place. Normally, I would buckle my own belt, but again I kept my arms at my sides to prevent wrinkles.

All that remained was The Old Guard equivalent of pre-combat checks. Sfc. Penrod had the soldiers pat me down with masking tape to remove wayward dust or lint, then he stared down every piece of metal on my uniform for smudges or fingerprints. He checked all the seams on my uniform, using the clippers to cut a string that had snuck out of the shoulder seam, then burning down the nub with the lighter. He inspected my saber one final time and slid it into the scabbard hanging from my belt. Sfc. Penrod, Cpt. Coutts, and Cpt. Beard took one last look as Cpt. Kaldahl approached in the distance. "You're good," Sfc. Penrod declared. "All right, Esquire," Cpt. Beard said, his nickname for me because of my past as a lawyer, "try not to pass out."

It was showtime. I gingerly stepped off the towel and onto the bricks. I was on the clock. Cpt. Kaldahl circled me, armed with a tailor's ruler and a clipboard, measuring and staring, sometimes just an inch away. He occasionally went over to the Charlie team behind me, where they spoke softly—too softly for me to hear— though I suspected that Cpt. Beard and Sfc. Penrod were "working the ref." Once I heard them start joking and talking sports, I knew the uniform test was over and I only had to finish the seventy-five-minute stand. Even if I had failed the uniform test, I would have the stand behind me.

"Okay, you can relax," Cpt. Kaldahl said, and I turned around, eager to hear the result. With no fanfare, he said I had passed the uniform test. He pointed out a few deficiencies—a press line here, a smudge there—but my grade was well above passing, a big relief. I loosened up my muscles and drank some Gatorade to prepare for the next six tests. The tests were sequential; I had to pass one to move on to the next. But it would all go fast from here. No single test takes more than ten minutes, and many take less than five.

First up would be voice commands. Cpt. Kaldahl and I moved onto the grass. The test was simple: he told me the command, then I issued it three times, maintaining ceremonial composure at all times. We completed this cycle fifteen times. The final task was condolences, which I executed perfectly—my practice paid off. Cpt. Kaldahl quickly tallied up his score sheet and said, "You passed."

"Esquire!" Cpt. Beard exclaimed. For good measure, he razzed Cpt. Coutts that I passed the voice test on the first try.

Up next was the saber manual test, the most commonly failed test aside from the chute. I stood on one of Summerall's small concrete pads, normally the commander's mark. Cpt. Kaldahl issued the commands and I executed them, three times each. As I stared straight ahead, he checked my tip height with a measuring stick. He made a few final notes on his score sheet, then said, "You're a go."

"Now it's getting real," Sfc. Penrod said, referring to the stakes for the next test. The first four tests are core Old Guard skills: uniform, voice, saber manual, and marching. The last three tests, by contrast, apply only to ceremonies. Once an officer completed the marching test, he could perform dependent funerals for the deceased spouse or minor child of a soldier eligible for burial in the cemetery. With only four other officers in Charlie, and Cpt. Coutts not yet certified for military-honor funerals, it would spread the workload significantly if I could perform dependent funerals. All I had to do was pass the marching test. And I did.

"Yes! Esquire in the cemetery!" Cpt. Beard yelled and pumped his fist.

I paused for a short break, drinking more Gatorade and collecting my thoughts. Though satisfied with my performance so far, now I wanted to finish it. I had worked toward this moment for two months—really for seven months since I had opened that email in Baghdad. I had not appreciated then, however, the time and effort it would take to get into the cemetery. But here I was, with the chance to get certified now. Seven for seven. Sfc. Penrod and I talked through the step counts for the NCO–Officer Exchange and dressing sequence. I aced those easy tests.

All that stood in my way now was the chute. The hardest test, it was also the shortest, and I was in control. Cpt. Kaldahl gave no commands, but merely observed at the reviewing stand and graded my three passes. I was playing with house money—few officers even reach this test on the first try—so I was loose and relaxed. "Whenever you're ready," he advised. I called, "Forward, march" and stepped off, saluting and "vacuuming the floor" as I passed the reviewing stand. I made a second pass. And a third. I turned and waited. We all did. Cpt. Kaldahl looked up from his clipboard, shrugged, and said, "You're good, congratulations."

As the Charlie guys celebrated, I was satisfied, as I had been when I passed my final patrol at Ranger School. I had not worried about passing the tests—almost everyone passes eventually. But for two months, I had been stuck at the barracks while my soldiers performed our mission in the cemetery. Now I could join them and lead them, as an officer should. I had earned the buff strap and now officially belonged to the oldest infantry regiment in the Army.

We walked back to Charlie's barracks together, led by an enthusiastic Cpt. Beard. He was excited, which he expressed not by praising me, but by joking that I had beat Cpt. Coutts. I did not join him, because I would not have gotten past the first test without Cpt. Coutts, Sfc. Penrod, and my soldiers squaring me away. Of course, when Cpt. Coutts passed the chute a few weeks later, I started teasing him about my "seven-for-seven," to which he always replied that Cpt. Kaldahl had pencil-whipped my test. Twelve years later, we still have the same debate whenever the topic comes up. (For the record, Cpt. Kaldahl insists that he never lowered the standard for anyone.)

Today, Old Guard officers must pass the same seven tests in the same sequence to earn their buff strap, but the testing program is more organized and structured than it was in my day. Back then, Cpt. Kaldahl was the only grader. Today three officers act as graders, and even more sergeants. We also scheduled our tests around our and Cpt. Kaldahl's availability, whereas today testing occurs every Thursday at 1300. The testing timeline is also more precise. In 2007, our manpower was so strained by Delta Company's deployment to Djibouti that I was not even aware of a timeline. The pressure to get new officers on the marks was so great that the standard was, in effect, "get certified, now." Today the target to complete testing is ninety days from the return of one's tailored uniforms. Some officers take longer, which is unpleasant for everyone from the regimental commander down to the struggling officer.

What have not changed are the standards. One of the graders, Captain Corey Morgan, joked, "I may be the most unpopular officer in the regiment." When briefing an officer for the standing-proficiency and uniform test, he cautions, "I can spot a toe wiggle from thirty feet away." He made no apologies for being such a stickler. "The standard has to be high because of the high-visibility missions. We can't screw up at the Pentagon or the White House, or make a mistake in front of a grieving widow. And now, with social media, online trolls are ready to spot-check the smallest deficiency." Col. Garkey backs up Cpt. Morgan and the other graders, just as our commander backed up Cpt. Kaldahl in my day, because a constant at The Old Guard over the years is the standard of perfection.

Organizing for War

Officer testing is more structured today because The Old Guard was itself restructured as a result of the 9/11 attacks and the wars in Afghanistan and Iraq. For most of the modern era, The Old Guard was really an oversized battalion—1st Battalion, 3rd Infantry—with a colonel in command, not a regiment with multiple battalions. As with so many things, all that changed on 9/11. The month of contingency operations at the Pentagon, daily funerals in Arlington, and heightened security at Fort Myer severely taxed The Old Guard and its troops. The Old Guard's senior leaders therefore prepared new contingency plans to respond to terror attacks around the capital. According to Col. Buche, they concluded that The Old Guard's structure and small headquarters staff would hinder its command-and-control capabilities in another attack, as large ceremonial events such as presidential inaugurations already did.

Moreover, The Old Guard would run out of troops during a major contingency operation. As on 9/11, the regiment had to prioritize funerals and secure Fort Myer, not only its home, but also home to some of the Joint Chiefs of Staff and other senior generals. Further, the pace of funerals continued to quicken as World War II veterans entered their eighties and Korean War veterans entered their seventies—and as casualties mounted from the War on Terror.

Shortly after Bravo Company deployed in 2003 to Djibouti, The Old Guard proposed to create a new battalion with head-

Captain Corey Morgan oversees officer testing as Lieutenant Mark Francour measures the saber tip height of Lieutenant Chris Caballero.

quarters staff, another infantry company, and an expanded logistics company. The Army approved the request, though not much had changed when I arrived in March 2007 because of typical bureaucratic delays. But when I returned to Fort Myer from Afghanistan in July 2009, the transformation was complete. The Old Guard had grown by almost three hundred troops and 4th Battalion—named in honor of its Vietnam-era predecessor—had a full headquarters just down Sheridan Avenue from Charlie's barracks.

"From my perspective, having two battalions made the regiment a lot more effective," said Col. Buche, the regimental commander who oversaw most of the growth. "We had three field-grade-officer staffs to plan and coordinate contingency operations, and also things like inaugurations and state funerals." At the battalion level, the restructuring reflected The Old Guard's core missions—memorial affairs and ceremonies—by assigning one mission to each battalion. Col. Buche especially thought "it made sense to have accountability for all the memorial affairs under one battalion commander" because funerals occur every day and depend so heavily on well-trained small units like casket teams and firing parties. Thus, 1st Battalion retained the three infantry companies dedicated primarily to funerals (Bravo, Charlie, and Delta) and added the new infantry company (Hotel), as well as the Caisson Platoon, which provides horses and caissons for funerals, and the Presidential Salute Battery, which fires the gun salute at funerals for high-ranking officials.

4th Battalion got everything else, both ceremonial and support units. The Commander-in-Chief's Guard and Honor Guard Company are the infantry companies dedicated primarily to ceremonies, and the Fife and Drum Corps is the regiment's marching musical unit. 4th Battalion also received the regiment's other specialty platoons—the Tomb of the Unknown Soldier Platoon, the Continental Color Guard, and the U.S. Army Drill Team— and its two support units. The 289th Military Police Company secures Fort Myer and marches in large ceremonies when needed; it also includes the 947th Military Police Detachment, one of the military's largest and most elite military-working-dog units. The 529th Regimental Support Company—named in honor of a famed Korean War–era logistics company—consolidated and expanded The Old Guard's medics, armorers, mechanics, cooks, and other support personnel.

The new structure also enabled better tactical training. Col. Garkey always stresses to his troops, "We are an infantry regiment first," as Col. Buche did in my day. Yet tactical training was very hard to fit into the calendar at The Old Guard in those days with Delta deployed. Today, though, each battalion can schedule tactical training more predictably around its core mission.

Not to say tactical training is easy to fit in or reaches the level of a normal infantry regiment. For instance, when I asked Cpt. Schaar, the Honor Guard Company commander, if he conducted regular tactical training, he laughed and said, "We schedule it." But he commended the support personnel at Fort Myer and Fort A. P. Hill who go the extra mile to help his troops stay tactically proficient up to the squad level, the nine-soldier unit that is the building block of the infantry. First Sergeant Raymond Wrensch of Charlie Company, who previously deployed nine times with the 75th Ranger Regiment and loves to teach tactics, acknowledged during a training exercise at Fort A. P. Hill that "memorial affairs and ceremonies are our priorities. As much as it hurts me sometimes to prioritize that over tactical training, that is our job."

Nevertheless, infantry training is essential to The Old Guard for several reasons. First, the regiment could hardly perform its other mission—defense of the nation's capital—if its soldiers' tactical skills atrophied. Second, getting back to infantry basics provides a morale boost for the troops. I heard often from junior soldiers a refrain familiar to Old Guard officers: "Sir, this isn't what I signed up to do." Even though they had volunteered for The Old Guard, they had also volunteered for the infantry, and weeks on the marks can wear down even the most motivated, dutiful soldier. Nothing improved their spirits like a few days of patrolling in the woods, putting rounds on targets, and blowing stuff up.

Finally, The Old Guard wants to train and retain soldiers for the Army. Major Eric Alexander, the regiment's operations officer, stressed that "we owe it to the Army to send back tactically proficient soldiers." Regrettably, though, good soldiers sometimes leave the Army from The Old Guard when their enlistment contract ends rather than transfer to another unit, because they fear being ill-equipped for a tactical unit. Yet the opposite is true— Old Guard soldiers learn intangible skills like attention to detail, poise, leadership, and problem-solving that often put them ahead of their peers at other units, even if they spend less time on the weapons range. It takes some convincing, though, and good squad-level training instills in junior soldiers the skills and confidence to succeed in the conventional Army.

But 1st Sgt. Wrensch is right. The Old Guard's main mission occurs not at Fort A. P. Hill, but ninety miles to the north on the sloping hills next to the Potomac River. Charlie Company's exhausted, dirty soldiers had spent a motivating week in the woods and on the range. Now Cpt. Harris and 1st Sgt. Wrensch loaded them onto buses. They would soon trade their dirty combat uniforms for pristine ceremonial uniforms. Arlington National Cemetery beckoned.

4

Inside Arlington
with The Old Guard

Dawn at Arlington is unforgettable, with pink and red hues backlighting the National Mall across the Potomac River. But we would not get to admire the sunrise this morning. It was the depths of winter in 2008, and in the frigid darkness, Charlie Company's leaders piled into a fifteen-passenger van, bundled in our fleeces, watch caps, and gloves. We drove away from our barracks for the morning recon, where we would inspect the grave sites for the full-honor funerals scheduled for that day.

We passed through Selfridge Gate in the low stone wall separating Fort Myer from Arlington. The cemetery began on this hilly high ground. We drove by the old, extravagant, custom-made headstones before descending down toward Arlington's flat river bottoms. These lands are the newer sections of Arlington, with the widely recognized white uniform headstones organized in clear, symmetrical lines. We performed most of our funerals down here.

We stopped in Arlington's southeast corner and hopped out into the biting cold. Sometimes the grave was easy to find because it was already excavated and had a metal platform above it. Other times, as today, it was not yet dug, and so we had to search the grave numbers on the headstones. We stumbled around in the dark with flashlights until someone cried, "Found it!" Our commander, Captain Dave Beard, and the casket-team leader went over to inspect the grave site for good footing and obstacles.

I would be the escort commander for this funeral, leading our marching platoon, color guard, and the band. The escort's position was the first priority at the grave site because we were the largest element in the funeral. While we normally stood opposite the family, forty-five degrees from the head of the grave, about forty to seventy-five yards away, we used the recon to identify trees that might obscure the family's view or other potential problems. We wanted everyone positioned where the family could observe the military honors.

"Switch!" Cpt. Beard yelled, both approving of our position and directing us to switch sides. At that hour, we did not know on which side of the grave the cemetery grounds crew would place the family's seats. Thus, we had to recon the grave from both sides. The firing-party commander and I jogged over.

"Mount up," said Cpt. Beard, signaling his approval. But First Sergeant Javy Montanez stopped us. As the noncommissioned-officer-in-charge, he performed several small but essential tasks to ensure the funeral would run smoothly. He pointed out a few gaps in the dense trees along the curbs through which we could march without interference. We then loaded into the warm van and drove to scout the next grave site.

I had no role in the next funeral, so I stayed in the van, watching as the others reconned the grave site. It took only two or three minutes, as ours had. But in those moments, we caught little details that might be the difference between a perfect funeral and a catastrophic mistake—a hole on the casket team's route to the grave site, for instance, which could have caused them to trip. While the morning recon might seem like a small thing, I had long ago learned to sweat the small things, which in combat can be the line between life and death—and in Arlington, the line between honor and failure.

★   ★   ★

Arlington is where heroes rest. Only those soldiers with the most distinguished or lengthy service are eligible for burial at Arlington by The Old Guard. And though The Old Guard has many responsibilities beyond military-honor funerals, there can be no doubt that its Arlington mission is preeminent. Even Old Guard soldiers who primarily work outside the cemetery in other ceremonies or support roles readily concede that "the cemetery comes first."

The duty to render the final honors to our heroes and their families weighs heavily on Old Guard soldiers, none more so than Lieutenant Colonel Allen Kehoe, the commander of 1st Battalion, which has primary responsibility for funerals. Though a veteran of the 75th Ranger Regiment with five combat tours, he admitted to me, "I've never experienced pressure like this anywhere else in the Army." After a pause, he reflected, "I know that sounds crazy." Perhaps to some, but not to me. I felt the same pressure every day in Arlington. Not from my commanders, to be clear, but from myself. And my soldiers, just like Old Guard soldiers today, felt the same way.

We held our nation's fallen heroes close to our hearts in everything we did. From the care of our uniforms to the precision of our marching to the grooming of our horses, it was our sacred duty to honor the fallen in ways big and small. Our standard was simple: perfection on every level. A funeral in Arlington is a once-in-a-lifetime experience for the family. And for us, service in Arlington National Cemetery was a once-in-a-lifetime privilege.

One Legion

1st Battalion is responsible for the conduct of military-honor funerals in Arlington. The battalion is known informally as "One Legion" in honor of President George Washington's brief reorganization of the Army as the "Legion of the United States" in the 1790s. The battalion works closely with Arlington National Cemetery, even receiving its missions—as funerals are known at The Old Guard—from the cemetery's civilian staff.

These missions come in three varieties, depending mostly on the decedent's rank: full honors, standard honors, and dependents. A full-honor funeral includes a casket team, firing party, marching escort, band, and horse-drawn caisson. These funerals begin at a transfer point, a traffic circle or intersection where the remains are transferred from the hearse to the caisson. The funeral procession then marches to the grave site, where the remains are carried to the grave. After the chaplain's brief service, military honors are rendered: three volleys from the firing party, Taps played by a bugler, and a folded flag presented to the next of kin. These full-honor funerals are authorized for sergeant majors and all officers with one significant exception: soldiers killed in action, regardless of rank.

This exception dates back only to 2009, after my tour at Arlington, and resulted from the efforts of an Old Guard veteran, Sergeant First Class Robert Durbin. In 2008, he lost a soldier in action with the 25th Infantry Division in Iraq. Knowing that his soldier would not receive full honors despite his battlefield sacrifice, Sfc. Durbin mounted a successful yearlong advocacy campaign with Army leadership to extend full honors to enlisted soldiers killed in action.

A standard-honor funeral is authorized for enlisted soldiers in the rank of master sergeant and below (and is also available to sergeant majors and officers if the family prefers the shorter wait time). Without the escort, band, and caisson, standard honors resemble the graveside service of full honors. Dependent funerals, usually for spouses, have no military honors, but 1st Battalion provides a casket team or urn bearer, along with an officer or sergeant to preside. The spouse (or dependent child) occupies the same grave as the veteran, with his or her name and dates of life engraved on the back of the headstone.

1st Battalion's infantry companies—Bravo, Charlie, Delta, and Hotel, commonly known as the "line companies"—perform all of these funerals, with support from the Caisson Platoon and the Presidential Salute Battery in full-honor funerals. These units have unique tasks and skills, which require specialized training before they can enter Arlington. A look behind the scenes at each demonstrates how much work goes into a funeral before the family even arrives at the cemetery.

Like any infantry company, the line companies have three platoons, but uniquely for the Army, these platoons have distinct specialties. The Escort Platoon provides the marchers and the four-man color guard that, along with the band, comprise the escort for full-honor funerals. The Firing Party Platoon supports full-honor and standard-honor funerals with eight-man firing parties (seven firers and one commander). The Casket Platoon carries the casket (or urn) and folds the flag.

New soldiers are assigned to a platoon based partly on manning needs, partly on their physique. In my day, 1st Sgt. Montanez sent "the big boys," as he called them, to Caskets and "the skinny kids" to Escort or Firing Party. The same holds true today. The platoon sergeant for Charlie's Casket Platoon is Sergeant First Class Bryan Dospapas, a former drill sergeant and veteran of the 75th Ranger

Regiment. "I want to see someone who could carry a five-hundred, seven-hundred-pound casket for one hundred meters and still show the family that it is done in a professional manner," he said, "not someone who is struggling." Captain Larry Harris, the company commander, agreed. "The skinny, runner-type isn't the right fit for Caskets," he said, adding that Caskets "has our most muscle-bound soldiers."

The line companies operate on an eight-week schedule that rotates them in and out of the cemetery for funerals and training or other missions. Each company spends four weeks at a time

A casket team carries the remains to the grave site during a snowy standard-honor funeral.

on funeral duty, alternating between "primary week," when it performs every funeral for which it has available personnel, and "backup week," when it supports the primary funeral company as needed. The company then spends four weeks off funeral duty, dedicated to ceremonies, tactical training, and training its funeral teams. This schedule is designed to keep the companies at peak performance in the cemetery, while also giving them ample time for funeral training and other missions. We aspired to this kind of schedule in my day, but with Delta deployed to Djibouti and Hotel not yet created, Charlie and Bravo essentially alternated weeks in the cemetery. We stayed proficient by performing.

Today's rotational calendar is a big improvement, because the line companies must train extensively before conducting a funeral. This is especially true for casket teams, firing parties, and color guards, which perform collective tasks as one organic unit—not as individuals. A casket team, for example, has a daunting number of tasks: removing the casket (or urn) from the hearse, transferring it on and off the caisson, carrying it to the grave, and folding the flag, all just steps away from the family. These teams cannot simply substitute one soldier for another. Even with experienced soldiers, changing just one member of a casket team or firing party necessitates several days of training to rehearse and synchronize tasks such as folding the flag or firing seven rifles as one.

All the time and effort dedicated to training may seem excessive, even obsessive, but the line companies know they have no margin for error in Arlington. "We may do twenty-two funerals in the cemetery in a day, and you may have guys doing six or seven," Lt. Col. Kehoe observed, "but to the individual family, that's the only funeral." Our young soldiers had those families in mind when they spent hours firing blanks in the parking lot behind our barracks or folding and refolding the same flag over and over again. A training aid out back stood as a somber reminder of our solemn responsibilities—a mock caisson and a casket filled with sandbags.

Key partners of the line companies in full-honor funerals are the soldiers and horses of the U.S. Army Caisson Platoon, the military's last full-time, equestrian-mounted unit. The horses and the caisson are throwbacks to an era before artillery was mechanized. Horses pulled artillery guns and caissons loaded with ammunition to the front lines and brought the wounded and dead back to the rear. Today the ammunition chests have been replaced with a flat deck and casket rollers; the caisson still transports our nation's fallen, not from the front lines but to their final resting place.

Caisson is "one of the most complicated platoons in the United States Army," said Lt. Col. Kehoe, who joked that he never expected to command an equine unit. The platoon includes fifty-six soldiers and three civilian experts—a herd manager and master farrier, a leather-smith, and a horse trainer—who train young soldiers as assistant farriers and leather-men, among the rarest jobs in the entire Army. The platoon also owns about sixty horses and accounts for about half the battalion's entire budget. By contrast, the platoons I led had about forty soldiers, a pittance of a budget, and the only animal I ever had was an angry goat once given to us by grateful Afghans.

By definition, Caisson's soldiers have no prior Army training in horsemanship, and few have any experience outside the Army, either. Most are infantrymen, though any Old Guard soldier can volunteer for tryouts. Caisson's leadership is typical of its soldiers. Neither Captain Mike Callender, the platoon leader, nor Sergeant First Class Chris Taffoya, the platoon sergeant, had any riding experience, though Sfc. Taffoya had served an earlier tour with

Caisson as a junior soldier during which he and I performed funerals together.

The training therefore starts from the ground up with the ten-week Basic Horsemanship Course at the platoon's stables at Fort Belvoir, about fifteen miles south of Fort Myer. On Day One, Cpt. Callender said, "the students report at 0430 in the morning. They have a layout of the packing list and they don't leave until Friday at 1700." Sfc. Taffoya added that the soldiers "literally sleep in the horse stalls"—though "not with the horses, obviously," Cpt. Callender interjected. "It's a large stable and the horses are usually in the pasture. But it's warm in there, and it's as good as a barracks."

During the course, soldiers learn the basics of equestrianism such as horse care and grooming, horse tack, and especially how to ride "The Old Guard way." While it might seem easier to perform funerals while mounted instead of marching, that is not the case. Caisson soldiers must maintain "ceremonial posture," essentially riding at the position of attention from the waist up. "It's just like marching," Sfc. Taffoya said. "You hear the term 'marching from the waist up.' " The technique strains the back and the pelvis, he said, "and the McClellan is not the most comfortable saddle," referring to the platoon's ceremonial saddle, modeled on the saddle that General George McClellan designed shortly before the Civil War.

Like their human teammates, Caisson horses undergo training at the Fort Belvoir stables. Caisson procures gelding draft horses, along with a few mares, from proven breeders across the country. Smaller horses are preferred, Cpt. Callender said, because they are less prone to illness and easier to care for. But "small" is relative; they still weigh on average between 1,200 and 1,400 pounds, with some as big as 2,000 pounds. The horses must be black or white—technically, gray, which means white fur and black skin.

They arrive "saddle-broken" but still need special training, just like soldiers. The horses must learn to work in pairs, pull the caisson, and operate comfortably around crowds. "Horses are just like soldiers," Cpt. Callender said. "They all have different personalities."

As their training progresses, horses and soldiers transition to Fort Myer, once the home of Army cavalry and 1,500 horses. Today, while most of the old stables have been converted to office space, Caisson still occupies two stables built in 1908. New soldiers and horses join one of the platoon's four squads, which have eleven soldiers and nine horses each. The squads operate on a four-week rotational schedule, with two weeks dedicated to full-honor funerals and two weeks for training, stables operations, and maintenance of the horses' tack, which is modeled on the Army's 1916 Field Artillery harness. The horses also get a week of pasture time at Fort Belvoir during this period.

In the cemetery, Caisson can perform up to eight full-honor funerals per day. The primary and backup squads each provide a seven-horse, four-soldier section and caisson. Six horses pull the caisson in three pairs of two, with one rider per pair. This technique is known as postilion riding, another link to the Army's past, when one horse carried the rider and the paired horse carried food and other provisions. The pair nearest the caisson, the wheel team, does most of the work pulling and stopping it. The middle pair is the swing team, which ensures that the caisson swings widely enough to make turns. The front, or lead, team controls the caisson's direction and distance from the marching escort. The seventh horse bears the section rider, the senior rider responsible for the overall mission. He and his horse are not hooked up to the caisson, allowing him to ride ahead to coordinate with other funeral leaders.

Caisson soldiers work one of the longest duty days in The Old Guard. At 0430, they wash the horses and prepare the tack. By 0730, the horses are hooked up to the caisson, and the section departs for the cemetery by 0800. After eight hours in the cemetery, the soldiers give the horses their second shower and clean the tack, leaving their animals and equipment ready for the next early morning of funeral duty.

In addition to Army full-honor funerals, Caisson also supports funerals for the other military services in two ways. First, the platoon provides the caisson for their full-honor funerals, since no other military service has horses. In February 2018, for instance, I attended the funeral for Colonel Leo Thorsness, who earned the Medal of Honor in Vietnam while also enduring captivity as a prisoner of war. While the Air Force performed the funeral—including a missing-man flyover—Army soldiers and gray horses transported the hero to his eternal home.

Caisson also provides the Caparisoned Horse for funerals for Army and Marine Corps colonels and generals. The riderless horse with boots reversed in the stirrups is an old cavalry custom, which once served the practical purpose of signaling the fallen commander's death to the rear headquarters. Today, the riderless horse is an evocative reminder that the fallen commander will never ride again. The horse walks behind the caisson, guided by a single soldier walking next to it and holding the reins. This Caparisoned Walker is a prestigious position in Caisson, reserved for the best soldiers.

Caparisoned Horses can serve for decades and garner worldwide fame, as happened with Black Jack, the feisty cap horse for President John F. Kennedy's funeral. Named for General John "Black Jack" Pershing, he also walked in the funerals for Presidents Herbert Hoover and Lyndon Johnson and General

Douglas MacArthur, as well as thousands of other funerals over twenty-four years of service. So beloved was Black Jack that he received a full-honor funeral himself when he died in 1976. He is buried at the south end of Summerall Field, a short walk from the Caisson stables. Today, the most famous Caparisoned Horse is Sergeant York, who walked in President Ronald Reagan's funeral. Named for Alvin York, a Medal of Honor recipient and among the most decorated soldiers in World War I, Sergeant York has served with Caisson since 1995—since before many Caisson soldiers were born.

Founded in 1953, the Presidential Salute Battery uses vintage M5 cannons to fire the gun salutes at funerals for generals and admirals, as well as major ceremonies around the capital. The M5 was a towed, seventy-five-millimeter antitank weapon deployed during World War II, but it fared poorly against German tanks. "It proved to be more effective at ceremonies than destroying tanks," joked First Lieutenant Dave Marthy, the Battery's platoon leader. "It's popular today at museums and veterans' halls, but far as we know, we've got the only operational ones in the world." The Battery, which has fired at every presidential inauguration since 1956, started with four guns and now has ten.

The Battery's soldiers are mortarmen, a small but critical specialty within the infantry that supports front-line troops with mortar fire. As with its infantrymen, The Old Guard recruits its mortarmen straight from basic training. They arrive trained to deliver precision fire, sometimes at a distance of several miles, and are thus prepared to execute the Battery's tactical mission as the regiment's mortar platoon. But like the regiment's infantrymen, they start from scratch on ceremonial training. The training to qualify as a loader or gunner on the M5 can last several months, and even longer for the five soldiers who stand behind the M5s to time the firing intervals, count the rounds, and give the fire commands.

While the ceremonial skills differ sharply from the tactical skills, both require discipline, poise, precision, and attention to detail. "The M5s are good weapons, but they're really old," Lt. Marthy told me. "They're going to misfire. It's just inevitable." The Battery's soldiers therefore train constantly to react to misfires, while keeping the guns firing at standard intervals of three or five seconds—three for ceremonies, five for funerals— with deviations of no more than two-tenths of a second. They also dedicate just as much time to maintenance to keep the guns in good working order. Because no one else in 1st Battalion can perform their mission-essential tasks, "we have to police ourselves," Lt. Marthy explained, adding that "if you're not going to do it, no one else will."

The Battery performs at only the highest-profile funerals and ceremonies, yet their role can sometimes seem like an afterthought. The platoon's motto is "Rarely seen, always heard," because their firing points are usually out of sight from the grave site. Lt. Marthy observed, "We really don't get thought about unless we screw up." Even so, the Battery's soldiers uphold the regiment's exacting uniform standards and extend those standards to the guns, which have a near mirror finish on the steel of the breech, as well as the black barrel, blast shields, and tow legs, simply "because it's the right thing to do," as Lt. Marthy said.

Though rarely seen by the individual families, the Battery's soldiers are some of the regiment's most visible soldiers in the cemetery because they often use a firing point between Arlington's most popular destinations, the Tomb of the Unknown Soldier and Arlington House. Sergeant First Class Josh Wood, the Battery's platoon sergeant, called his soldiers "ambassadors in the cemetery" because visitors stumble upon them and invariably stop to talk. "They ask who we are and what we're doing, so we talk to them about our history and The Old Guard," he explained, adding that "the old veterans and young kids especially love to look at the guns, and we encourage them." Lt. Marthy added that "civilians see The Old Guard at three places in the cemetery"—funerals, the Tomb of the Unknown Soldier, and the Battery's firing points—"but we're the only ones who talk to them. They keep a respectful distance from funerals and silence is enforced at the Tomb. We have a unique opportunity to tell The Old Guard story."

One Legion's training discipline and its pursuit of perfection is all the more remarkable for a simple reason: Old Guard soldiers typically know very little about the veteran for whom they render military honors. Rank, first initial, last name—that was all the information we had. Our limited knowledge consistently surprises those who ask me about The Old Guard, then and now, probably because it contrasts so sharply with the normal experience of attending funerals for loved ones and close friends. In my opinion, though, the detachment between the soldiers and the fallen only underscores The Old Guard's ethos of honor for our fallen and their families.

There are also practical reasons The Old Guard stands at a distance from the fallen and their families. One is historic practice. The Old Guard has conducted funerals in Arlington since well before the internet, when biographical details were much harder to come by. Another is the sheer workload that more familiarity would create. Arlington's administrative staff already works long hours with families and local funeral homes to coordinate funerals in the cemetery, and asking them to compile biographical vignettes for The Old Guard could overwhelm these dedicated professionals.

Beyond these practical reasons, the distance helps Old Guard soldiers render military honors in the most professional way possible. When I discussed it with the regiment's memorial-affairs experts, both from my days and today, they stressed that every funeral matters as much as the next. Captain Gary Kaldahl, 1st Battalion's memorial-affairs officer during my tour, said, "My personal view is even if the information were available, I would want each soldier to put forth their best effort regardless of whether it was a general or a private." Captain Zach Kennedy, the regiment's memorial-affairs officer today, agreed: "We want to treat all these families with the same amount of respect" no matter their loved one's rank or heroics.

Moreover, the lack of knowledge about the decedent allows the soldiers to maintain ceremonial composure and emotional distance. Reflecting on the "raw emotion" at the grave site, Lt. Col. Kehoe acknowledged that "you don't necessarily have to be disconnected from it, but you have a part to play in military honors. And that part is an emotionless part." Harsh though it may sound, a display of emotion or loss of composure in front of the family is just as bad as a ceremonial mistake.

Even so, we were not always in the dark about the decedent's life or his military service. We occasionally got snippets from the chaplain or the cemetery representative while we waited for the funeral to begin. When I presided over funerals at the head of the grave, the casket team and I could hear some of the chaplain's eulogy if the wind was calm and airplanes from Reagan National Airport were not flying overhead. But these occasions were rare enough that I cannot recall many specific funerals even though I performed more than four hundred—nor can other Old Guard veterans with whom I have spoken.

What we all can recall, with as much clarity as any combat experience, are the rituals of our daily life in Arlington. Early morning recons. Talk-throughs. Funeral sequences. While my marching and saber skills long ago atrophied, the rituals of Arlington are as fresh in my mind as they were a decade ago. And they demonstrate in ways both big and small the respect, the honor, and the love that we felt for every soldier who rests in Arlington.

The Rituals of Arlington

These rituals begin not in the verdant hills of Arlington, but in the Memorial Affairs Section's small office at One Legion's headquarters on Jackson Avenue in Fort Myer. Captain Greg Rhodes leads the seven-soldier section. "We build redundancy into every step of funeral planning," he explained, "because these are no-fail missions. It has to be perfect." The redundancy of the planning process, far from needless Army bureaucracy, is just another example of The Old Guard's devotion to our nation's fallen and their families.

"We have direct access to the ANC database, so we use that to plan and deconflict missions a couple weeks out," Cpt. Rhodes continued. "Most days are straightforward, but a big funeral or a sensitive one takes some extra work." When 1st Battalion performs a funeral for a senior official, as it did for former Secretary of the Army Togo West in April 2018, for instance, it has to put most of its soldiers in the cemetery—not just two companies as usual. Likewise, a soldier killed in action is entitled to an expedited full-honor funeral within two weeks of death, which can require a third caisson section. "We can support those funerals," Cpt. Rhodes said, "but the companies need as much advance notice as possible."

The Memorial Affairs Section produces two mission orders that drive the funeral-planning process. Each Tuesday, the section issues five days' worth of draft funeral orders for the following week. The "MA Draft," as it is known, is a single page that includes every detail for every Army funeral: time, place, honors to be rendered, religion, and the decedent's rank, first initial, and last name. But the MA Draft is only provisional and my work in Arlington revolved around the MA Final, which I carried in my ceremonial cap every time I entered Arlington for funerals, as leaders do today. I depended on it to be flawless.

It falls to the Memorial Affairs Section to be sure the MA Final is perfect. "We build a whole new MA Final off the ANC database—we don't just make changes to the Drafts. It's just another redundancy to avoid errors," Cpt. Rhodes said. His section issues the MA Final in early afternoon the day before the funerals to the units responsible for them: the primary and backup funeral companies, Caisson, the Salute Battery, and the 529th's Transportation Platoon, which drives the soldiers into the cemetery on buses. These units also send a representative to the daily clearing meeting at 1500.

The clearing meeting is essential for coordinating the next day's funerals. Timelines are validated and funerals are assigned to the primary or backup company. The meeting also covers special circumstances such as a double interment of a veteran and spouse or a funeral in what is known as "Hollywood," the older sections of the cemetery near the Tomb of the Unknown Soldier and the JFK Gravesite. While funerals are uncommon there, when they occur the clip-clop of the caisson's horses and the clicking of soldiers' steel shoes attract tourists like flies to honey. I performed a few funerals in Hollywood, and each had hundreds of onlookers, some of whom walked right up to me to take pictures. The additional soldiers assigned for crowd control during a funeral in Hollywood politely asked them to stand at a respectful distance.

After the clearing meeting, funeral planning shifts to the

companies. I recall 1st Sgt. Montanez returning each day from the meeting and huddling with our platoon sergeants around a unique Old Guard institution: the Tag Board. Our Tag Board was twenty feet long and four feet tall with hundreds of hooks, arrayed in the formations used in funerals and ceremonies. 1st Sgt. Montanez and the platoon sergeants used little card-stock key tags bearing each soldier's name to assign them to upcoming missions. "Tagging out" the day's missions is essential for accountability and just another example of the extreme care given to each mission. "Don't touch my Tag Board!" was a common refrain from 1st Sgt. Montanez in Charlie's hallways. I joked with other officers about moving tags just to provoke him: "I know that officers aren't out there touching my tags!" 1st Sgt. Montanez's theatrical attitude reflected how seriously we took our missions. I have never seen anything like a Tag Board outside The Old Guard. Like the MA Final and the clearing meeting, the Tag Board is part of an unseen ritual directed toward the singular pursuit of perfection in the cemetery.

With the missions tagged out, I released our soldiers, but reminded them to take it easy so they were rested for the next day's funerals. As firing-party members, they were less prone to falling out or heat casualties than was the escort, but a fallout in the cemetery was a serious matter for soldiers and leaders alike. As for myself, during primary week I typically skipped my evening workout, ate a healthy meal, laid off alcohol, and went to bed early. The demands of honor even followed us home.

Our early-morning rituals in Charlie were a flurry of last-minute preparation. Junior sergeants accounted for their troops, ensuring they were present—and had followed orders about resting the night prior. Our officers, senior sergeants, and funeral team leaders met to confirm one last time which teams had which missions,

Charlie Company soldiers review the Tag Board, which shows the assignment of each soldier in the company to current and upcoming missions.

yet another redundancy against failure. When the Memorial Affairs Section representative picked us up for the morning recon, we gave him the MA Final with the key leaders' names penciled in so they could track funerals all day.

While the usual Army custom is for soldiers to exercise in the morning, even this yielded to the dictates of the cemetery. The first funerals started at 0900 and we loaded buses at 0800, leaving no time for exercise and requiring an afternoon workout instead. We grabbed a quick breakfast, had our coffee and Gatorade, and did final uniform and equipment checks. Even those with a later start were restricted—no long or hard runs to start the day. If I was not performing a funeral at 0900, I might lift weights at the gym, or check the news and tackle paperwork.

We also got the day's uniform call from headquarters. Because our soldiers might not return to the barracks all day, they had to wear or carry all the uniforms they might need depending on the weather. On warm and clear days, we could wear the blouse all day. But if rain was in the forecast, the call was blouse/carry-raincoat. Or the reverse, if rain was in the area, but clearing off later: raincoat/carry-blouse. From the late fall to the early spring, moreover, we might have to wear or carry the overcoat, the uniform when the temperature fell below forty-five degrees. Add a chance of rain and the soldiers joked that the uniform call was "blouse/carry-wall-locker."

Around 0740, the firing parties began to warm up out back, the crack of the rifle serving as an impromptu alert to us in the barracks. We filtered outside, and junior leaders did final checks of their men and equipment—and squared away officers when we needed it. By 0755, we loaded the "Myer Flyers," as the buses are called, and rolled out, meeting The Old Guard standard to depart the barracks no less than one hour before a funeral, leaving plenty of time to get on site and get ready. We usually ended up with a lot of standing-around time, but that was fine with us. We knew this moment had been a lifetime in the making for the family.

As we stepped off the buses at the transfer point, a reverential air descended upon our rituals. We now stood on hallowed ground. We talked, but the conversation was muted and focused on the mission: honoring the fallen and giving the family one final, perfect memory of the Army in which their loved one faithfully served.

Our first step was the key-leader talk-through, a rapid-fire verbal rehearsal. No matter how seasoned we were, every funeral still began with a talk-through of the key commands and cues. My role was escort commander, so I played a key part at the talk-through with the help of my guidon bearer. The guidon bearer played a critical role, quietly relaying cues when my back was turned to the grave. But he also assisted new officers who forgot the script. More than once, I heard a whisper over my shoulder like, "Sir, face about. Say, 'Order arms.' " Soon enough, though, I could conduct a talk-through in my sleep. Even today, observing Charlie's talk-throughs on my visits to the cemetery, I can still recite most of the escort commander's cues.

Putting on our ceremonial belts—or "blousing up"—was a two-person operation. My guidon bearer pulled the pleats of my blouse tight in the back, I buckled my belt, and then he smoothed the fabric under the belt and tucked away excess material. I did the same for him, as the other soldiers did for each other. Once bloused up, the soldiers got in formation and warmed up, running through the basic rifle manual for the funeral. As with our talk-through, the soldiers could execute these movements in their sleep, but we never left anything to chance or mere habit.

What came next exemplified The Old Guard's dedication to honoring our nation and those who served it. As the escort commander, I led the daily ritual of posting the colors, during which we saluted the flag together and then the color guard fell into formation. We could have skipped this step; no one was watching, after all. But the veterans buried in Arlington had worn that flag on their uniform, and many had fallen in combat underneath it. By honoring the flag, we also honored them and the cause for which they fought. I never once heard a soldier ask why we went to the trouble each morning.

At the transfer point, we also linked up with the other funeral participants. First among those was the chaplain, who performed the genuine rituals. Arlington has about ten active-duty chaplains—the majority from the Army—who perform a religious service upon the family's request. Major Eric Bryan is one of them. Like many chaplains I knew, he had an unusual path into the clergy. A West Point graduate, he left the Army after fulfilling his initial obligation and became a minister. But he decided to rejoin, this time to minister to soldiers. (The Old Guard has its own chaplains, but they work at Fort Myer and minister to its troops.)

The chaplains are the Army's main liaison to the family. About a week out, Chaplain Bryan calls the next of kin to prepare for the service. "I introduce myself. I ask them if they have any questions about the day and the service," he explained. "And then I ask them the question, 'Tell me more about your husband, or your wife, or your loved one.' " He uses that conversation to select the scripture and prepare the service.

Although the chaplains are assigned to the cemetery and not The Old Guard, we worked together constantly and shared the same ethos. They prepare their uniforms to Old Guard standards. They approach each funeral with equal reverence. "Each person is so incredibly unique and every American has a beautiful and different story," Chaplain Bryan reflected. He keeps a journal with notes from each funeral. He recalled the funeral for a widow who lost her husband in their twenties more than seventy years ago and never remarried just as quickly and movingly as he recalled the soldier with eight Bronze Stars, a Silver Star, and a Purple Heart. The chaplains understand what the moment means to the family: "You look into the eyes of a beautiful, eighty-five-year-old woman who is just so thankful, so thankful, that the nation remembers." And they understand what a privilege it is to serve in Arlington. "The blessing here significantly outweighs the hardship," Chaplain Bryan volunteered. "It is by far the best assignment I think I've ever had, and ever will have in the Army."

Besides the chaplain, we also joined forces at the transfer point with The U.S. Army Band, known as "Pershing's Own" for the great general who ordered its creation in 1922. The Band has more than 250 musicians and ten ensembles. Along with The Old Guard's Fife and Drum Corps, Pershing's Own is "the most highly educated unit in the United States Army," as Pershing's successor, General Mark Milley, likes to say. Most of its soldier-musicians have a master's or doctorate in music, often from prestigious conservatories like Juilliard.

One of the ensembles in Pershing's Own is The Ceremonial Band, which performs funerals in Arlington with The Old Guard. Though formally under my control as the escort commander, the drum major directed the musical performance. During funerals, the band plays musical selections whenever the remains are in motion and during the casket team's flag-folding sequence. They tend to play a handful of classics, such as "America the Beautiful" and "Mansions of the Lord." The band also provides the bugler, who steps out of their formation to play Taps.

The caisson section arrived next at the transfer point, about fifteen or twenty minutes out. As they approached, the section rider galloped ahead of the postilion riders, saluting the officer-in-charge as he passed. The officer returned the salute, dropping it once the caisson was where he wanted it to stop. This silent signal was the first of many that occurred during the funeral.

The last key player to arrive was the Arlington representative. The "ANC Rep," as we referred to this role, was responsible for scheduling the funeral with the family, providing them with instructions, answering questions, and guiding them during the funeral. The ANC Rep also drove by the transfer point (or the grave site for a standard-honor funeral) a few minutes before the funeral to brief key leaders about the number of attendees, the route of the procession, whether the casket (or urn) was heavy or oddly shaped, and any tensions within the family, which can regrettably occur in Arlington just like at any other funeral.

In my time in the military and government, ANC Reps stand out alongside soldiers as some of the most respectful, professional public servants. They take great pride in their highly sensitive job, remaining unflappable in moments of high emotion, extreme weather, or family strife. Many have dedicated a career to Arlington and, before that, the military. Joe Mercer is a case in point. He served nine years with The Old Guard, from 1985 to 1994, and has worked at Arlington ever since. "It is a no-fail," Mercer stressed, "because you only get one chance to get it right." I worked dozens of funerals with Mercer, and he exhibited tenderness and grace, while also moving the funeral efficiently along—the Reps, like the soldiers, perform several funerals a day. Yet he did not miss an opportunity to reinforce the meaning of each funeral. "It's so important that they understand or at least get a little impression in their mind of just how much their loved one's service to our country means," Mercer explained when recalling that he tried to position young children where they can see the military honors. "After they're gone, this is what we do for them because they have served their country and their country owes this to them."

"Visual!" That command, yelled by the first soldier to see the ANC Rep's black sedan leading the procession, started the funeral. But in the rituals that followed, only one voice would be heard: mine as the escort commander, and only a few times. A silent cue or a whispered word triggered most of the action as we strove to uphold the solemnity of the moment and to preserve a reverential silence around the family. These silent rituals were, in no small part, why we trained and rehearsed so much, even talking through the cues beforehand. We all had to know the funeral sequence without fail, and focus intensely throughout the mission.

When the funeral procession approached, I commanded the escort to attention and saluted, along with the casket-team leader and the officer-in-charge, usually Cpt. Beard. The ANC Rep zoomed through the transfer point, parked, and hopped out to direct traffic. As with the caisson a few minutes earlier, Cpt. Beard dropped his salute as the silent cue to stop the hearse. Now we waited for the ANC Rep to direct the family and mourners to park and exit their vehicles. This moment was my closest look at the family, no more than twenty to thirty yards away. Whether a small, staid funeral for a World War II veteran or a large, emotional funeral for a soldier killed in Iraq a few days earlier, some things were common across funerals. The family members hesitated, deferring to the ANC Rep. They glanced over at me and the escort after looking at the casket team. And they were transfixed by Old Guard soldiers in action.

Once the ANC Rep positioned the family and mourners where they could see the transfer, he slightly nodded his head to Cpt. Beard, who made eye contact with the casket-team leader and nodded imperceptibly. The casket team stepped off and halted at the hearse's door, where the "drag man," who pulls the casket out of the hearse, stepped in and bent over, ostensibly to blouse the flag but actually signaling me to order the escort to salute. Because I was already facing the escort, the guidon bearer relayed the cue at a whisper. After I gave the command, I turned to face the casket and gave a solo saber salute, cuing the band to start a hymn and the casket team to start the transfer.

We held the salute and the band played until the casket team had loaded the casket onto the caisson, which was the rule at every funeral: when the remains were being carried, we rendered honors with a salute. Once the casket team secured the casket with clamps and straps, the ANC Rep directed the family and mourners back to their vehicles for the procession to the grave site. With another silent nod from the ANC Rep, Cpt. Beard stepped off, saluting the flag and remains as he walked ahead of the procession. I commanded the escort to fall in behind them, in front of the caisson and the family.

The march to the grave site could vary a lot, from barely a quarter mile to more than a mile if the family had requested a chapel service at Old Post Chapel on Fort Myer to precede the funeral. The best conditions for a funeral were mild and clear weather, though I personally enjoyed marching in the snow; muggy heat or rain, less so. Regardless the conditions or length, though, I surveyed the scene—spotting the position we had identified at the morning recon, marching the escort onto the grass and around the headstones, then waiting for the caisson and family to arrive.

I missed much of what came next because I still faced the escort, but I knew what to expect from all the rehearsals and talk-throughs. The silent rituals started again. Cpt. Beard stopped the caisson with another salute. The ANC Rep positioned the family and nodded to Cpt. Beard, who signaled my guidon bearer with a big, exaggerated nod, visible at the distance. The guidon bearer whispered updates to me along the way, concluding with the cue to order the salute—sometimes at a loud yell to overcome the wind or airplanes from Reagan National Airport. As at the transfer point, my solo salute cued the band to play, and then the casket team to remove the remains and carry them to the grave site.

Cpt. Beard followed them to the grave, as I watched, still saluting. The family and mourners followed, while the caisson section rode away. As the casket came to rest on the platform above the grave, Cpt. Beard dropped his salute, my cue to end the escort's

A caisson section transports the remains during a full-honor funeral. Members of the casket team march beside the caisson.

salute and put them in the position of parade rest. Now we waited for the family to be seated and for the casket team to pull the flag taut, silently cuing Cpt. Beard to step backward so the chaplain could step in for his remarks.

Although I never served as the officer-in-charge of a full-honor funeral, I did so often in standard-honor funerals. The graveside service is similar for both, and the chaplain's role is identical. At these funerals, I could at times hear the chaplain's words and thus learn more about the decedent. While I cannot recall specific

An escort platoon salutes during the graveside service of a full-honor funeral.

stories, the tenor was often the same: amazing valor by humble heroes. Paratroopers who jumped into Normandy. Rangers who fought in Vietnam. Clerks thrust into combat. And all stoic and reserved for decades about their heroism.

After the chaplain finished his remarks, the spotlight shifted back to The Old Guard for the formal military honors. Cpt. Beard stepped back to the head of the grave and saluted, my signal to bring the escort to attention, order them to salute, and command, "Firing Party, fire three volleys." The firing-party commander directed his troops through the volleys, with the goal—usually achieved—of seven rifles sounding like one. Next came the bugler, who had stepped out of the band's formation to play the mournful notes of Taps. After the last note, I ended our salute and put the escort at parade rest again. When I assumed that position myself, the band started its final hymn, putting the casket team on the clock: it had one minute, fifty-five seconds to fold the flag perfectly, without voice commands and just steps from the family. Once it was folded, the "present man" presented the flag to Cpt. Beard—hence, the name—and then the team silently marched off. Cpt. Beard turned to the next of kin, usually a widow or adult child, presented the flag, and offered condolences and then one more salute, before returning to the head of the grave.

One last Old Guard soldier now approached the next of kin, with an elegantly attired woman on his arm. She had appeared earlier, almost like an angel, to greet the caisson at the curb, then followed the family to the grave site. She and her soldier stood at a respectful distance during the service and the honors. Although she displayed no emotion—her job was to honor, not to grieve— her kind, gentle countenance contrasted with our studied reserve. Now she spoke softly to the next of kin, offering condolences and passing two notes, one on behalf of the Army Chief of Staff and one from her. This is the ritual of an Arlington Lady.

In 1973, Julia Abrams, the wife of Army Chief of Staff General Creighton Abrams, organized the Army Arlington Ladies program, modeled on an Air Force program to ensure no soldier would be laid to rest alone. An Arlington Lady represents the Chief of Staff at every Army funeral, offering condolences to the family, or accepting the flag on their behalf if they could not attend due to weather, illness, or infirmity. The Old Guard provides three soldiers to the Ladies as drivers and escorts. Each Lady, who volunteers without pay, is either a veteran herself or an

Army wife. For example, the Abramses' daughter-in-law, Connie, became an Arlington Lady when their son and her husband, General Robert Abrams, was stationed in the Washington area (today he commands U.S. Forces Korea). Another Arlington Lady is Lt. Col. Kehoe's wife, Christie.

"I had always heard of the Arlington Ladies," Christie recounted, and when her husband was assigned to The Old Guard, she thought, "Oh, this will be fantastic if I ever get the opportunity to join." But she "didn't know whom to ask about doing it or how you got involved." Then, "as if by divine intervention," her Bible study leader happened to be an Arlington Lady and invited Christie to join when she learned that Lt. Col. Kehoe commanded 1st Battalion. Christie now works in the cemetery a few days a month. "It's a really amazing privilege" to serve alongside her husband's soldiers, she said, "just amazing to see the precision and the gratitude and the honor they give each one of our fallen service members."

As the Arlington Lady stepped away, the funeral concluded—but our work did not. Even in our departure, we upheld the highest standards of dignity and honor. I commanded the escort to march off with a low conversational tone, in contrast to my usual command voice. We walked on the grass as much as possible to avoid heel clicks. At the bus, soldiers maintained ceremonial composure as they loaded up, while the key leaders gathered for the after-action review, a final ritual illustrating The Old Guard's dedication to the nation's fallen and their families. An outsider might call it nit-picking, but we always sought to sustain and improve our performance. The casket team, for instance, might have carried the casket at a slight angle up a hill. No matter how imperceptible, no miscue was too small to correct before the next funeral.

Yet not every mistake was small or imperceptible. The worst

I witnessed was a fallout in the escort on a hot, muggy afternoon. Out of the corner of my eye, I could see the soldier slowly fall on his face, like a tree falling to the ground. I did not break ceremonial composure, nor did the other escort soldiers. We had a contingency plan for these moments. The assistant noncommissioned-officer-in-charge, an all-purpose utility player for the funeral, silently walked over, picked up the soldier, and carried him away. Then the "supernumerary," an extra soldier for the escort platoon, stepped out from hiding behind a nearby tree. Already bloused up, he marched into position and picked up the fallout's rifle. We were displeased at the after-action review, to say the least, but further investigation—and a fallout always resulted in an investigation—revealed that the soldier was getting sick. He had skipped sick call that morning because he did not want to let down his platoon. Good initiative, bad judgment.

Even in error, the character and the honor of The Old Guard and its soldiers shines through. Lt. Col. Kehoe shared one especially telling story with me. Staff Sergeant Patrick McAllister from Charlie Company erred in condolences when presenting the flag in late 2018. The condolences start with the presenter saying that he acts "on behalf of the President of the United States, the United States Army, and a grateful nation." Ssg. McAllister inadvertently started with the Army, but caught himself and included the president. It was a minor mistake, noticed by neither the family nor the ANC Rep. Nevertheless, "I was kicking myself all the way to the bus," he recalled, and he promptly reported himself to the Memorial Affairs Section. Cpt. Rhodes recommended decertification. "I'm the MA standard-bearer and I have to enforce the standards," he explained, though he commended Ssg. McAllister's "impeccable integrity." Lt. Col. Kehoe settled on requiring him to retest on condolences, milder discipline than full decertification.

But the story does not end there. Lt. Col. Kehoe wanted to make an example of Ssg. McAllister—a positive example. He addressed all of Charlie Company and presented Ssg. McAllister with his commander's coin for excellence, no doubt puzzling some young soldiers. "I'm not encouraging people to make mistakes, don't get the wrong message," he explained. "I'm rewarding this guy for his commitment to excellence. Because that's our job." For his part, Ssg. McAllister downplayed what he had done: "I don't see the big deal. I did the right thing. That's how I was raised and what we expect of Old Guard soldiers." When I asked Lt. Col. Kehoe to reflect on the incident, he said, after a long pause, "The Old Guard is an incredible place to serve. I am so proud of my soldiers."

On these rituals went, for the rest of the day. Those soldiers who had performed the 0900 full-honor funeral remained together for the other three full-honor funerals at 1100, 1300, and 1500. The two standard-honor funeral teams also remained together, often conducting a funeral on the hour, every hour. The only exception was Charlie's officers. Like marchers in the escort, our roles were interchangeable, so we could move among the various funerals. For example, after marching as the escort commander in the 0900 full-honor funeral, I might get dropped at the grave site for an 1100 standard-honor funeral over which I would preside as the officer-in-charge, then wait with the casket team to conduct a dependent funeral at 1300, and finally return to the barracks.

But our soldiers generally stayed in Arlington all day, with only the Myer Flyer as something of an oasis. Out of public view, soldiers could talk, use iPods and smartphones, nap, and drink and eat. One thing they could not do, however, was sit down while in uniform, which was prohibited in order to prevent wrinkles on the blouse and the trousers. As a workaround, many soldiers wore shorts so they could strip down and rest between funerals. We spent hours in the press room so families would see a razor-sharp uniform—not accordion wrinkles behind the knee.

The day's last funerals began at 1500, after which soldiers rode back to Fort Myer—but not before one final ritual in the cemetery. Just as we posted the colors in the morning, we retired the colors after the last full-honor funeral. The ceremony was a simple salute from the troops to the flag. Again, we could have skipped it; no one would see, by design. But we went the extra distance to honor the flag—the flag worn by the soldiers we buried that day, the flag that adorned their remains, the flag that their loved ones now carried back to their home.

By 1600, a company's worth of foot-sore soldiers—hot, sweaty, cold, or wet, as the season and weather may be—had reached the barracks, but the day was far from over. 1st Sgt. Montanez had returned from the clearing meeting, and he and the platoon sergeants tagged out missions for the next two days. The officers discussed which funerals we would each perform the next day. Funeral teams with any deficiencies from the day's funerals—a loose volley from the firing party, for instance—conducted retraining out back. And we worked on our uniforms after a day of wear and tear, the last ritual of the day.

Uniform maintenance was a daily constant at The Old Guard, with some days easier than others. After mild days, I could restore my uniform in fifteen minutes. I wiped my shoes' Corfam uppers with Windex and applied another coat of edge dressing to the steel plates and the soles—including the bottom of the soles to avoid "flashing" the family with pale soles. My blouse had two hot spots: the right sleeve from saluting and the waistline from the ceremonial belt. I removed those wrinkles in a few minutes with a garment steamer. For good measure, I locked clamp hangers upside-down onto the sleeves and hung shoes from the hooks; the weight pulled the sleeves taut overnight. I did the same with my trousers, hanging them upside down from the ankles, letting the weight of the pockets and belt line pull out the fabric.

But not all days were so easy. After a muggy summer day, only the press machine could restore the razor-sharp crease in my sleeves. Likewise, after a rainy day, both my raincoat and trousers needed a new press, and my saber and scabbard required anti-rust polish. But I could hardly complain. The escort and firing party marched and fired all day long, wrinkling both sleeves and the shoulders. And the casket team sweated through their blouses while carrying the casket—all while working next to horses that shed a lot and relieved themselves with no regard for ceremonial composure. In no case, though, did we leave for the day until our uniforms were ready for the next day's missions, a final display of respect for the fallen.

Day after day, we carried out the rituals of Arlington. By Friday afternoon, we were exhausted. Marching and standing in steel-plated shoes took a toll on one's knees and back. Moreover, five days of intense mission focus was mentally draining. Yet we could not simply punch out for some well-deserved weekend rest and relaxation. Sometimes, we returned to the cemetery on backup week, or even a second consecutive primary week because of Delta Company's deployment. Otherwise, we started a week of support for ceremonies, with rehearsals often beginning on Monday. Thus, primary week ended with one last round of uniform maintenance and tagging out the next week's missions. While the venue shifted from Arlington to the parade field, our expectations did not. We would be ready to hit the marks—without fail.

5

IIIII

Standing on Ceremony

"It's already miserable out here," I thought to myself as sweat streamed down my face while hundreds of troops milled about on Macomb Place, a small street just off Summerall Field, the main parade ground on Fort Myer. It was a little after 0900 on June 26, 2007, but the heat index was already well over ninety degrees, with no cloud cover in sight. We were staging for the change-of-command ceremony, officially known as an Army Full Honor Review. Colonel Bob Pricone was transferring command of The Old Guard to Colonel Joe Buche. And I was marching in my first ceremony.

"Key leaders!" someone yelled from down the street. As with funerals, the key leaders huddled up and talked through the entire ceremony beforehand. But for ceremonies, these huddles were much bigger because the sequences were longer and more complicated, and many of us performed them infrequently compared to funerals. I joined and focused sharply, not wanting to make a mistake in front of my soldiers and my new commander.

Meanwhile, the soldiers did a "box-up," The Old Guard's equivalent of pregame warm-ups. The platoons faced each other and executed the commands of a senior sergeant standing in the middle of the box. These exercises got them loose, while also synchronizing the movements of nearly two hundred soldiers in ceremonial uniforms. Even forty yards away from the audience, the soldiers' white gloves against their dark blue blouses would magnify the slightest mistake.

As the talk-through and the box-up concluded, I heard Command Sergeant Major Russell McCray shout, "Listen up, listen up!" We all gathered around The Old Guard's senior enlisted soldier, the chief enlisted advisor to Col. Pricone and soon to Col. Buche. "This is your commander's day! Get out there, stand tall, look sharp for him! And no fallouts!"

The pep talk motivated the soldiers, but I had my doubts about not having fallouts. We were already soaked in sweat. It had been hotter last year in Baghdad, of course, but somehow it seemed worse in my heavy wool uniform than it had in my combat gear. And while this ceremony was my first, the seasoned sergeants had predicted at both rehearsals that "they'll be dropping like flies out there."

Strangely, I felt more anxious about this first ceremony at Fort Myer than I had felt last year about my first patrol in Baghdad. I knew why, or at least I thought I did. Over there, I had trained for more than a year to lead in combat, I led battle-hardened soldiers, and we operated on our own, with no one looking over our shoulder. Today, by contrast, I had only a few weeks of training, my soldiers were great but could not help me once the ceremony began, and we were performing for a large audience.

But a bugler sounded "Attention," our cue to march on, so the time for butterflies had ended. I stepped off with my soldiers and we reached our marks, a mixture of permanent concrete blocks and temporary stakes, invisible to the audience. Over the next hour, I hit my cues and felt strong, if hot and soaked. Unlike a funeral, the ceremony lasted more than an hour; a few soldiers fell out during the speeches, though a nice breeze minimized the casualties (while testing the flag bearers). As we marched by the reviewing stand and off the field, I was proud of all my troops, who stood tall, honored Col. Pricone, and welcomed Col. Buche. And I was glad to get out of the sun.

★ ★ ★

While funerals take first priority among The Old Guard's missions and are most closely associated with its public identity, ceremonies are also central to the regiment's role in the Army. Lieutenant Colonel Todd Burroughs, the commander of 4th Battalion, which has primary responsibility for ceremonies, described them as the Army's "strategic messaging" to the American people and the world. First Sergeant Matt Craig has spent eight years in The Old Guard over two tours, worked in the cemetery for years, deployed with Bravo Company to Djibouti, and now is the senior enlisted soldier in Honor Guard Company, the regiment's main ceremonial company. He summed up the two functions simply: "face to the family and face to the world."

As the Army's strategic messenger, The Old Guard delivers a variety of messages to many audiences, whether in person or through its popular social-media sites. Old Guard troops express the Army's gratitude to retiring soldiers for dedicating a career of service to the nation. They wear colonial uniforms and march to colonial music to connect today's Army back to our founding, a reminder not only of The Old Guard's history, but also our founding principles and why they are worth fighting for. They travel the country on outreach missions to deliver these messages. Along with their four sister services, they deliver a simple message to allies and adversaries alike: our military is full of equally disciplined and skilled troops ready to defend our nation and our friends.

The soldiers of 4th Battalion who deliver these messages are among the Army's best, serving in some of the Army's most unique units. They range from young soldiers with the strength and stamina of professional athletes to world-class musicians. They operate in the highest-profile settings, yet often work as small, independent teams with only a young sergeant in charge. What they have in common is that they are the best in the world in their missions.

Continental Color Guard

The busiest ceremonial unit in The Old Guard is the Continental Color Guard, which performs in more than seven hundred events per year, even though it has only twenty-five soldiers. Known as CCG, its missions range from serving as the color guard in a large ceremony with hundreds of troops to sending a four-man color guard to a banquet at a local hotel. Given the number and complexity of its missions, the platoon's operations resemble an overseas deployment, and it requires mature soldiers who can act responsibly and perform without supervision.

"They're working decentralized all the time, crazy hours, working with random people, and they never falter," is how Sergeant First Class James McFatridge, CCG's platoon sergeant, described his young soldiers. Many previously served as guidons or in color teams in their line company. More than that experience, though, Sfc. McFatridge looks for motivated soldiers with "high character" who want to succeed: "If I'm going to be a guidon, I'm going to be part of the color team, why don't I go be part of the premier color-guard team?" The result is that CCG is full of "eager beavers," he explained. "They all tried out to be here, they all want to be here, and they will all want everything big."

But even with that attitude, the attrition rate for CCG training exceeds 80 percent because of the platoon's extreme strength and endurance demands. For example, Sfc. McFatridge was the

Personal Color Bearer for President Donald Trump at the White House arrival ceremony for French President Emmanuel Macron in April 2018. He carried the National colors while standing at attention for more than an hour just behind the American president. Another example is the weight of the Army colors, with its 190 battle streamers. When the Army colors dip to salute the National colors, these top-heavy streamers weigh the equivalent of eighty-eight pounds, causing even the strongest bearer's right arm to quiver by the end of the National Anthem. More challenging still is a ceremony with a foreign dignitary when the anthems are played in sequence. When Secretary of Defense Jim Mattis hosted a Pentagon arrival ceremony for the Ministers of Defense of Sweden and Finland in May 2018, the anthems lasted for more than three and a half minutes, an eternity when holding eighty-eight pounds with an extended arm.

These tasks may seem obscure, yet the settings are anything but. CCG soldiers perform routinely for the president, heads of state, and worldwide television audiences. Because of this spotlight, CCG cannot have a fallout. In fact, CCG does not use supernumeraries, unlike other Old Guard units. "We don't have supers," Sfc. McFatridge stressed. "We don't have fallouts. Period." No one at The Old Guard could recall a CCG fallout, or had even heard of one. According to the platoon's operating manual, "CCG has never had a ceremonial fallout," which it calls "a great source of pride within the platoon."

This zero-defect standard demands the highest levels of physical fitness, and a soldier who reports to the three-week training cycle with anything less is likely to fail. Soldiers start with a ten-mile run from Fort Myer to Washington National Cathedral and back, one of the steepest hills in the capital. Along the way, they stop frequently for calisthenics and repeats of the "Exorcist steps," the narrow stairway in Georgetown where a famous scene from *The Exorcist* was filmed. They also must complete a five-mile run carrying a nine-and-a-half-foot flagstaff, stopping along the way to perform upper-body exercises. And they conduct two standing-proficiency tests, one holding colors for ninety minutes and one at attention for three hours in a room brought to more than ninety degrees with sauna-like humidity to simulate an outdoor summer ceremony. The soldiers who pass these intense physical tests are, in Sfc. McFatridge's word, "beasts." (He is no slouch himself, at six-one and 230 pounds, with the build of an NFL linebacker.)

Soldiers must also demonstrate proficiency in CCG's basic tasks: the manual of arms for the M1903 A3 Springfield, the rifle carried in Joint Armed Forces missions; the manual for flagstaffs; and ceremonial sequences. "The standard is extremely high" for these tests because, according to the platoon's operating manual, "failure to meet the standard could result in serious embarrassment not only to the individual, but the CCG, United States Army, and our Nation." The soldiers who pass these tests join CCG on a probationary status, with further evaluations after thirty and sixty days.

Once qualified, soldiers specialize based on the missions they perform and the uniforms they wear. 2nd and 3rd Squads wear the normal ceremonial blue uniform and often march with the other four services as part of an eight-man Joint Armed Forces Color Guard in Armed Forces missions, such as the Macron arrival. CCG provides the National Color Bearer, the Army Color Bearer, and one of the armed guards. (The other services carry their colors and the Marines provide the second guard.) By contrast, 1st Squad wears the distinctive 1784 Continental Infantry uniform—commonly known as "colonials" or "wigs and tights"—which George Washington approved during the Revolutionary War and The Old Guard wore when it was activated in

Section 60, the eternal home at Arlington National Cemetery of soldiers killed in the War on Terror. When I arrived at The Old Guard in early 2007, much of Section 60 was an open green field. Today, the section is nearly filled with headstones. *Elizabeth Fraser/Arlington National Cemetery*

The 2018 official photograph of The Old Guard on Summerall Field, the main parade field at Fort Myer. The regiment includes soldiers in colonial uniforms, horses and caissons, and military working dogs. *The Old Guard*

The American Soldier, 1786, by H. Charles McBarron, illustrates the uniforms worn by the First American Regiment, The Old Guard's forerunner, during the founding era. Commanders used musicians in the era to communicate with their soldiers, thus the musicians' uniform featured the reverse colors seen on the drummer and fifer (upper right corner) to allow for quick identification in battle. *U.S. Army Center of Military History*

Master Sergeant Mark Metrinko leads the Fife and Drum Corps during an Army Full Honor Arrival ceremony on Whipple Field, with the National Mall on the horizon. FDC wears the 1779 Continental Musician uniform to commemorate the heritage of Army musicians. *Specialist Gabriel Silva/TOG*

Captain Andrew Talone leads the Commander-in-Chief's Guard on a bayonet charge during Twilight Tattoo on June 6, 2018. CinC Guard wears the 1784 Continental Infantry uniform to honor its predecessors in the First American Regiment. *Sergeant George Huley/TOG*

Just off the bus in Arlington National Cemetery one morning in late 2007.
Tom Cotton

A rare action shot of me leading the escort during a full-honor funeral in early 2008.
TC

Lieutenant Colonel Todd Burroughs leads Representative Warren Davidson and me on the inspection of troops during a ceremony in May 2018 to commemorate the seventieth anniversary of The Old Guard's reactivation as the Army's official ceremonial unit. Rep. Davidson also served with The Old Guard. *Sergeant George Huley/TOG*

My wife, Anna, and I attend the 4th Battalion ball in February 2019. To our right is the battalion commander, Lieutenant Colonel Todd Burroughs and his wife, Svetlana; to our left is his senior enlisted advisor, Command Sergeant Major Lee Ward, and his wife, Tanya. *TOG*

Sergeant First Class James McFatridge bears the National colors behind President Donald Trump and Specialist Zachary Beard bears the French colors behind President Emmanuel Macron at a White House arrival ceremony on April 24, 2018, while Captain James Rojek (center, background) commands the fifty-six state and territorial flags lining the South Lawn driveway. *Stephanie Chasez/White House*

Colonel Jason Garkey, The Old Guard commander, leads President Trump and President Macron on the review of troops. Lieutenant Harrison Barber, the platoon leader (facing away), commanded "eyes, right" as they approached the formation, the soldiers' cue to snap their heads to the right and follow the reviewing officials back to the front. *Joyce Boghosian/WH*

Old Guard soldiers prepare to draw their bayonets and fix them to their rifles. The Old Guard marches with bayonets fixed in honor of its bayonet charge at the Battle of Cerro Gordo in the Mexican War. Soldiers fix bayonets to a seven-count drumbeat without verbal commands. Even at a distance from the audience, the soldiers' white gloves against their dark blue uniforms highlight the precision of their movements. *Specialist Lane Hiser/TOG*

The U.S. Army Drill Team performs on Soldier Field during halftime of a Chicago Bears game on Veterans Day 2018. The Drill Team travels nationally and internationally to showcase the U.S. Army through precision-based drill routines. *Specialist Jacob Plank/TOG*

Sergeant First Class Allen Addison follows his casket team off an aircraft at Dover Air Force Base during the dignified transfer of remains on May 3, 2018, for Specialist Gabriel Conde, who was killed in action three days earlier in Afghanistan. The Old Guard has conducted the dignified transfer at Dover since 2003. *Sergeant George Huley/TOG*

General Mark Milley (left), the Army Chief of Staff, and Sergeant Major of the Army Dan Dailey (center) salute as Old Guard soldiers carry the remains of Specialist Conde to a waiting transfer vehicle. "If I'm in Washington," Sgt. Maj. Dailey told me, "I go to every dignified transfer of remains. I will cancel everything on the schedule to get to Dover." *Sergeant George Huley/TOG*

An Old Guard soldier places a flag at a headstone during Flags In, when the regiment places a flag at every grave site in Arlington National Cemetery on the Thursday before Memorial Day. We used our foot to estimate distance from the headstone and a bottle cap in our hand to push the flag. *Specialist Gabriel Silva/TOG*

An Old Guard soldier carries a rucksack full of flags during Flags In. With nearly a quarter million grave sites to honor, Flags In is a major operational mission for The Old Guard and its soldiers. *Specialist Sarah Pond/TOG*

An Old Guard officer leads the escort in a full-honor funeral. Consisting of The U.S. Army Band, an Old Guard color team, and an Old Guard platoon, the escort leads the funeral procession from a transfer point, usually a traffic circle or intersection where the remains are transferred from the hearse to the caisson to the grave site. *Rachel Larue/Arlington National Cemetery*

An Old Guard caisson section of seven horses and four riders transports the casket from the transfer point to the grave site. The eight-man casket team marches alongside the caisson. *Elizabeth Fraser/ANC*

An Old Guard color team salutes during a full-honor funeral. The Old Guard's regimental colors are topped with fifty-five campaign streamers to reflect its history of battlefield valor. *TOG*

Old Guard soldiers with the Presidential Salute Battery fire a gun salute during a funeral in Arlington National Cemetery. The Salute Battery performs in funerals for general officers and senior government officials, as well as ceremonies around the capital region. *Specialist Brandon Hutchinson/TOG*

Colonel Jason Garkey, The Old Guard commander, follows an Old Guard casket team to the grave site at the funeral for former Secretary of the Army Togo West on April 26, 2018. While junior officers usually serve as the officer-in-charge of full-honor funerals, Col. Garkey performs this role for the highest-ranking officials. *Elizabeth Fraser/ANC*

An Old Guard firing party fires the three-volley salute during a full-honor funeral. All eyes turn during the volley to the seven-member firing party and its commander as the soldiers endeavor to make seven rifles crack as one. *Rachel Larue/ANC*

Colonel Jason Garkey salutes as the casket team holds the flag taut and a bugler plays "Taps" at the funeral for Secretary West. *Elizabeth Fraser/ANC*

Sergeant Major Jasper Johnson awaits as an Old Guard casket team folds the flag at a full-honor funeral. The casket team conducts the fold to the rhythm of "Army Blue" for West Point graduates or "America the Beautiful" for other soldiers, both of which last one minute, fifty-five seconds. *Rachel Larue/ANC*

Staff Sergeant Justin Courtney, a Sentinel at the Tomb of the Unknown Soldier, buckles his ceremonial belt while another Tomb guard blouses the fabric of his raincoat and two more guards pat him down with masking tape to remove lint or dust. The Tomb guards go to the greatest lengths behind the scenes to perform their singular mission to the standard of perfection. *Sergeant George Huley/TOG*

A Tomb guard shines his Tomb Badge. The guards dedicate hours to uniform maintenance every night to restore their uniforms to pristine condition for their next duty day. *Sergeant George Huley/TOG*

Corporal Matthew Koeppel (center) conducts the Changing of the Guard, relieving Private First Class William Jeffs (left) and posting Private First Class Trevor Drahem (right). The Tomb has been guarded twenty-four hours a day nonstop since 1937, rain, snow, or shine. *Specialist Gabriel Silva/TOG*

Old Guard soldiers salute during a wreath-laying ceremony at the Tomb of the Unknown Soldier, while the Tomb guard salutes from "the box," the green canvas hut on the edge of the Plaza. *Rachel Larue/ANC*

Specialist Colin Martin walks a Caparisoned Horse out of Arlington National Cemetery after a full-honor funeral. The riderless horse with boots reversed in the stirrups once signaled a commander's death on the battlefield to the rear headquarters. Today, the Caparisoned Horse honors the fallen commander's service one final time on the avenues of Arlington. *Elizabeth Fraser/ANC*

1784 as the First American Regiment. The uniform consists of a long blue coat with a red collar, cuffs, and lapels; tan wool pants and vest; a ruffled neck beard; black leather shoes; a black ammo pouch and a red canteen; white gloves; and, most famously, a black tricornered hat and a white wig. Given this unique uniform, 1st Squad performs only in Army missions.

But all squads execute the platoon's most common mission, the "color shot": a presentation of the colors for the National Anthem in settings as high-profile as the Capitol and as routine as a conference at a hotel. Color shots account for more than 80 percent of the platoon's missions, they last only five to ten minutes, and they can occur in either colonials or ceremonial blues.

A color shot that illustrates CCG's unique mission and the quality of its soldiers is the July Fourth Celebration at the National Archives, which houses the original Declaration of Independence. On Independence Day each year, the Archives hosts a dramatic reading of the Declaration on its steps along Constitution Avenue. 1st Squad presents the colors each year, and I joined them in 2018. We linked up at the platoon's off-post room at Fort Myer, where soldiers store their uniforms and prepare for their missions—five alone on July 4. Corporal Chandler Kelley, the noncommissioned-officer-in-charge, did a quick equipment check, then the four soldiers loaded into a van. After the short drive to the Archives, Cpl. Kelley called his point of contact a few times—"It's pretty common that they're hard to reach," he observed—and the team followed her into a holding room. After they stored the colors and their garment bags, they reconned the mission site and sequence of events from the steps of the Archives.

Common sense, perhaps, but few units besides The Old Guard would entrust such a prominent mission to a corporal, the lowest-ranking noncommissioned officer. In most Army units, a senior sergeant or officer would lead this mission. But as Sfc. McFatridge stressed, his soldiers have to operate without supervision, which Cpl. Kelley appreciated. "I couldn't imagine being anywhere else now that I've been in CCG," he said, "because we get treated like adults, we don't have higher breathing down our neck."

The Archives mission is also a good example of the opportunities afforded to CCG soldiers. As we reentered the Archives, I asked the soldiers if they had seen the original Declaration, Constitution, and Bill of Rights. None had, so I encouraged them to do so. In the empty Rotunda, security guards and docents welcomed the young soldiers, who were giddy throughout their exclusive tour. Cpl. Kelley exclaimed, "This is so amazing, what a great part of our history." Specialist Mario Arias responded, "It's hard to believe that we just saw our founding documents for the first time on the Fourth of July." Not every mission has such memorable moments, but CCG performs often enough at major sporting events, the White House, the Capitol, and other landmarks that most of its soldiers have experiences that few Americans ever will.

Back in the holding room, the soldiers began the colonial-uniform version of blousing up—putting on their vests and coats, hanging their tricorns around their necks, and unfurling the colors. As they walked outside, heads turned and spectators gawked. "This always happens," Cpl. Kelley explained. "A big part of our mission is outreach and representing the Army and The Old Guard to the public," so they go out early just to interact with the public. Within a few minutes, a young girl asked for a picture. Cpl. Kelley answered, "Of course you can take a picture!" For the next twenty minutes, happy families mobbed these young soldiers in colonials as if they were Mickey Mouse at Disney World.

All that remained was the mission itself. The team donned their wigs and tricorns five minutes out and lined up on Constitution Avenue. They marched into the performance area to a drumbeat and Cpl. Kelley called, "Present arms." Private Khalif Kroma, a giant young soldier, held the eighty-eight-pound Army colors motionless as the singer belted out the National Anthem. They marched off, the mission complete in less than three minutes. Back inside the Archives, they posed for a few more pictures, never missing an opportunity to put a human face on the Army for our citizens.

Fife and Drum Corps

On Constitution Avenue, though, the mission continued for the United States Army Old Guard Fife and Drum Corps. FDC, as it is commonly known, had provided the drummer for CCG's presentation of the colors. Now a twelve-soldier group—four fifers, four buglers, three drummers, and one drum major—played a medley of colonial music selections in a ten-minute marching concert. The crowd delighted as they watched what is perhaps the most exotic unit in not only The Old Guard, but the entire military.

The Fife and Drum Corps' unique character starts with its uniform. They wear the 1779 Continental Musician uniform, which resembles CCG's infantry uniform with one key difference: the musician's uniform coat is red with blue trim. Military commanders in the revolutionary period used musicians for signaling, thus they wore reverse colors so commanders could identify them quickly on the battlefield. (Today the coats cause many spectators to mistake FDC for British redcoat reenactors.) The drum major's uniform is even more distinctive. He wears the period's light-

The Fife and Drum Corps performs at Fort Monroe, Virginia.

infantry cap, which is a leather cap with a long bear-fur Mohawk from the bill to the base of the neck. And he carries an espontoon, a seven-foot spear used to give silent commands. Because the espontoon does not leave his right hand, the drum major is the only soldier in the Army authorized to salute with his left hand.

Yet their uniforms and equipment are perhaps the least distinctive things about the Fife and Drum Corps. A case in point is the drum major for the Archives mission, Sergeant Major Billy White. He has served with FDC since he enlisted in 1994. Though Sgt. Maj. White has the most tenure in FDC, his longevity is not unique. Unlike nearly all Army units, FDC is a permanent duty station; once assigned its soldiers can stay for the remainder of their careers, making it one of the Army's most stable and experienced units.

In part because of this stability, FDC is unquestionably the best marching unit in The Old Guard. "No matter how rusty the other companies are at rehearsals, you know FDC will be wired tight," noted Captain Zach Kennedy, the ceremonial expert in the regimental headquarters staff. Captain Corey Morgan, the expert in the 4th Battalion headquarters staff, agreed: "FDC always hits their marks and crushes it." Yet Sgt. Maj. White stressed that their marching excellence is by design, not just years of repetition. "One of the things that I think is unique about the Fife and Drum Corps as an Army band is that we take the visual representation just as seriously as we take the music." FDC is the only Army band that does not play while seated and does not use sheet music: "Everything we do is on our feet." Thus, they put the highest priority on marching. Sgt. Maj. White recalled his first trainer, who told him a quarter century ago, "Most of your audience is going to hear with their eyes." A perfect musical performance, in other words, cannot overcome a marching mistake. "Our average audience will see mistakes," he said, "but they won't necessarily hear mistakes."

FDC's marching expertise is just one way The Old Guard benefits from their experience. They teach the other units how to maintain and care for the colonial uniforms and wigs—not exactly a common skill in the Army. Also, FDC's long-tenured and senior sergeants can be informal advisors and sounding boards for the regiment's other leaders. For instance, I got to know Sgt. Maj. White during my tour because we both ran marathons in those days. He was a trusted expert at our rehearsals, as well as a source of institutional knowledge and sound judgment. And FDC provides experience and continuity for presidential inaugurations and state funerals—rare events that have a global spotlight.

Because soldiers often spend their entire career at FDC, its leadership carefully screens and auditions aspiring members, who can be current soldiers or civilians. When an infrequent vacancy occurs in the seventy-member band, the competition is intense. Applicants must submit a résumé, cover letter, reference letters, photographs, and a video recording of a musical performance. Only the most talented performers will make the cut, and talent alone is rarely enough. Most applicants will have years of experience and advanced education. In fact, FDC is one of the most well-educated units in the Army. Most members have a master's degree—including Sgt. Maj. White, in American history—and some soldiers even have doctorates in music.

From this applicant pool, FDC invites the most competitive applicants for a rigorous two-day on-site audition at Fort Myer. A committee then selects the new member, who must complete four to six months of training to master both marching and music. During that time, they will be promoted to staff sergeant if they have not yet attained that rank; this accelerated promotion is a recruiting tool and also reflects their specialized skills and education. (In the infantry, by contrast, a soldier needs many years to obtain and then exceed the rank of staff sergeant.) Upon promotion, new soldiers earn the buff strap and begin to perform FDC's other basic missions. For example, FDC buglers play for military funerals outside Arlington National Cemetery in the Washington area. When the training cycle ends, new soldiers integrate into the full range of FDC missions.

FDC performs more than five hundred missions each year, primarily ceremonies and special shows. FDC participates in most Old Guard ceremonies and many Armed Forces ceremonies in which they play "functional music," as Sgt. Maj. White explained, to provide marching cues for the rest of the regiment. They also twice "pay honor to the reviewing official" with marching medleys. But the special show, in Sgt. Maj. White's opinion, "is of the most benefit to The Old Guard, in terms of what we do that is unique to the Fife and Drum Corps." These shows come in many varieties, including the twelve-soldier performance at the Archives and the twenty-six-soldier performance in the parade that followed. FDC performs these shows in settings as humble as local parades and as august as the Super Bowl.

Whatever the occasion, Sgt. Maj. White observed, "the Fife and Drum Corps is one of the best tools that the Army has for getting out in the American public and reminding the American public about our founding values, those core principles that America was founded on." The core mission of the Fife and Drum Corps and the Continental Color Guard is to call forth the memories of our founding in the minds of our fellow Americans. And that is the real purpose of the colonial uniforms and music. "These uniforms and the old music we play just sets people in that frame of mind," Sgt. Maj. White explained, "and then we use that as our entrée to talk" about the founding and provide a few simple reminders: our founding principles are noble and just, our ancestors fought for those principles, and we ought to be ready to fight for them, too.

Commander-in-Chief's Guard

The Old Guard has one other unit that wears colonial uniforms: the Commander-in-Chief's Guard, modeled on General George Washington's hand-selected personal guard during the Revolutionary War. CinC Guard also maintains proficiency in the weapons and tactics of the era. Thus, they carry Brown Bess muskets and march to unique voice commands that distinguish them from other Old Guard units. Like the Continental Color Guard and the Fife and Drum Corps, CinC Guard's "primary mission is outreach," in the words of its commander, Captain Dick Tallman.

But unlike those units, CinC Guard is also a regular infantry company—officially Alpha Company of 4th Battalion—with about 130 soldiers. When new Old Guard soldiers report to CinC Guard after completing the Regimental Orientation Program, they must further train on the musket manual and complete a "black powder" certification because CinC Guard's muskets are functional and fired in demonstrations. Because soldiers do not apply to CinC Guard, unlike the regiment's other specialized units, some "think they got stuck in the strangest unit in the Army," chuckled Cpt. Tallman. But most "buy in to the purpose of reaching out to the American public." And the company's leaders love the mission. "I would rather be in CinC Guard than any other company," Cpt. Tallman's executive officer, Captain Zach Watts, opined.

CinC Guard's most important outreach event is Twilight Tattoo. While they march in other Old Guard ceremonies, Twilight Tattoo is not only the central mission of CinC Guard, but also one of the biggest annual events for The Old Guard, something I did not appreciate when I first reported to Fort Myer. The only tattoos in my military experience were the ones my soldiers had, not a musical and marching extravaganza.

The origins of tattoo date to the seventeenth century and to that most soldierly tradition of drinking beer. Dutch military commanders sent a drummer and bugler into the streets to recall their troops from local taverns by playing a tune known as *doe den tap toe*, which is Dutch for "turn off the tap." As British and American commanders adopted the practice, the tune's final two Dutch words were combined and altered into "tattoo." By the nineteenth century, tattoo had evolved into a kind of evening entertainment, a custom that continues today with military tattoos around the world.

The Old Guard's tattoo began in 1961 under the name Torch-light Tattoo, a reference to the torches used for lighting at the Sylvan Theater on the grounds of the Washington Monument, which once hosted the show. Twilight Tattoo took its current name in 1983. Over the years, The Old Guard has performed the show at the Jefferson Memorial, the Ellipse, and the White House. Today, Twilight Tattoo occurs at Fort Myer.

More than anything, Twilight Tattoo resembles a Broadway musical. The purpose of Twilight Tattoo, according to the show's written operation order, is "to relate the Army story to the American people and personally connect the nation to the soldiers who serve them." Twilight Tattoo showcases soldiers with historically accurate uniforms and weapons. These soldier–actors "tell the Army's story from the beginning of the Army and nation to to-day," as Cpt. Watts put it. The U.S. Army Band and the Fife and Drum Corps support the historical vignettes with musical performances and underscores.

CinC Guard dedicates the better part of the year to Twilight Tattoo. The planning process starts in December with script and graphics preparation, casting calls, musical arrangements, and show scheduling. Rehearsals begin in March, with soldiers breaking out authentic uniforms and weapons from every major conflict throughout our history. CinC Guard is responsible for the weapons and blank ammunition, so its arms room includes not only modern infantry weapons and the Brown Bess muskets, but also weapons as diverse as the 1795 Springfield musket from the War of 1812 and the Thompson submachine gun from World War II.

Twilight Tattoo begins its fifteen-week run in late April. The show occurs on Wednesday nights at no expense to the public with different weekly hosts, from the Secretary of Defense to Army

*Lieutenant Colonel Todd Burroughs (left) and Captain Travis Womack
(right) stand at ceremonial at-ease during the "Salute from the Chief"
Twilight Tattoo on June 6, 2018. The Continental Color Guard appear
in the background in the 1784 Continental Infantry uniform.*

generals. Each season, the Army Chief of Staff hosts a "Salute
from the Chief" to recognize civilian honorees for their support
to the military. On June 6, 2018, I attended this special Twilight
Tattoo hosted by General Mark Milley on Whipple Field, a small
parade field named for the Union general who led the defense of
Washington in 1862 and later died at Chancellorsville. Whipple
has the most majestic natural vista in the Washington area, with

the Lincoln Memorial, the Washington Monument, and the Capitol lined up in perfect order.

Just off Whipple, Lt. Col. Burroughs led the talk-through and encouraged his young soldier-actors, many of whom rarely perform for the public. For instance, Private First Class Logan Stack, a human-resources specialist, was making his debut as a World War I actor. I asked him why he auditioned for Twilight Tattoo. "I love it here at The Old Guard, sir, but I don't get to do our mission much," he explained. "Twilight gives me a chance to get out of the office, get away from paperwork problems, and get on the marks." This motivation is common among the non-infantry actors, according to 4th Battalion's Command Sergeant Major, Lee Ward. "My soldiers love Twilight Tattoo," he said, "because they get to do The Old Guard mission. CinC Guard marches in ceremonies all the time. But I've got all these cooks and medics and mechanics; they support us, but they never get to do our core mission."

Meanwhile, down a steep hill in a grove of trees, several dozen CinC Guard soldiers with nonspeaking roles seemed to have stepped out of a malfunctioning time machine. A colonial soldier chatted with a World War I doughboy. A Union soldier relaxed with a poncho-wearing Korean War soldier, while a Confederate lounged next to a Vietnam-era soldier. I spotted a group of soldiers wearing World War II uniforms with the 101st Airborne's Screaming Eagle patch, which I wore in Iraq. I commented that soldiers in that uniform had jumped into Normandy seventy-four years ago today. Several soldiers knew that and said they wished they could have been there.

Up the hill, we heard the pre-ceremonial concert end and the Fife and Drum Corps marching on, the equivalent of the curtain rising on Broadway. Over the next ninety minutes, The Old Guard and The U.S. Army Band's jazz and vocal ensembles, The U.S.

Army Blues, and The U.S. Army Voices, would dazzle hundreds of spectators with the Army story. "George Washington"—Chief Warrant Officer Scott Sobataka of the Caisson Platoon—rode his large gray horse onto the field as CinC Guard soldiers fired their Brown Besses and charged with bayonets fixed. "The Star-Spangled Banner" followed the story of the Battle of Fort McHenry in the War of 1812, Francis Scott Key's inspiration for his poem that became our National Anthem. Mounted Civil War soldiers—in blues and grays—rode onto the field as Sergeant Major Greg Lowery from the Voices sang "Arlington," a song from the perspective of "one of the chosen ones" who "made it to Arlington" after dying in battle. When the World War I actors appeared, Stack nailed his debut performance, as another soldier sang the jaunty World War I song "Over There."

After the World War II and the Korean War vignettes, Captain Travis Roland, the executive officer of Honor Guard Company, led the Vietnam-era troops as "Hal Moore," a famed commander and author of the best-selling memoir *We Were Soldiers Once . . . and Young.* "He's a great actor and he gets totally into character," Cpt. Morgan said. "He wears his Vietnam uniform all day on Wednesdays and he signs his emails as 'Hal' now." Even better, Cpt. Morgan laughed, Cpt. Roland carried dumbbells to each show and did curls right before his performance. Cpt. Roland later explained, "I like to get a good pump, where the sleeves are tight, looking nice and vascular." When Cpt. Morgan told me about Cpt. Roland's secret trick, a young woman in front of us turned around and said, "You better put that in your book!" Cpt. Morgan responded, "That's his wife, Callie."

The show's finale featured the U.S. Army Drill Team and modern soldiers reciting the Soldier's Creed. As all the soldier-actors returned to the field, the announcer encouraged the spectators to meet the soldiers, an opportunity they seized. Vietnam veterans

Captain Travis Roland performs during Twilight Tattoo as "Hal Moore,"
while other Old Guard soldiers in Vietnam uniforms reenact a first-aid scene
in the background.

sought out "Hal Moore" and his troops. History buffs examined
the period weapons. Teenage girls took pictures with young soldiers not much older than they were. The mounted soldiers and
their horses were a particular fan favorite.

Though the show had ended, these last moments with CinC
Guard and other troops embodied its purpose. As Cpt. Tallman
explained of the audience's reaction, "It blows their mind. They
love it. You get that reaction every single time." The spectators
"love interacting with the soldiers in colonials. It just makes

people want to talk. It really does." As the sun set on Whipple, CinC Guard had once again told the Army story in vivid fashion.

CinC Guard soldiers performed Twilight Tattoo for another two months until the 2018 season ended in early August, when they began something of an "off season." They still marched in Old Guard ceremonies and performed at special events like Washington's Birthday at Mount Vernon. But CinC Guard could dedicate much of the fall and winter to tactical training up to squad live-fire exercises—a great source of motivation for these infantrymen before their next star turn in Twilight Tattoo.

U.S. Army Drill Team

There is no off season, however, for the U.S. Army Drill Team, the Army's premier precision-marching unit. The Drill Team performs not only at Twilight Tattoo, but also for special events year-round. The Drill Team travels extensively to fulfill its "primary mission of showcasing the U.S. Army both nationally and internationally through precision-based drill routines with bayonet-tipped 1903 Springfield rifles," according to the platoon's operating manual. In fact, Twilight Tattoo is the rare occasion when the Drill Team performs with other Old Guard units; it plays no role in memorial affairs, nor does it march in other ceremonies. The team performs up to 150 times per year, often in public settings around the capital like the Jefferson Memorial and sports venues such as Nationals Park. But they travel for up to a third of their missions. In 2018, for instance, the Drill Team performed at the Alamo for Fiesta San Antonio and for the Army–Oklahoma football game in Norman, Oklahoma.

With such a high profile at such a distance from Fort Myer, the Drill Team needs especially disciplined and motivated sol-

Lieutenant Adam Scheenstra, the Drill Team Commander, marches through "the Arch" during the "Salute from the Chief" Twilight Tattoo on June 6, 2018.

diers. First Lieutenant Adam Scheenstra is the Drill Team's platoon leader, also known as the Drill Commander. (The platoon sergeant is known as the Drill Master.) He said that the regimental chain of command "expects maturity obviously, and they expect a high level of responsibility, from not only me, but from the soldiers because of how far away we are from the flagpole." The Drill Team also looks for extroverts because its soldiers are expected to engage the public at all times, not just through their performances.

Of course, the Drill Team also screens for the mental and physical ability to learn and perform the team's intricate precision drills—all done silently, with no voice commands. The candidates volunteer from within The Old Guard; some joined the regiment specifically for the opportunity to try out. The training cycle for these aspiring drillers lasts for three weeks and the attrition rate ranges from 50 to 75 percent for soldiers on their first try, but motivated candidates often succeed in subsequent attempts.

But even successful candidates are still a long way from a public performance. They must pass periodic tests to become "drill certified" and then challenge a regular driller to a competition before an event. If the trainee wins, he "breaks drill" and earns his spot in the performance and the regular drilling roster. On average, trainees take about six or seven months to break drill, though superior performers have earned a spot in as little as two months.

A regular driller then can train and test for one of three specialty roles: thrower, catcher, and soloist. The throwers and the catchers, as the names suggest, throw and catch the rifle during the Drill Team's signature maneuver, the Front to Rear Overhead Rifle Toss. The soloists are the most skilled drillers in the platoon; Lt. Scheenstra likened them to scouts and snipers, who are usually the most talented and skilled soldiers in an infantry battalion.

The platoon attempts to maintain at least four soldiers in each specialty, with the soloists and the senior thrower and catcher in charge of training both their positions and the full team on its drill sequences.

The Drill Team choreographs these sequences into three kinds of public shows: full drills, sports drills, and solo missions. The full drill lasts about ten minutes and includes the most sequences. Lt. Scheenstra prefers the full drill, "so we can show the most stuff." But when time is tight, the sports drill is a shorter version of the full drill, lasting about six minutes, typically to fit into a pregame or halftime show. Both drills usually consist of sixteen drillers and either the Drill Commander or the Drill Master.

Both full and sports drills include the team's most popular sequences. One is the Arch, in which the Drill Commander marches between two rows of drillers facing each other as they spin and toss their rifles, bringing them into crossed-bayonet "arches." Another crowd pleaser is the Line, when the soldiers line up for a series of rifle and hand movements that ripple up and down the line. The Line is also an opportunity for "flair" like fist bumps and shoulder brushes. "We incorporate flair for less formal crowds, something like Twilight, where we have families and kids," Lt. Scheenstra explained. "It makes the drill a little more accessible." Whichever sequences are chosen, most drills conclude with the Overhead Rifle Toss.

Solo missions, which last four to five minutes, can be incorporated into a full drill or sports drill or performed separately. At the Salute from the Chief, for instance, the soloists performed during the pre-ceremonial concert, while the team conducted a sports drill during the show. Solo missions consist of up to four soldiers performing precision rifle movements, and also surrounding the Drill Commander and tossing their rifles just inches away from him. These solo missions are the team's most gripping performances. Almost without fail, the crowd gasps when the first bay-onet passes within inches of the Drill Commander's face, then breaks into applause with each dramatic toss and spin around and over him.

The solo performances also capture the true significance of the drill routine and why the Drill Team trains so hard to perfect them. The team's announcer compares the soloists to soldiers deployed in combat zones: "Soldiers often face life-and-death situations. Like our soloists, they're relying on the performance of the soldiers to their left and right." Most spectators who see the Drill Team will never see our soldiers fight on the battlefield. For them, as the announcer puts it, "the Drill Team embodies the characteristics found in our soldiers around the world." Indeed, the drillers wear uniforms without nameplates or medals partly for safety, but also to epitomize all soldiers regardless of identity. Because the Drill Team is ultimately showcasing not itself, but the trust, bravery, skill, discipline, and professionalism of the American soldier.

Honor Guard

If the Drill Team is The Old Guard's showcase ceremonial unit, then Honor Guard Company is its workhorse. Honor Guard marches in almost every Old Guard ceremony. When The Old Guard provides troops for Armed Forces ceremonies, they will come from Honor Guard. For the highest-profile missions at the White House and the Pentagon, Honor Guard will represent the Army. More than any other unit, Honor Guard executes The Old Guard's role as "the Army's official ceremonial unit and escort to the president."

Yet, Honor Guard may be the least remarkable of The Old Guard's specialty ceremonial units. Honor Guard—officially,

Echo Company of 4th Battalion—has no tryouts and no special uniforms, weapons, or marching style. They wear the ceremonial blue uniform and carry the M14 rifle, just like other infantry companies. One thing chiefly distinguishes Honor Guard from The Old Guard's other infantry companies: Honor Guard is very, very tall.

"We really get them because they are tall," explained Captain Rob Schaar, Honor Guard company commander, when I asked if his soldiers were selected for a special skill or talent. "This is the first unit that I've come to and felt short," joked the six-two, 220-pound former college football player. Cpt. Schaar himself went straight to Honor Guard when he arrived at Fort Myer, with no ceremonial experience, which he attributed to his "physical stature" and his reputation as "a hard driver." I suspect Cpt. Schaar is right, because the same thing happened to me. Not long after I reported to Charlie Company, I was offered a spot at Honor Guard with no apparent qualifications besides my height. I declined, mostly because I was already surrounded by good soldiers and leaders, but the offer to lead troops in the Army's premier ceremonial company was tempting, to be sure.

The Old Guard's demanding, hectic schedule would be hard to manage without such a dedicated ceremonial company. While some ceremonies are regularly scheduled or planned well in advance, others come with only a few days' notice and often involve a visiting foreign dignitary. These short-notice missions would disrupt the companies performing funerals or other ceremonial missions without a dedicated ceremonial company to march in them. Honor Guard plays this role, which gives it a highly unpredictable schedule and keeps it on the marks every week.

Because of that dedicated ceremonial role, Honor Guard gets the regiment's tallest soldiers so as to project a certain appearance and bearing at high-visibility events. When I take civilians to

Old Guard ceremonies, they marvel at Honor Guard's extreme height. I explain that the troops are selected for their height because we want foreigners to believe that the Army has a million more giants under arms, ready to fight. As Secretary Mattis told Cpt. Morgan during a Pentagon arrival ceremony, "You guys look good out there today. You look intimidating; that's what we're trying to do."

Even within Honor Guard, soldiers are assigned partly by height. Honor Guard platoons specialize by ceremonial function, with 1st Platoon serving as the marching platoon. If a ceremony requires a platoon, 1st Platoon will be on the marks. The platoon's minimum height is six-three, though height alone is not enough; a soldier must also demonstrate superior marching ability. Even within 1st Platoon, the very best, and the very tallest, are assigned to 1st Squad, the front rank of the formation. "One of the highest honors in 1st Platoon," according to Cpt. Schaar, "is to march front rank because that is the face of the Army."

The other two platoons also have ceremonial specialties. 2nd Platoon is responsible for carrying the fifty-six state and territorial flags for major ceremonies. 3rd Platoon fills the gaps when 1st and 2nd Platoons need additional manpower, and also serves as the second marching platoon behind 1st Platoon for large outdoor ceremonies. Finally, 3rd Platoon provides the Army personnel for smaller missions, such as honor cordons for state dinners at the White House or for visiting defense ministers at the Pentagon. Thus, 3rd Platoon's well-earned nickname is "the Jack of All Trades."

With this variety and frequency of ceremonial missions, Honor Guard troops quickly become ceremonial experts and they share that knowledge widely. On Mondays, for instance, the regiment holds training sessions known as Sword and Saber Training and Regimental Parade Training. At these sessions, Honor Guard trains alongside the other companies, yet its soldiers can also act as peer coaches for less experienced soldiers. "If we can help make it look better," Cpt. Schaar explained, "that's our ultimate goal. It's all about the look and showing perfection." Honor Guard soldiers also assist other troops at rehearsals. Whenever I had a question at a rehearsal about my step counts, commands, or anything else, I knew that the Honor Guard officer would probably have the answer because he marched in ceremonies almost as often as I performed funerals.

Army Ceremonies

The whole regiment joins together in Army ceremonies to honor Army personnel and special occasions. In addition to The U.S. Army Band, these ceremonies feature 1st Battalion's infantry companies, Continental Color Guard, Fife and Drum Corps, Commander-in-Chief's Guard, and Honor Guard. The Old Guard conducts three main kinds of Army ceremonies: retirements, reviews, and arrivals.

These ceremonies share a common structure and rhythm, but honor different people and serve different purposes. Retirements are the most common ceremonies. The Old Guard performs a group retirement each month for retiring soldiers in the rank of colonel and below; I have seen retirements with up to eighty soldiers. Most months, the regiment also performs one or two retirements for a general officer. A review welcomes or bids farewell to a senior Army official or recognizes a special occasion. For instance, The Old Guard welcomed Secretary of the Army Mark Esper with a review in November 2017 shortly after we had voted to confirm him in the Senate. Likewise, The Old

Guard performed a review for the seventieth anniversary of the regiment's reactivation last year, a memorable ceremony for me because I was the reviewing official along with Representative Warren Davidson, another Old Guard veteran. Finally, an arrival welcomes a visiting foreign dignitary, usually the counterpart to our Secretary of the Army or Chief of Staff. These ceremonies often occur on Whipple Field with its grand view of Washington.

Aside from a ceremony's length—usually determined by the length of the speeches—for the soldiers the biggest difference is whether a ceremony occurs outdoors or inside Conmy Hall. Sometimes Mother Nature decides the question, pushing a ceremony indoors for rain and in the winter. But on fair days, the honoree can request a ceremony on Summerall Field. While Conmy Hall has Broadway-quality lighting and sound plus air-conditioning, nothing beats an outdoor ceremony on the thick green grass of Summerall, under a brilliant blue sky, with flags waving in the breeze, and against the backdrop of Fort Myer's redbrick, colonial-style homes. But outdoor ceremonies also have their drawbacks. For one, they require more than 450 soldiers— versus about 250 indoors—to fill the bigger space on Summerall. Another drawback, of course, is the heat and humidity. At the rehearsal for the change-of-command review for Colonel Jason Garkey and his successor, Colonel Jim Tuite, 1st Sgt. Craig joked that "tomorrow will be like the Bataan Death March." Sure enough, with a heat index well over ninety and no cloud cover or breeze, fourteen soldiers fell out of formation.

Whether indoor or outdoor, and whatever the occasion, The Old Guard prepares with the same pursuit of perfection for which it strives in Arlington. After the rehearsal for Col. Garkey's change of command, for example, Cpt. Kennedy reminded soldiers to hydrate, eat well, and get plenty of rest given the forecasted heat.

I used to stress the same things to our soldiers the night before a long stand. As during primary week in Arlington, the dictates of honor followed us home. I stayed off my feet the night before a ceremony, ate a big pasta dinner, and drank lots of water and Gatorade. On the morning of a ceremony, we had a big breakfast, drank more Gatorade, and did some final uniform work before reporting to Conmy Hall or Summerall a little more than an hour before the ceremony for the box-up and the final talk-through. These dutiful preparations occur out of the public eye, another testament to The Old Guard's professionalism.

For prominent events, though, the spotlight turns on early as guests start to arrive during the talk-through. At the retirement in honor of Lieutenant General H. R. McMaster, the outgoing National Security Advisor to President Trump, Conmy Hall was already half full and would soon be standing-room-only. "Normally it takes seventy retirees and their families to turn out this kind of crowd," Cpt. Morgan marveled as he scanned the seats. An actual spotlight quieted the crowd when it illuminated The U.S. Army Band for a pre-ceremonial concert. While The Old Guard units stood in the hall's darkened corners, the band played four selections, including "Hit the Leather and Ride," the official song of the 2nd Cavalry Regiment, with whom then–Captain McMaster served during the famous Battle of 73 Easting in 1991, where he earned the Silver Star for valor. The meaning was not missed by the dozens of 2nd Cavalry veterans in attendance.

With the concert complete, the ceremony begins. The Continental Color Guard anchors the middle of the formation, wearing colonial uniforms and carrying the National, Army, and regimental colors, symbolizing the historic use of colors on the battlefield. To the right is The U.S. Army Band and two companies in ceremonial blues, usually from 1st Battalion. When I marched in ceremonies, I would lead one of these two companies. To the left of the colors is Honor Guard's 1st Platoon, CinC Guard, and Fife and Drum Corps.

But first the troops must get on the marks. Military music controls the ceremony in these opening sequences. The Band or the Fife and Drum Corps play a series of bugle calls—Attention, Adjutant's Call, Officer's Call, and Fix Bayonets—that direct the troops to march on, conduct a dressing sequence to get aligned, and fix bayonets to their rifles, all without voice commands. These bugle calls and various drumbeats are what Sgt. Maj. White of FDC called "functional music" and are more than mere procedures to get the ceremony started; they connect today's Army to its history. Like colonial uniforms, Sgt. Maj. White explained that the bugle calls and drumbeats hark back to "what field music would've done in the eighteenth and nineteenth century for the Army, providing signals for the regiment to execute its maneuvers and its drills."

Formation complete, the host welcomes the honoree and The Old Guard conducts the honors. If the honoree's rank or office warrants, the band will play Ruffles and Flourishes, followed by a musical selection while the Presidential Salute Battery fires a gun salute. For instance, Secretary Esper received a nineteen-gun salute and Gen. McMaster received a fifteen-gun salute. (For indoor ceremonies, the guns are displayed on Conmy Hall's large video screens.) After an invocation, the Fife and Drum Corps marches past the reviewing stand with a medley known as "Sound Off," a way to honor dignitaries in the eighteenth century—another homage to The Old Guard's heritage. Finally, the commander of troops returns his saber to his scabbard and leads the honoree on a walking inspection of the troops. "This is where it gets dicey," Col. Garkey explained, "because the dignitary isn't used to it." For example, at his retirement ceremony Gen. McMaster turned

Colonel Jason Garkey (left) leads Lieutenant General H. R. McMaster (right) on the inspection of troops during Gen. McMaster's retirement ceremony in Conmy Hall on May 18, 2018.

the wrong way at the end of the formation until Col. Garkey corrected him, prompting laughter from his old friends in the stands and a smile from Gen. McMaster himself. But they also gave him "very loud, unusually loud, sustained applause," in Cpt. Morgan's opinion.

After the honors and inspection come the speeches and awards, which present a different kind of challenge. For twenty minutes, the soldiers have stayed active, but now they face thirty to sixty minutes of standing still during all the remarks. To minimize fallouts, the troops "exercise" during transitions among speakers, with the commander of troops calling them to attention from ceremonial at-ease and quickly putting them back at ceremonial at-ease, just to get the blood moving. These moments are one reason why we all had to pass long standing-proficiency tests during our initial training.

That training paid off at Gen. McMaster's retirement. Gen. Milley spoke for twenty-four minutes, then Gen. McMaster rushed the podium before his introduction and started speaking as the applause died down. "He jumped the exercise!" I whispered to Cpt. Kennedy and Cpt. Morgan, who looked stricken. But Col. Garkey, who had about-faced to issue the commands, took it in stride. He turned to face the front and went back to ceremonial at-ease—a good example of how leaders must stay alert and occasionally improvise. After Gen. McMaster's thirty-two-minute speech, the troops had stood at ceremonial at-ease for fifty-six minutes, "the longest time I've ever seen," according to Cpt. Kennedy. Yet no Old Guard soldier fell out. "They did great," Cpt. Morgan said. "I'm very proud of them."

When the last speech ends, the troops march by the reviewing stand for the pass-in-review and off the field. This is the "chute" to which I and so many officers dedicated long hours of practice. Behind the infantry comes the Fife and Drum Corps performing a "troop step," a slow, exaggerated march with pointed toes that concludes with "Yankee Doodle," always a crowd pleaser. Sgt. Maj. White described it as "another eighteenth-century means of honoring a dignitary." At the end come any special troops, such as three military working dogs and their handlers from the 947th Military Police Detachment and nine horses from the Caisson Platoon for Col. Garkey's change-of-command ceremony. "For once, it'll be a literal dog and pony show," Lt. Col. Burroughs had joked at the rehearsal.

But as with funerals, The Old Guard's work is not done until key leaders gather for an after-action review. I have participated in dozens as both a soldier and an observer over the last year, none so enthusiastic as the one after Gen. McMaster's retirement. Gen. McMaster is beloved by the troops and their mood after the unexpected fifty-six-minute stand was proud and ebullient. "This is the best ceremony we've done yet," Col. Garkey praised. "A lot of people here don't get to see the Army, and you impressed them today." He was right. White House officials, cabinet secretaries, lawmakers, old friends, and many others had already formed a receiving line for Gen. McMaster. But he ran over to the huddle to thank the soldiers. We embraced, and I told him how he had jumped the exercise. Gen. McMaster, who knew I was writing this book, laughed and joked, "I just wanted your Old Guard troopers to show everyone how tough they are!" And, indeed, when the spotlight was on, they had done just that.

Armed Forces Ceremonies

In addition to Army ceremonies, The Old Guard performs in Armed Forces ceremonies alongside its four sister services. These high-visibility ceremonies are reserved for the president, the Secretary of Defense, and the Chairman of the Joint Chiefs of Staff and their visiting foreign counterparts. While The Old Guard may appear at first glance as just one of five services, with Honor Guard's 1st Platoon standing alongside the Marine Corps, Navy, Air Force, and Coast Guard, behind the scenes and on closer inspection The Old Guard plays an outsized role in these joint missions.

This responsibility derives partly from the Army's status as the oldest service, but mostly from The Old Guard's unique capabili-

ties. The sheer size of The Old Guard—more than double the size
of the other four services' ceremonial units combined—brings
with it additional duties. The 529th Regimental Support Company provides logistical support for large joint ceremonies. The
289th Military Police Company assists with security. The Old
Guard's large headquarters staff supports the Military District of
Washington with command and control of large events. Honor
Guard squares away its sister services where needed, just as it does
for other Old Guard units. The Fife and Drum Corps offers rich
institutional knowledge because of its soldiers' longevity, especially for the biggest and rarest ceremonies, such as White House
arrivals, presidential inaugurations, and state funerals.

The Old Guard's central role in Armed Forces ceremonies also
appears on and off the parade field in many ways. The commander
of troops is always an Old Guard leader, from Col. Garkey commanding at the Macron state arrival ceremony at the White House
to a junior lieutenant leading a nineteen-man honor cordon at the
Pentagon. Three members of the eight-man Joint Armed Forces
Color Guard come from the Continental Color Guard, including
the National Color Bearer, the place of honor in a color guard.
An Old Guard officer always leads the troops carrying the state
and territorial flags and the Presidential Salute Battery always provides the gun salute. While the band rotates among the services,
the Fife and Drum Corps performs at the highest-profile events,
like the Macron state arrival. On the sidelines, The Old Guard's
headquarters staff serve as liaisons with White House or Pentagon
officials, adjusting timelines or providing cues from their radio
earpiece—usually a discreet thumbs-up or salute—to the commander of troops or the drum major. Finally, The Old Guard
also fills the support roles on the periphery: the setup detail, au-
diovisual support, the announcer, route restrainers, medics, door
openers, umbrella bearers, and award bearers.

While Armed Forces ceremonies resemble Army ceremonies—minus the allusions to The Old Guard's history—the mix of ceremonies is different. For instance, the joint force does not conduct retirement ceremonies. Only the Chairman of the Joint Chiefs would warrant one, and that event is also a change-of-responsibility review with the incoming Chairman, as when Army General Martin Dempsey transferred responsibility to Marine General Joe Dunford in 2015 on Summerall. Armed Forces reviews are also rare, used mostly as farewell ceremonies for the Secretary of Defense and the president. Both President Barack Obama and Secretary of Defense Ash Carter were honored at reviews in Conmy Hall in January 2017.

Arrivals, by contrast, are the most common and significant kind of Armed Forces ceremony. The Chairman hosts chiefs of defense at Whipple Field, the Secretary hosts ministers of defense at the Pentagon, and the president hosts heads of state on the South Lawn of the White House. These arrival ceremonies are among the best examples of what Col. Garkey and Lt. Col. Burroughs call The Old Guard's "strategic messaging." When Secretary Mattis hosted the Ministers of Defense from Sweden and Finland in May 2018, it did not escape notice in Washington—or Moscow—that two non-NATO allies in Europe received the honor of a Pentagon arrival ceremony. Secretary Mattis called Col. Garkey the next day to thank The Old Guard's soldiers and explain that the ceremony "played across every major media outlet in Sweden and Finland and sent a very strong message about their status as American allies." Col. Garkey added, "Our ceremonies send a message that extends beyond the parade field," and Secretary Mattis "wanted to ensure that our troops understood how they supported our greater diplomatic efforts."

The biggest stage for strategic messages is a White House arrival ceremony. "We don't do them very often, but the lights are on the brightest," observed Col. Garkey, who has marched arrivals for the last three presidents in his multiple Old Guard tours. For the Macron arrival, he estimated that they rehearsed twelve hours on both the South Lawn and Summerall. "It was very important to us to recertify after being off the South Lawn for eighteen months," he recalled. No detail is too small when the stakes are so high. For example, Old Guard soldiers known as drafters placed a mark in advance on the South Lawn for every person in the ceremony. By contrast, Summerall has marks only for key leaders and the first, middle, and last man in each rank.

Captain Rob Schaar (left) commands an honor cordon at the White House for a credential ceremony for newly appointed ambassadors.

These rehearsals and this attention to details pay off when it counts, as evidenced at the Macron arrival. When President Macron finished his remarks, Col. Garkey needed about forty-five seconds to bring the formation to attention, salute President Trump, and say, "Mr. President, this concludes the ceremony." But President Trump immediately departed the reviewing stand with President Macron and their wives. Fortunately, Lieutenant Colonel Derrick Shaw, the Director of the U.S. Army Herald Trumpets, recognized what had happened and commanded the trumpeters to begin playing as the two presidents and their wives ascended the South Portico stairs. No one not in uniform noticed—including me. "It happens, we're used to it," a nonplussed Col. Garkey later explained. "It's why we stress staying on your toes. Colonel Shaw did a great job of picking it up."

All was well that ended well, and President Trump improvised the ending, too. After halting on the terrace and waving as the ceremonial script called for, he came to attention and unexpectedly saluted. "I was touched that the last thing he did was salute the troops," Col. Garkey recalled. "I had never seen that before, so I just returned the salute." They deserved the commander-in-chief's salute. "The soldiers did great, the execution was almost flawless." Col. Garkey beamed. "The guys were pretty excited and there was a lot of high-fiving in the after-action review."

A final, special kind of Armed Forces ceremony, perhaps the only one comparing to a White House arrival, is a presidential wreath ceremony at the Tomb of the Unknown Soldier on Memorial Day and Veterans Day. When the cameras are rolling, the ceremony is short—barely five minutes—and simple. The president walks onto the Memorial Amphitheater Plaza, salutes for the National Anthem, lays the wreath, salutes during Taps, and departs for his remarks in the Amphitheater.

Behind the scenes, though, the ceremony is one of The Old Guard's largest, most complicated missions. A presidential wreath ceremony requires more than five hundred personnel. The Old Guard provides more than half the troops, including a 120-man honor cordon on the streets of Arlington National Cemetery through which the presidential motorcade passes. The planning process begins four months out, and on-site rehearsals occur at dawn since the cemetery opens at 0800. Further, a wreath ceremony is trickier than most because of the terrain. The Tomb sits on a hill, with steps leading down to a grassy mall. The Plaza is also the smallest venue for any ceremony, and the Tomb splits the only natural location for the formation, the last landing on the stairs. As a result, the Tomb sits in the middle of the platoons, with three on one side and two on the other. From the mall below, the troops march up the steps to the Tomb, a slow and arresting visual seen at no other ceremonial venue.

Given these complications, The Old Guard and its sister services benefit from performing more Armed Forces wreath ceremonies than just the ceremonies for the president's biannual visits to Arlington. Two or three times per month, they conduct a wreath ceremony for foreign dignitaries such as defense ministers and chiefs of defense. These smaller ceremonies are virtually identical to the presidential wreath ceremony, simply without the publicity and all the support troops. Thus, Honor Guard's 1st Platoon maintains the highest proficiency in wreath ceremonies, always ready to perform when the lights are brightest on Memorial Day and Veterans Day. (The joint force can also perform a wreath ceremony on the Tomb's mall side for heads of state, but these occur only once or twice per year.)

Whatever the occasion, though, wreath ceremonies begin and end with the same silent reminder of why the ceremony happens at all: the commander of troops faces the Tomb and renders a solo saber salute. One could easily miss the salute and its meaning. Three American soldiers "known but to God" are buried under that Plaza, each a Medal of Honor recipient. Military custom dictates that all soldiers, no matter the rank, salute a Medal of Honor recipient. The commander of troops upholds that custom by beginning and ending each wreath ceremony with his silent salute.

Each ceremony also has the same postscript, another silent reminder of the sacred ground on which it occurs. Throughout the ceremony, a lone soldier stands in what is known as "the box," a green canvas hut about the size of a telephone booth on the edge of the Plaza. He was in the box when the troops marched up the steps. He executed the commands during the ceremony. And he remained in the box when the commander of troops saluted the Unknowns and marched off the Plaza. Ceremony now complete, this soldier puts on his sunglasses, steps out of the box, and marches onto the Plaza. He is a Sentinel of the Tomb of the Unknown Soldier, resuming the post that he and his forebears have guarded without fail for eighty-two years.

6

||||

The Unknowns

As I parked my car and stepped into the crisp spring night, I gazed at the glimmering headstones of Section 46. Like most people, I had never entered the cemetery at night, so I had never seen how the moonlight illuminates Arlington's white marble headstones like the smooth surface of a still lake. Above them soared a memorial with the mast of the U.S.S. *Maine*, whose sinking into Havana Harbor 109 years earlier had sent my new unit on its first overseas deployment to Cuba. The nighttime scene was beautiful.

It was the spring of 2007 and I was still new to The Old Guard. I was not yet certified to march in ceremonies or perform funerals, so I was not much use to anyone. But I could pull regimental staff duty. The Army never "closes" and the staff-duty officer holds down the fort, so to speak, on nights and weekends when everyone else is off duty. The staff-duty officer has to "do rounds" to check on the unit's buildings and soldiers. At The Old Guard, that meant driving from Fort Myer into the cemetery to check on the Tomb of the Unknown Soldier and its guards.

After taking in the beauty of Section 46, I walked down the sidewalk to the Tomb Quarters underneath the Memorial Amphitheater. As I did, I noticed Section 35 on the south side of the Amphitheater was pitch black, as dark as the farm where I grew up during a new moon. The effect, I realized, was the result of its sharp downhill slope and a thick tree canopy.

Around the corner, I heard the unmistakable sound of steel-plated ceremonial shoes clicking on marble. I walked out to the Plaza, where the Tomb is located, and saw a young soldier in an unusual uniform combination: combat fatigues, white gloves, a ceremonial M14 rifle, and black dress shoes. He was practicing his marching when he saw me and walked over.

"Hey, sir. Staff duty?" he asked, inferring this from my own fatigues, which bore The Old Guard's shoulder patch.

"Yes," I replied. I had visited the Tomb and seen the Changing of the Guard a few times, but only during the day. Now the Plaza and the Tomb were bathed in a spotlight. In the distance, the yellow glow of city lights illuminated the Potomac River and the Capitol. The young soldier now still, the silence was stark.

"The rest of the guys are downstairs," the guard said, pulling my attention back from the horizon and pointing toward the south end of the Plaza. "Just walk down those stairs and ring the buzzer."

I asked, "I guess you don't wear ceremonial blues at night?"

"Nah, once the cemetery shuts down, the new men just come out to train in our steels."

"Got it," I replied. "Don't let me interrupt. I'm just doing my rounds." I walked back to the Quarters and rang the buzzer. The door clicked and I walked in. The walls were covered with plaques, headstone rubbings, and pictures from the Tomb's history. A few soldiers were busy shining shoes or bayonet scabbards; one was practicing the rifle manual in front of a mirror. A staff sergeant introduced himself as the relief commander, telling me the men and weapons were all accounted for and everything was quiet. After verifying all that with a quick inspection, we talked for a few minutes about their duty schedule, the training regimen, and life at the Tomb. I was fascinated and could have stayed for hours, but I had to finish my rounds.

As I walked back to my car, I was greeted again by the inky darkness of Section 35 and the brilliance of Section 46. What a special place, I thought, and what a unique unit.

★ ★ ★

The Tomb of the Unknown Soldier is the most famous and popular destination within Arlington National Cemetery. More than four million visitors pass through the cemetery gates each year; most will climb the hill to the Memorial Amphitheater to watch the Changing of the Guard at the Tomb. "The Tomb of the Unknown Soldier is the most highly visible guard post in the United States," in the words of the operating manual for the Tomb of the Unknown Soldier Platoon.

Like the Tomb itself, the Tomb guards are the most famous and iconic troops within The Old Guard. When my service with The Old Guard comes up, most people assume I guarded the Tomb. I joke that I was not a Tomb guard because I was an officer and officers cannot be trusted to execute such a sensitive duty. That is a lighthearted quip—officers have in fact served at the Tomb—but the question illustrates the fame and prestige of the Tomb guards. To many Americans, the Tomb guards *are* The Old Guard.

In fact, the Tomb Platoon is the most specialized unit in The Old Guard. While the majority of Old Guard soldiers train for and perform a variety of funerals and ceremonies, Tomb guards have only one mission. Likewise, no Old Guard soldier guards the Tomb except the Tomb guards. This separateness, along with their fame, creates a mystique about the Sentinels, as guards who have completed training are known. Some of that aura is an urban legend. According to internet myths, guards take a vow of silence for their first six months and an oath never to swear or drink alcohol again. None of that is true. A guard cannot lay a wreath or perform many other tasks without speaking. I have heard guards swear like any other soldier, though never in public. And when off duty, I have known guards to enjoy a beer or three.

But much of the mystique is justified. Over many weeks at the Tomb, I encountered some of the most disciplined and motivated soldiers I have ever known. The Sentinels strive for perfection in everything they do, even—especially—when no one would notice, all to honor the Unknowns. Their dedication to that mission transcends duty into love for three Unknown Soldiers who, in a phrase I heard often, "didn't just give up their lives, they gave up their identities." That supreme sacrifice, so that we might live in freedom, has driven the Sentinels every minute of every day for eighty-two consecutive years as they stand watch over America's most sacred shrine to our fallen war heroes.

History of the Tomb

The story of the Tomb of the Unknown Soldier begins on the battlefields of Europe as the guns fell silent on the eleventh hour of the eleventh day of the eleventh month of 1918. The American Expeditionary Forces had proved decisive in World War I, the Great War that would shape so much of the coming century. But despite its late entry, the AEF lost more than 116,000 troops. Thanks in part to the recent introduction of identification tags, though, fewer than two thousand remained unidentified. Thus, for the first time the nation faced the question of how to handle large numbers of identified remains in an overseas war.

Senior Army leaders generally preferred not to disturb the dead, but war mothers and war widows wanted their late sons and husbands returned home. Not surprisingly, Congress sided with them and most Gold Star Families brought their loved ones home, though nearly 31,000 Americans remained in Europe in eight newly established cemeteries, where they still rest today under the care of the American Battle Monuments Commission.

This policy left unsettled the question of what to do with the unidentified remains. Some advocated for a memorial to an unknown soldier who would represent all the unknown fallen, but some Army leaders resisted such proposals. On Armistice Day 1920, however, France and Great Britain buried an unknown soldier at the Arc de Triomphe and Westminster Abbey in elaborate funerals before vast crowds. The pageantry and emotion of the day galvanized American public opinion. General John Pershing, who had led the AEF, testified to Congress in favor of a memorial for an unknown soldier, as did other senior military officers. Congress quickly passed legislation to honor an unknown at Arlington and President Woodrow Wilson signed it on his final day in office.

The funeral would occur on Armistice Day 1921, giving the Army's Graves Registration Service in Europe eight months to select the remains of an unknown soldier. They went to great lengths to ensure anonymity, exhuming four unknowns from four cemeteries, destroying all related records, and even rearranging the caskets in secret shortly before the selection. Sergeant Edward Younger, who had served in the AEF's biggest campaigns, made the selection on October 24 by laying white roses on a casket. America's Unknown Soldier then crossed France to great fanfare before departing for home the next day aboard the U.S.S. *Olympia*, Admiral George Dewey's flagship in the Battle of Manila Bay.

Meanwhile, the Military District of Washington prepared a welcome befitting a General of the Armies for the Unknown's arrival on November 9. A large ceremonial procession escorted him from the Washington Navy Yard to the Capitol Rotunda, where he lay in state on the Lincoln Catafalque and received visits from

The World War I Unknown is laid to rest during the committal service at the Tomb of the Unknown Soldier on Armistice Day, November 11, 1921.

President and Mrs. Warren Harding and senior officials from all three branches of the government. When the Capitol's east doors opened the next morning, thousands of soldiers, veterans, and fellow citizens were gathered to pay their final respects—including Gold Star Families of missing or unidentified soldiers, perhaps wondering if it was their son or husband or dad resting in that casket. By midnight, nearly one hundred thousand people had passed through the Rotunda to honor the Unknown.

On the morning of Armistice Day, the Unknown was honored with a funeral procession from the Capitol to Arlington. Alongside the military escort, President Harding and Gen. Pershing led hundreds of dignitaries, including Supreme Court justices, cabinet officials, governors, legislators, Medal of Honor recipients, and other soldiers and veterans. Inside the Amphitheater, President Harding gave an emotional address and decorated the Unknown with the Medal of Honor and the Distinguished Service Cross. After a committal service on the Plaza, the Unknown was lowered into the Tomb, a bugler sounded Taps, and the artillery fired a final twenty-one-gun salute. The Unknown now rested in his eternal home, the high ground of Arlington.

Within a year, the absence of a guard at the Tomb began to generate controversy. Some contrasted the Tomb unfavorably with the guarded unknown shrines in Europe. Senior Army leaders declined proposals for a guard, however, with one senior quartermaster explaining "there is no place at the Amphitheater where a sentry may be quartered, and the posting and relieving of guards would probably be inconvenient at Fort Myer." Having walked too many times to count from Fort Myer to the Tomb and beyond—usually in steel-plated ceremonial shoes—I must say this argument is not terribly persuasive.

Even stronger opposition came from the commander of the Military District of Washington, whose opinions sound an ironic note given the Tomb's popularity today. He contended that "the placing of an armed sentry at this tomb during the day would not lend dignity to the shrine." Besides, he believed, "the average American visitor to the tomb would not be impressed, or would probably not even notice the fact that a sentry was stationed nearby." He also observed that visitors to Washington "can reach the distantly located tomb only with great difficulty" and further predicted that the Tomb "is not and never will be visited by the thousands of visitors as is done in England, France, and Italy."

In 1923, though, the Army reacted to negative newspaper reports of photographers "soliciting business" at the Tomb, "laughing, thoughtless women," other tourists "laughing and talking," and men not removing their caps, among other offenses. A senior quartermaster instructed the cemetery's superintendent to direct the "watchmen at the Amphitheater" to stop professional photographers and prevent anyone from sitting or leaning on the Tomb. Another quartermaster noted that a "neat picket fence now protects the Tomb from encroachment."

A picket fence and an Amphitheater guard—there matters stood until the Army, responding to more negative publicity and congressional inquiries, assigned a civilian guard specifically to the Tomb for the first time on November 17, 1925. Sensing momentum, the advocates for a military guard redoubled their efforts, and a resolution was introduced in Congress calling for "a special guard armed and equipped as for field service during the World War" to guard the Tomb "from sunrise to sunset." Within days, President Calvin Coolidge settled the matter, ordering a military guard to be posted when the cemetery was open. On March 25, 1926, soldiers from the 3rd Cavalry at Fort Myer assumed responsibility for guarding the Tomb, with occasional support from other nearby Army units.

The Army may have lost the battle over a military guard at the Tomb, but it did not come away empty-handed because it requested and received $50,000 to complete its construction. The original Tomb was modest, no more than knee-high, which is why visitors could sit on it. The plans for the Tomb had always called for a larger, grander structure, but Congress had never appropriated the money.

Now bidding and construction could move ahead. Any Tomb Sentinel not only knows that architect Lorimer Rich and sculptor Thomas Hudson Jones won a prolonged competition in 1929, but also can describe their design. The Tomb is eight feet wide, thirteen feet long, and eleven feet tall. The six wreaths—inverted to represent mourning—on the north and south sides stand for six major campaigns in World War I. The eastern front contains three classical figures: Victory, holding a palm branch; Peace, holding a dove; and Valor, holding a sword. And the western facade bears only the famous inscription seen by visitors the world over: HERE RESTS IN HONORED GLORY AN AMERICAN SOLDIER KNOWN BUT TO GOD.

The marble for the Tomb came from the Yule Marble Quarry outside Marble, Colorado, the same source for the Amphitheater and the Lincoln Memorial. After a yearlong search for the seven massive pieces of marble that would become the Tomb, the marble went to Rutland County, Vermont, home of some of the country's finest stoneworkers. They cut and polished the marble pieces, which arrived for assembly at Arlington on August 29, 1931. But an imperfection in the base halted work for three months as a new piece repeated the journey. Workers then moved quickly to construct the Tomb, placing the cap on New Year's Eve 1931—no doubt giving everyone involved good cause to celebrate that night. Now Jones and his team could finally start carving and sculpting the design into the Tomb. They completed their work and the new Tomb was unveiled to the public on April 9, 1932.

Throughout it all, the 3rd Cavalry continued to guard the Tomb during the day, with support from other units at nearby Fort Washington and Fort Belvoir. Eventually, the 3rd Cavalry extended their guard duty beyond the cemetery's hours of operation. At midnight on July 2, 1937, they posted a guard and ever since, for eighty-two years and counting, not a minute has passed without a military guard on the Plaza. In December 1940, the 12th Infantry joined the 3rd Cavalry. For the next year, the 3rd Cavalry stood guard the first half of the month and the 12th Infantry the second half. All that changed after Pearl Harbor, however, as both regiments were reassigned to other bases to prepare for World War II. During the war, the Military District of Washington maintained a small ceremonial detachment to guard the Tomb and to perform funerals and ceremonies.

Upon its reactivation at Fort Myer in 1948, The Old Guard assumed responsibility for guarding the Tomb, which it has done now for seventy-one years. While the Tomb Platoon has a meticulous daily log starting in 1959, no one seems to know who served the first guard shift for The Old Guard. But not much has changed over the years, as the Tomb guards attest. Staff Sergeant Shane Vincent, a two-time Sentinel, explained to me that "the standards are pretty much the same since 1948. Old Sentinels return and recognize pretty much everything." Gavin McIlvenna, a Tomb guard from 1997 to 1998, retired as a sergeant major and now serves as President of the Society of the Honor Guard, Tomb of the Unknown Soldier, the platoon's alumni organization. He confirmed to me that video recordings as far back as 1960 reveal the same basic sequences for guarding the Tomb and the Changing of the Guard. Likewise, the Tomb guards' uniforms and weapons have evolved along with those of the broader Army. The guards started in the Army's classic World War II–era "pink and green" uniform, whereas they now wear the ceremonial blue uniform. The platoon adopted the M14 rifle in 1964 in place of the earlier M1903 Springfield and M1 Garand, then added the Beretta M9 in 1988. As the Army switched from the M9 to the

SIG Sauer M17, the Tomb Platoon had a small ceremony in October 2018 with SIG Sauer to accept four new pistols, custom-made for the Tomb guards.

The most meaningful change to their uniforms was probably the introduction of the Tomb Badge—or more precisely, the Guard, Tomb of the Unknown Soldier Identification Badge. The badge, designed by early guards based on the Tomb, is silver and approximately two inches in diameter, with an inverted wreath around the Tomb's eastern front above the words HONOR GUARD. The Army authorized it for wear on February 1, 1958, and the first badge was awarded six days later to Master Sergeant William Daniel, a prisoner of war in World War II and the Sergeant of the Guard for more than three years. He returned that original badge to the Tomb Platoon in 1996 and it now hangs prominently in the Tomb Quarters. Msg. Daniel passed away in 2009 and now rests in Section 35, just a few steps south of the Tomb.

While the badge was initially limited to Sentinels serving at the Tomb, the Army authorized it in 1963 as a permanent award. Thus, a Sentinel who completes training and serves at least nine months at the Tomb may wear the badge forever, much as the Ranger Tab and the Parachutist Badge are permanent awards once earned. With only 666 Tomb Badges awarded to date— each badge's number is engraved on its back—the Tomb Badge is among the rarest skills badges in the Army, second for many decades only to the Astronaut Badge. (And as a common joke among the Sentinels goes, who joins the Army to be an astronaut?)

Unusually for a skills badge, though, the Tomb Badge may be revoked for bad conduct, even after a badge-holder leaves the Army. Under Army regulations, The Old Guard commander is the revocation authority. Colonel Jason Garkey, the regimental commander, explained to me that "a revocable offense is anything that would bring discredit on the Tomb Platoon and the Unknowns." The punishment might seem harsh, but it simply reflects the highest standards of integrity that we, as a nation, expect from the soldiers guarding our Unknowns. I never spoke with one Sentinel who disagreed.

Yet the introduction of the Tomb Badge was not the most significant event at the Tomb in 1958, for on Memorial Day of that year, the Unknowns from World War II and the Korean War were interred. Congress and President Harry Truman had provided by law for a World War II unknown in June 1946, but those plans stopped when the Korean War broke out in June 1950. By 1956, Congress passed and President Dwight Eisenhower signed a new law providing for a double interment of a World War II and a Korean War unknown.

The selection process for both unknowns mirrored the rituals used for the World War I Unknown. The Army selected two finalists for a World War II unknown, one each from the Atlantic and Pacific theaters, and selected the Korean Unknown at the same time. All three sets of remains were transferred to the U.S.S. *Canberra* off the Virginia coast on May 26, 1958, where Hospital Corpsman 1st Class William Charette, a Navy Medal of Honor recipient from the Korean War, chose the World War II Unknown by placing a wreath on one of the caskets. The two Unknowns then sailed for Washington, while the other World War II finalist was buried at sea. Upon arrival, the two Unknowns were escorted to the Capitol Rotunda. Vice President Richard Nixon led the large party of dignitaries and laid a wreath in honor of the Unknowns. They lay in state for two days and took turns on the Lincoln Catafalque. Again, more than one hundred thousand people paid their respects.

On Memorial Day, the Unknowns had another grand procession from the Capitol to Arlington, this time with caissons from The Old Guard and an honor cordon of Old Guard troops. The procession crossed Memorial Bridge, which had opened in 1932. Awaiting the Unknowns at the Amphitheater was President Eisenhower, the Supreme Allied Commander in World War II. He paid them tribute and presented them with the Medal of Honor, then the Unknowns moved a final time to the Plaza. Rather than new tombs, the Unknowns would lie in crypts on the Plaza by the original Tomb. After the committal service, Old Guard troops closed out the ceremony: the Presidential Salute Battery fired the twenty-one-gun salute, a firing party rendered the traditional three volleys, and a bugler played Taps. The casket teams folded their flags and presented them to President Eisenhower and Vice President Nixon, who stood in as next of kin for the Unknowns. The funeral concluded and the dignitaries departed, while Old Guard troops guided members of the public who wished to pay respects.

Three days later, the two crypts were sealed with a marble top inscribed with dates and nothing more: 1941–1945 and 1950–1953. On the same day, the dates 1917–1918 were carved into the stone in front of the Tomb. Now, three Unknown brothers-in-arms commanded the high ground above Arlington.

As the new Unknowns arrived at their eternal home, American troops were arriving in Vietnam. Over the next seventeen years, a small advisory mission became a major conflict. Within months of the Paris Peace Accords in 1973, Congress directed an unknown soldier from the Vietnam War to be buried at Arlington. A crypt was built for a Vietnam unknown the next year, between those for the World War II and Korean War Unknowns. But the story of the Vietnam Unknown would be longer and more complicated, as was the war itself. And the story ends not with an

*The Old Guard and its four sister services march in the procession for the
Vietnam Unknown on Memorial Day 1984.*

unknown soldier resting in Arlington, but a quarter century later with the exhumation of First Lieutenant Michael Blassie.

Blassie was shot down in May 1972, and his remains were tentatively identified when recovered five months later. But forensic experts later reclassified the remains as unidentified—one of very few from the war, given scientific advances—and they ultimately became the Vietnam Unknown. Thus, the newest Unknown began a two-week journey from a Hawaii laboratory to Arlington in May 1984, with the highest military honors at every step—many rendered by Old Guard soldiers, caissons, and artillery guns. On Memorial Day, after lying in state for three days, the Unknown moved in a funeral procession from the Capitol Rotunda to the Amphitheater, where President Ronald Reagan consecrated the Unknown's sacrifice and presented him with the Medal of Honor. After the committal service on the Plaza, a twenty-one-gun salute from the Presidential Salute Battery, and Taps, President Reagan stood in as next of kin and accepted the flag. Later that night, cemetery workers lowered the casket into the crypt and sealed it with a marble top again inscribed with dates and nothing more: 1958–1975.

But the crypt would not remain sealed. Ten years later, after evidence of the Unknown's identity surfaced, the Blassie family asked the Air Force to reopen the matter, without success. Then, *CBS Evening News* examined the controversy in January 1998. The Department of Defense ordered an investigation and decided to exhume the Unknown for DNA testing.

The night of May 13–14, 1998, was unlike any other in the Tomb's long history. A wall was placed around the three crypts to shield the dignity of the site. The Sentinels continued their vigil as workers cut into the Vietnam crypt with a diamond-tipped saw. A few minutes after midnight—0029:25, down to the second, as any Sentinel can recount today—the Unknown was exhumed, draped with a flag, and placed on a catafalque. That morning, with the Tomb and the Plaza restored to immaculate condition, Secretary of Defense William Cohen hosted a brief removal service. The Unknown departed in a hearse, bound for Walter Reed. A few weeks later, DNA testing made known the Unknown. Michael Blassie was returned to his family and he received a full-honor funeral at the Jefferson Barracks National Cemetery outside St. Louis, near his childhood home.

The saga of the Vietnam Unknown has long generated controversy, strong emotions, and even ill will, which I believe is unfortunate. Because in the end, the story of all the Unknowns is a love story—the love we hold in our hearts for the men and women of our Armed Forces who have given their lives to protect our nation. We venerate the Unknowns, including Michael Blassie for fourteen years, not merely as representatives of the unknown dead from four wars, but as heroes who embody the courage and sacrifice of all our war dead, from Lexington and Concord to Iraq and Afghanistan. As President Reagan said when the Unknown lay in state, "This American hero may not need us, but surely we need him." That love is why the Vietnam crypt now reads, HONORING AND KEEPING FAITH WITH AMERICA'S MISSING SERVICEMEN, 1958–1975. That love is why the Sentinels keep a framed rubbing of Michael Blassie's headstone at Jefferson Barracks in their Quarters. And indeed, that love is why we as a nation have committed to guard the Tomb without fail for eighty-two years—a symbol of our boundless love for America's fallen heroes.

The Changing of the Guard

Twenty-one. The number is central to the Tomb. While the Tomb guard walks the sixty-three-foot black rubber mat on the

Plaza—"walking the mat," as it is known—he takes twenty-one steps. Where he halts is known as the "twenty-one block." There, he faces the Tomb and stands at attention for twenty-one seconds. He faces back up the mat and shifts the rifle to his shoulder opposite the Tomb—or nearest the visitors, as a symbol of his duty to protect the Tomb. He stands at attention for another twenty-one seconds before he steps off for another twenty-one steps. The guard repeats that sequence, over and over, back and forth, an endless vigil for the nameless dead.

Why twenty-one? It symbolizes the love we feel for our war dead, and the honor we pay them. The twenty-one-gun salute is the highest military honor, otherwise reserved for presidents and foreign heads of state. A gun salute reflects a universal custom of rendering one's weapon inoperable to demonstrate peaceful intent. As long as men have fought wars, this custom has appeared, be it an American soldier in Iraq putting his rifle muzzle into the ground or a warship firing cannons out to sea when entering a harbor. The origins of the number of guns are, to a degree, lost to the mists of time. Some say it reflects the number seven, the number of days in which God created the Earth, multiplied by the number three, the Holy Trinity. Others say it relates to the number of cannons on early warships. In any case, the twenty-one-gun salute was established by the late nineteenth century as the highest military honor between two nations and for a head of state. As one Sentinel put it to me, whatever its origins, the symbolism of twenty-one reflects our nation's commitment to pay the highest honor to our war dead.

The Tomb guard walks the mat until the Changing of the Guard, which occurs on the hour during the winter and on the half hour during the summer. The Amphitheater's bells signal the start of the ceremony. On the first gong, the door to the Quarters opens and out comes the changer, as the guard who conducts the ceremony is known. A civilian security guard usually clears visitors out of the Foyer by the door. If not, as I occasionally witnessed, the changer immediately directs them to "step aside" in the guards' icy, intimidating command voice.

As he ascends the steps and turns east toward the Plaza, visitors scramble to get a glimpse. I attended dozens of changes this past year, observing the Tomb guards and also the visiting crowd. Familiar scenes recur throughout the day and across the seasons. Visitors rush to the south side of the Amphitheater when they hear the changer's steel-plated shoes on the marble, then slowly follow him to the Plaza. Parents explain the Tomb and the guards to a son or daughter. Schools and youth groups gather in matching colored shirts. Some visitors are overcome with emotion, perhaps remembering a lost loved one. Hundreds of smartphones take pictures or record the ceremony. I know of no other place in the nation's capital where so many people focus so reverentially on a single thing. And it happens ten times a day in the winter and nineteen times a day in the summer.

But many visitors will witness this one Changing of the Guard and never see it again. Although the Tomb guards stressed to me that they strive for perfection to honor the Unknowns, they understand that many visitors will see the next change and only that one. They therefore want to leave the visitors with a perfect image of their mission at the Tomb. They remind me of our commitment at Charlie Company to conduct flawless funerals that leave the family with the best possible memory of the Army.

On Flags In Day in 2018, I hosted Vice President Mike Pence at the Tomb. At a lunch with other senators earlier that Thursday, I had explained Flags In and encouraged them to drop by on the way home. The vice president was at the lunch and decided to go. After placing flags in Section 60, we went to the Tomb. The soldiers were prepared for him, even though they had only a few minutes' notice. He toured the Quarters, took photos with the guards, and signed the platoon's daily log book for history.

Vice President Pence and I went to the Plaza at 1625 to watch the Changing of the Guard. As we stood in the press pit, near the Tomb and opposite the stairs where most visitors stand, there were lots of waves and pictures. Meanwhile, Private Trevor Drahem was the walker, as the guard on the mat is known, and he went straight to "the box," the small green canvas hut just north of the Tomb. He called down to Quarters on the hotline, as I explained to the vice president that walkers use the box to wet their gloves, adjust their uniforms, or call for guidance. I told him that Drahem, a young soldier still in training, was probably surprised that the vice president had just appeared on the Plaza. But Drahem told me afterward, "I didn't recognize either of you, so I called to ask if I should remove you from the pit." When I told Vice President Pence that story a few days later, he said, "Good for him, he was doing his job!"

By the time Drahem got back on the mat, Staff Sergeant Craig Hudson was making his way to the Plaza. I explained to the vice president that much of the ceremony is silent, conducted off unspoken cues and silent counts. Indeed, when circumstances dictate— say, a funeral is occurring near the Tomb or the National Anthem is playing during an event in the Amphitheater—the Tomb guards can conduct the entire Changing of the Guard silently, going off only cues and counts. As Ssg. Hudson's feet passed the ground-level window into the Quarters, for instance, the oncoming walker took that as his cue to go "out the door." And within a few moments, Staff Sergeant Garrett Golden rounded the corner.

Once Ssg. Hudson turned onto the Plaza, I pointed out to the vice president that he scraped his steel plate on the first and eleventh steps, which signals to the off-going walker that the changer is present and ready to step off in cadence. I told the vice president that Ssg. Hudson's first act would be to salute the Tomb, since the Unknowns are all Medal of Honor recipients. Likewise, I explained that Ssg. Golden wore no rank on his sleeve because the Unknowns have no rank and no walker may outrank them.

After Ssg. Hudson introduced himself and the ceremony to the crowd, the vice president and I positioned ourselves next to the inspection block, one of the easily recognizable rust-colored spots on the marble where the changer and the oncoming walker have stood for decades. Ssg. Golden brought his M14 rifle to port arms and Ssg. Hudson snapped it out of his hands to begin the rifle and uniform inspection, the most iconic part of the ceremony. The inspection takes two minutes and forty-five seconds, with no voice commands. The guards operate entirely off a silent count, I explained, while also pointing out that Drahem used the pop of the rifle in Ssg. Hudson's hands or a nod of his head as a cue to start walking on the mat.

With the inspection complete, Ssg. Hudson fell in next to Ssg. Golden and commanded, "Forward march." As they passed Vice President Pence and me, Ssg. Hudson again scraped his shoe. The vice president asked, "What does that one mean?"

"He's saying hi," I whispered.

"Really?"

"Yes. They scrape their shoes as a way of saying hello, or thank you, or good job. So he's just acknowledging us."

As we whispered, the three soldiers converged on the Tomb, saluted the Unknowns, and changed out.

"Pass on your orders," Ssg. Hudson commanded.

"Post, and orders remain as directed," Drahem replied.

"Orders acknowledged," answered Ssg. Golden.

After one more salute of the Unknowns, Ssg. Golden stepped onto the mat and assumed responsibility for the Tomb. All three soldiers now marched together to the south, with Ssg. Golden stopping in the twenty-one block while Ssg. Hudson and Drahem continued to the fallout block, another easily recognizable rust-colored spot on the marble surface. Ssg. Hudson inspected Drahem's rifle through a silent, seven-count sequence, which I whispered to the vice president. Drahem faced south to walk off the Plaza on Ssg. Hudson's command of "fall out" and Ssg. Hudson followed shortly behind him, acknowledging us again with a scrape.

Vice President Pence and I walked off the Plaza behind them and said our good-byes. Col. Garkey escorted the vice president to his motorcade. I turned back to the Quarters, where the mood was enthusiastic. Ssg. Hudson was talking through what had happened during the change. He saw me and said, "Sir, I could see your lips counting in the fallout block. You almost threw off my count!"

"Sorry about that," I apologized. In fact, however, I had not observed a single deficiency among any of the three guards, despite the vice president's presence. And that itself was a telling detail; the Tomb guards are so accustomed to worldwide attention that no one and no moment seems to fluster them.

Meanwhile, back on the Plaza, Ssg. Golden continued his vigil, walking the mat to the rhythm of twenty-one, back and forth until the next change. The crowd at 1700 was sparse, but the Tomb guards executed the ceremony with the same professionalism and precision that they had thirty minutes earlier for their vice president.

Introduction to the Tomb Platoon

As with the Changing of the Guard, the leadership, structure, and daily rhythms of the Tomb platoon have remained largely unchanged for decades. And like the Tomb's public duties, its hidden life differs in key ways from that of most of the Army.

Unlike most Army units, which are led by an officer, the Tomb Platoon's leadership typically consists of the Sergeant of the Guard and the Assistant Sergeant of the Guard. The Sergeant of the Guard is a sergeant first class and often has demonstrated leadership ability at another unit in The Old Guard. But he is expected to qualify as a Sentinel and perform at the Tomb, most notably in wreath-laying ceremonies for the president. The Assistant Sergeant of the Guard is a staff sergeant and usually is a Sentinel promoted from within the platoon.

This is not to say the Tomb platoon never has an officer in charge, known as the Commander of the Guard. Fifteen officers have earned the Tomb Badge, including Jim Laufenburg, who later returned to The Old Guard as the regimental commander. Indeed, Captain Vic Farrar became Commander of the Guard in 2018 after successful stints with Charlie Company and Honor Guard Company. One reason he wanted to be the Commander is that his father was a Sentinel, so the Tomb was a special place for him growing up. Col. Garkey encouraged Cpt. Farrar to extend his Old Guard tour by a year to take the job. "Vic is one of my best, most experienced officers, plus you've got the great family connection with the Tomb," he explained. But the Tomb usually goes without a Commander for two reasons: guard duty in the Army is primarily the responsibility of sergeants, and sergeants cannot substitute for officers in funerals and ceremonies, so The Old Guard needs officers there more than the Tomb needs a platoon leader.

The platoon is organized into three squads, known at the Tomb as reliefs. The relief is the basic element of the Tomb platoon: its training, operations, and schedule all revolve around the relief. Like an infantry squad, each relief is led by a staff sergeant. Rather than "squad leader," the title for this job is Commander of the Relief, or simply relief commander. Although their backgrounds vary—and not all are infantrymen—the relief commanders typ-

ically have five to ten years of Army service and usually have
served outside The Old Guard as well. For example, Staff Sergeant Kevin Calderon had five years in the Army and Ssg. Golden
had eight before they reached the Tomb. In addition, each relief
has an assistant relief commander, typically a sergeant.

The size of a relief varies, depending on the platoon's overall
manpower. In good times, a relief might have nine to eleven soldiers. In lean times, a relief might have only five to seven soldiers.
Four is the absolute minimum to function—three to conduct guard
changes and one to remain in charge of Quarters. As important
as the number of soldiers, though, is the number of fully trained
Sentinels, because they can perform all the platoon's duties under
any conditions. A relief with multiple "new men," as guards still in
training are known, has less flexibility in executing its mission.

The Tomb Platoon's home is the Quarters, underneath the Amphitheater. Just as the Tomb is guarded twenty-four hours a day,
the Quarters are always open and manned. Outside the door is
the Foyer, which includes a glass display case of Tomb memorabilia and other items. Just inside is the Brief Room, so called because Sentinels use it for public briefings. Although the Quarters
are not generally open to the public, the Sentinels welcome dignitaries there and can invite family, friends, or other visitors for
a briefing. For instance, on a slow Saturday afternoon, I walked
into a briefing that Specialist Mike McCutchen was conducting
in German because Specialist Antonio Garcia had heard a group
of German tourists and offered them a briefing in their native lan-
guage. Because of these visits, the Brief Room contains historic
photographs and memorabilia, plus a Badge Board that contains
the names of all past and current Sentinels.

On the other side of the Brief Room is the Ready Room, the
central hub of the Quarters. Guards rehearse and inspect each

other in front of its many mirrors. Ceremonial M14 rifles—with black slings to symbolize mourning—rest in a weapons rack. Shelves known as the "ready rack" contain the "last-minute items": ceremonial cap and belt, scabbard (or holster), gloves and keepers, and sunglasses. A whiteboard lists the day's critical information: weather, uniform, expected visitors, and so forth. A closed-circuit television provides a live shot of the Plaza to observe for irregularities and threats. A hotline is connected directly to the box on the Plaza. A large conference table provides space for the relief commander and other Sentinels to work and eat.

One thing that struck me about the Ready Room was the lack of distractions and the mission focus. I have spent many hours in

The Ready Rack in the Tomb Quarters holds the Sentinels' "last-minute items," such as sunglasses, scabbard (or holster), cap, belt, and gloves and keepers. On the top shelf rests the platoon's custom-made M17 pistols.

Army command posts, and it is common to see televisions tuned to sports, iPods playing music, and magazines and books lying around. But I never witnessed these distractions at the Tomb, only soldiers focused on their job. I asked Ssg. Calderon if his relief used the large television and DVD player in the corner. He answered, "Maybe after 2300, once we're done with training and Taps, the guard who has charge of Quarters will watch a movie. But not while we're working." When duty calls, the relief is single-minded in its dedication to that duty.

The rest of the Quarters is located down a long hall off the Ready Room and resembles a cross between Home Depot, Hobby Lobby, and a locker room. The Supply Closet is like an arts-and-crafts exhibit with medals, ribbons, and other uniform items. The Badge Holder Locker Room contains a locker for each Sentinel; new men who have completed the first two months of training use the Locker Room next door. The Rouge Room is named for jeweler's rouge, which guards apply to a buffing machine used to shine metal. The room also contains a workbench for sanding rifle stocks, unit citations, and the heel plates on their shoes. The Press Room holds the same industrial press machine used by the rest of the regiment. Wreaths for upcoming ceremonies hang in a small side hall. The Gym has a pull-up bar and a few free weights, most of which remain unused during the platoon's busy days. Finally, the New Man Locker Room has temporary lockers for new men in the first two months of training.

The round-the-clock nature of the Quarters sets the stage for the relief's duty day. An old joke that the Army fits more than twenty-four hours into the day is the official standard at the Tomb. The duty "day" actually runs for twenty-six hours, from 0430, when soldiers from the oncoming relief arrive for their morning workout, to 0630 the next day, when those same soldiers have cleaned the Quarters and transferred them to the next relief.

A relief's twenty-six-hour duty "day" is part of its nine-day "work set." A relief is on duty and guarding the Tomb for Days One, Three, and Five of the work set. The twenty-two hours on Days Two and Four between duty are hardly "off" days, as most soldiers prepare their uniforms and train on ceremonial skills. These five days shape the workweek for the relief, as Staff Sergeant Justin Courtney described to me: "It doesn't matter what the calendar says, Day One is Monday, Day Five is Friday."

Which would mean, as Ssg. Calderon joked, "Day Six is great, it's like Saturday. The only thing better is Day Eight, since you're coming off Day Seven." If Days Six and Eight are like the weekend, Days Seven and Nine are like half days. On Day Seven, the relief meets in the morning for organized physical training, usually a run, so the relief commander can keep his troops in peak physical shape. Because of their unusual nine-day schedule, reliefs exercise together about sixty fewer days a year than a regular infantry squad, so every day counts. On Day Nine, the relief starts the day with refresher ceremonial training on the Plaza while the cemetery is still closed. After a couple of hours, the relief conducts physical training again before soldiers are released.

For new men, though, these four days present an opportunity. Garcia explained to me that he came to Quarters every day for five months to prepare for his next test and to improve his skills by learning from guards on the other two reliefs. Other Sentinels had similar stories. While in training, they viewed these four days not as a break, but as time to get ahead of the curve. Not surprisingly, they earned the Tomb Badge and became Sentinels, not washouts.

The Making of a Sentinel

While guarding the Tomb is the platoon's public mission, the making of new Sentinels is its central mission behind the scenes. The meticulous training cycle can last up to a year, and the attrition rate historically approaches 90 percent. Those who make the cut join one of the military's smallest and most honored fraternities.

The Tomb Platoon recruits only within The Old Guard, and thus its new soldiers generally meet the regiment's basic standards for height and weight, physical fitness, and so forth. New men usually have at least six months with the regiment before trying out for the Tomb Platoon, but not always: I met several guards who came straight to the Tomb upon arriving at The Old Guard. Tomb guards need not be infantrymen. During the time I spent with the platoon, it included two medics, a military-police officer, a mechanic, and a driver.

And despite the old term "new man," female soldiers are eligible for the Tomb. Over the last twenty years, four female guards have earned the Tomb Badge, most recently Sergeant Ruth Hanks in 2015. Though the female guards can be striking to visitors—they wear the same uniform as do the male guards, but the hair bun is the immediate giveaway—the Sentinels make little of it. Sgt. Hanks trained Ssg. Golden, who called her "an amazing Sentinel and a great leader—she's the only reason I passed training." McCutchen said, "She set the standard for the platoon." For her part, Sgt. Hanks downplayed the accomplishment, emphasizing that "I always try to bring it back to the Unknowns."

What all new men have in common is that they volunteered for the Tomb. In fact, some guards joined the regiment specifically to try out for the Tomb Platoon. Ssg. Calderon explained,

"I came here to The Old Guard just to become a Tomb guard." He pressed for two years before he finally got to try out. Despite the long wait, he never gave up. "I wanted to be part of the best of the best," he said, so that "when my kids grow up, they have something to be proud of their father for." Others overcame initial reservations about serving at the Tomb. Staff Sergeant Dallas Kempo, a recently departed Sentinel whom I met while he was visiting his old friends at the Quarters, recalled that when he first observed the Changing of the Guard as a teenager, "I was awestruck." He later enlisted and deployed to Iraq with the 82nd Airborne, then joined The Old Guard. But he hesitated to try out for the Tomb Platoon because he was newly married and the platoon's hours can be hard on families. After two years with Bravo Company, he finally joined the platoon.

Some guards are not quite "voluntold," to use the old Army joke, but they do get strong encouragement to volunteer. Garcia was a top performer in Bravo Company and wanted to go to Ranger School. But he recalled, "One day, my first sergeant called me into his office and said, 'Guess where you're going.' I got so happy and said, 'Ranger School?' And he said, 'No, the Tomb.' I guess I was shocked; I just stood there silent. He said, 'You'll do fine there, and you can still go to Ranger School.' " Once Garcia got over the initial surprise, his mind-set was simple: "I never fail at anything and I always give 110 percent." And he did not fail. Garcia earned his Tomb Badge in barely five months, the fastest of any Sentinel in recent memory. His first sergeant was also vindicated: Garcia completed Ranger School and Airborne School in late 2018.

The Sentinels quickly assess whether these new recruits are suited to become a Tomb guard. Within a few days, the platoon's leadership evaluates their aptitude, physical fitness, mental abilities, and motivation. The platoon uses a "whole soldier" concept, as Ssg. Vincent put it, asking, "Does this soldier have what it takes to continue and succeed in training?" Those who lack potential are sent back to their units in the first week. Those who make the initial cut proceed into the platoon's training cycle. The details of this training regimen have evolved over time—the first two months today are known as the Tomb Guard Qualification Course—but the standards and expectations have not.

The first two weeks of training, which occur at night from 1900 to 0700 under the watchful eye of a senior Sentinel, act as another screen to identify new men with the right stuff. The new men do not have Tomb uniforms yet, so they focus on "outside performance," or walking the mat and changing the guard, and knowledge of the cemetery and the Tomb. While new men cannot march or handle a rifle up to the platoon's standards after two weeks, they should be able to show some progress and memorize the ceremonial sequences. And the platoon's required knowledge is a good proxy for work ethic and discipline, according to Ssg. Calderon. "Our test scores are high enough that we can all learn the knowledge; it's just a question of wanting to. If you don't learn it, you just don't want to be here." After these two weeks, new men must pass their first test to continue the qualification course.

With that test behind them, the new men return to the Central Issue Facility at Fort Myer, where they receive their new uniforms. While the Tomb Platoon uses the same basic uniform as does the rest of The Old Guard, there are some critical differences. First, Tomb guards get more of everything—blouses, trousers, caps, and so forth—because service at the Tomb subjects the uniform to more wear and tear. Second, the guards get a few Tomb-specific items, most notably leather shoes, a personal bayonet scabbard (or pistol holster), and sunglasses. Third, the tailors alter Tomb uniforms in slightly different ways. For instance, the blouse sleeves are longer to ensure that no skin is visible when a guard moves his rifle.

Fourth and most significant, the Tomb guards modify their uniforms in ways not permitted to other Old Guard soldiers. For example, they "gut the blouse" by removing its nylon liner and they cut the pockets out of the trousers, both of which allow for a smoother, cleaner press on the exterior wool. They also seal the trouser pockets and the chest-pocket pleats with Stitch Witch, a fusible bonding tape that melts under the heat of the press machine. These modifications are a good illustration of the Tomb Platoon's unique standing within The Old Guard: what Tomb guards are required to do would result in any other soldier being fined for destruction of government property. The contrast underscores how far The Old Guard will go to honor the Unknowns.

New men spend the next four weeks getting their uniform up to standard. While regular uniform items are straightforward—in fact, a gutted Tomb blouse is easier to press than a normal one—the Tomb-specific items can take hundreds of hours. Every guard with whom I spoke agreed that the leather shoes and bayonet scabbard are by far the most labor-intensive items. I could prepare my glossy Corfam shoes in two minutes with Windex and edge-dressing. By contrast, when I asked Ssg. Golden how long it takes to finish a pair of Tomb shoes, he laughed and said, "You never do." The shoes must be repeatedly "sanded and built up," using fine sandpaper and layer upon layer of polish on the leather uppers and the soles. The scabbard, which starts in the Army's standard olive-drab green, undergoes a more dramatic transformation still. The new men disassemble it, polish the metal to a high shine using the rouge machine, sand down the sheath and spray-paint it black, and then polish it just like the shoes. The end result for both the shoes and scabbard is a brilliant, onyx-like surface with a near-mirror finish.

The shoes and scabbard are so time-consuming that guards often take them home, which requires creative ways to protect them in transit. The preferred technique is to convert clear document boxes into a carrying case. For the shoes, guards bolt or tape four magnets to the bottom, which then secure the steel plates on the soles. For the scabbard, they use cotton balls and rags to create a protective cocoon inside the box. Ssg. Calderon recalled his first trip to a nearby Container Store when he asked a clerk for a document box and magnets, to which she replied, "Oh, you must be one of the Tomb guards."

During these four weeks, the new men also continue to practice their outside performance. They work inside the Quarters on their rifle manual, usually in front of its many full-length mirrors. Mirror Time, as it is called, is essential for a new man to gain the skills and confidence in handling the M14 according to the platoon's standards. Garcia explained that one reason he earned his badge so quickly is that he came to the Quarters on off-duty days for extra Mirror Time.

The "training relief," as the Sentinel trainer and his new men are known, has responsibility for guarding the Tomb from 2200 to 0700, so they also train outside on the Plaza. These hours allow the new men to learn the unique marching style of a Tomb guard out of the public eye. The goal is for nothing above the guard's waist to bob up and down, so the top of the ceremonial cap stays perfectly still and level to the Plaza. The guards achieve this gliding effect by "rolling" along the outside of the sole of the shoe, from the heel to the side to the balls and toes. They also swing their arms mostly to the rear, in contrast to our natural swing and also to the Army standard of "nine to the front and six to the rear." This is much harder than it probably sounds, and the mat is the best place to practice because that is where they will walk during the day. Train like you fight, as the Army says.

The training shifts to the daytime during the final two weeks of the qualification course. By this point, the new men's uniforms should meet the platoon's standard and the men should be proficient in walking the mat and the change sequence. Now their goal is a Day Walk, guarding the Tomb while the cemetery is open. The first step, though, is a BOLO, short for "be on the lookout" for unauthorized persons present while the cemetery is closed. These walks are conducted in ceremonial uniform and to the normal ceremonial standard but occur in the hour before the cemetery opens and the hour or two after it closes, when stragglers may still be present around the Plaza. During these two weeks, the training relief's shift is noon to midnight, allowing the new men to earn the evening BOLO, after which they can earn an afternoon Day Walk.

New men earn their walks through a "Quarter Till" and a "Three Minute, Go." Fifteen minutes before the Changing of the Guard, the new men line up in front of a three-way mirror called the "Knowledge Corner" and call out "Quarter Till, may I earn this walk?" The relief commander then quizzes them on their knowledge. If a new man answers enough questions—and had passed the daily uniform inspection and has satisfied the platoon's leadership with his outside performance—he will be told, "Three minutes, go." This drill requires the new man to change into ceremonial uniform in three minutes, an important skill for all guards to be prepared for contingencies such as a turn in the weather or uniform malfunctions. The new man races back to the Ready Room, where the relief commander inspects him and then tells him to blouse up and get out the door.

These first walks are major milestones for a new man. Sergeant Jeff Dickerson recalled his first BOLO, saying, "Of course, I was super nervous." He described it as "my most memorable moment" and choked up as we talked. Halfway through the BOLO, a Sentinel "came out and he said, 'Hey, man. Congratulations. You're a Tomb guard now.'" That moment, Sgt. Dickerson said, "is when I probably felt like I had done something with my career." Other Sentinels reflected on their first Day Walk, when the public is present. Ssg. Golden said, "It was one of the most terrifying but rewarding moments of my life." Ssg. Hudson's first Day Walk came after a morning BOLO. He returned to the Quarters and then earned the very next walk. "When I went back out," he said, "I couldn't believe how many people were there. It was crazy. I was only gone for twenty minutes, but it was like the cemetery opened the gates and everyone raced straight to the Tomb."

Given the stakes—and the nerves—the element of last-minute surprise to the BOLO and Day Walk works to the new man's benefit. In these final two weeks of the qualification course, a new man knows that his BOLO and then his Day Walk are approaching, but he still must earn them. He could fail the quiz at the Quarter Till or the uniform inspection after the Three Minute, Go, and all that happens within ten minutes of the walk or less. "It's probably for the best that it's kind of a surprise," Ssg. Golden observed, "so you don't sit around and get wound up."

The new men who pass the qualification course by earning and successfully performing a Day Walk next join one of the platoon's three reliefs. While these new men—or, in some cases, given attrition rates, the new *man*—are far from earning the Tomb Badge and becoming a Sentinel, they now integrate into a relief's daily operations. Each new man is assigned a Sentinel mentor on the relief and they work together to hone the new man's craft. The new man's daily life also begins to reflect his status as a Tomb guard, not a trainee. For example, new men assigned to a relief move down the hall to the more spacious Locker Room. When on duty but not walking or changing, they can wear "Tomb attire"—a polo shirt and slacks—instead of the less comfortable Army Service Uniform—a short-sleeved dress shirt and dress blue trousers, also known as "Class Bs." This may not seem like much, but as Garcia remarked, "it's such a morale booster when you're in training." New men get at least one scheduled walk a day and perhaps more based on their performance. They also can earn additional walks through Quarter Tills and try to earn wreath-layings.

As these new men continue to improve their skills, they progress toward the three remaining tests to earn the Tomb Badge. The tests are essentially the same, only with higher standards. For example, a new man can pass the uniform portion of Test 1 with seven minor deficiencies, but with only five on Test 2 and just two on the Badge Test. Likewise, new men must memorize eleven pages of knowledge by Test 1, but all seventeen pages by Test 2. The all-day tests are also administered in the same way, starting with a uniform inspection at 0630. Ssg. Hudson estimated that the inspection takes about thirty minutes, though he quipped, "It can be done in thirty seconds." Either way, the new man is scheduled into the relief's daily walking rotation; he does not have to earn walks on test day. Once the cemetery closes, the new man has time to eat and prepare for the knowledge test.

These tests, though useful as checkpoints, simply reflect a new man's work ethic, discipline, and reverence for the Unknowns. There is no last-minute cramming at the Tomb. New men have two months to pass Test 1 and another two months for Test 2, then six months to take the Badge Test, but the most motivated and talented young guards can move much faster. Likewise, the Sentinels will have taken a good measure of the new men by Test 1, so the results are rarely surprising. By Test 2, they should demonstrate not only the skill of a Sentinel, but also the same maturity, initiative, and responsibility. As Ssg. Calderon put it, "Test 2 is when I expect them to meet the standard of a badge-holder." The new men who reach this point in the training cycle rarely fail. One young Sentinel, Specialist Cameron Payne, recalled that "it's smooth sailing after Test 2—the job is harder, but the training is easier."

The last step of training is the Badge Test. In a way, the test is anticlimactic, because it resembles the other tests and guards are highly proficient by this point. But of course earning the Tomb Badge and becoming a Sentinel is a life-changing moment. As I listened to the Sentinels' stories about receiving their badge, I heard tales with jokes and laughs, tears and hugs. In fact, many Sentinels choked up as they remembered the moment, and I must confess it was hard not to tear up myself as I relived it with them.

Right after the Badge Test, the Sentinels will often imply that the new man failed the test before revealing the good news. Ssg. Golden recalled fretting for hours, thinking he had failed, and even dozing off. He awoke with Sergeant First Class Paul Basso, then the Sergeant of the Guard, in his face saying, "PTs, three minutes, go." That was a good sign, he assumed, as was Sfc. Basso's order to get three specific headstone rubbings and then go to his favorite headstone, that of Sergeant First Class Paul Ray Smith, the first Medal of Honor recipient of the Iraq War and a veteran of Ssg. Golden's old unit. The relief was waiting for him, but Ssg. Golden was too exhausted to realize that the grave numbers on the rubbings added up to 651, his badge number. Sfc. Basso told him to look behind the memorial headstone. Ssg. Golden said, "I look and there's my badge sitting there. I just took a knee and started tearing up." As Ssg. Golden remembered the moment, the Sentinels "gave me a big old group hug," then

Sfc. Basso "called me his brother, told me he loved me," and "I just started crying, I couldn't help myself."

Occasionally these moments are genuine family affairs. When Ssg. Kempo finished his Badge Test, he believed that he had passed, but then his trainer sent him on a headstone run to the grave of Chaplain (Major) Charles Watters in Section 2. Ssg. Kempo explained, "Chaplain Watters's grave is my favorite, so I was worried the run was supposed to boost my morale and remind me of why I was doing this after failing the Badge Test." Ssg. Kempo had chosen a very noble grave: Chaplain Watters earned the Medal of Honor posthumously for heroism in Vietnam after repeatedly exposing himself to enemy fire, unarmed, so he could provide aid to the wounded and administer last rites to the dying. Ssg. Kempo had visited his grave many times throughout training. But this time, he said, "as I ran up to the grave, I saw my wife, Caroline, and my son, Connor. That's when I realized I had passed. Sure enough, they were holding my badge. I just hugged them and cried."

Not every Badge Test is so poignant. Corporal Matthew Koeppel recalled Ssg. Golden trying to lead him on, but "he couldn't even keep a straight face, he just said, 'No, you passed.' " Still, Cpl. Koeppel recalled fondly "the rite of passage." He said, "They told me to get into PTs, and said, 'You have a surprise waiting for you at the flagpole, you have one minute to go get it.' " He sprinted to the flagpole, only to find two forty-five–pound weights, which he dragged to the Quarters. The relief laughed and Ssg. Golden said, "Where did those come from?" He sent Cpl. Koeppel back to the flagpole, where he found a badge box and raced back to Quarters with it, only to open it and find it empty. At that point, the Sentinels challenged him to a race to the water fountain. Cpl. Koeppel continued. "I beat them, of course, and they said, 'Yep, okay, you get your badge.' I asked, 'Okay, where is it?' They said, 'I think I see something shining in the water fountain over there.' " Even though it was nighttime in February, Cpl. Koeppel jumped in and retrieved his badge. He came out and they all hugged and congratulated him for "bathing off the new man, coming out a Sentinel."

The final, celebratory step in becoming a Sentinel is the Badge Ceremony, usually a few weeks after the Badge Test to coordinate schedules for the new Sentinel, his family, and the chain of command. The ceremony occurs in the Display Room, the museum-like room above the Quarters and just off the Plaza. At Cpl. Koeppel's ceremony, the room was full of family, friends, and Old Guard soldiers. The entire Tomb Platoon aside from one guard on duty and one in charge of Quarters was also present, one of the few times the platoon gathers as a whole. The ceremony was short and dignified. Col. Garkey described what the Tomb and the Sentinels mean to visitors, from foreign heads of state to Gold Star Families. Then Cpl. Koeppel's grandfather pinned the badge on him while the orders were read. After the Sentinel's Creed, the other Sentinels filed by to shake hands and happily smudged the highly polished badge with their thumbs.

I would have enjoyed the ceremony under any circumstances, but I appreciated it still more for the weeks I spent with the Tomb Platoon. Cpl. Koeppel had spent hours the night before preparing his already immaculate uniform and rehearsing a creed he had recited hundreds of times. Afterward, he admitted that the ceremony "was nerve-racking." Those nerves and his extra rehearsals reveal, in my opinion, a loving dedication to the Unknowns that is as much the culmination of the making of a Sentinel as the ceremony itself.

Daily Life at the Tomb

From an outsider's perspective, a relief's day might seem repetitive, even monotonous—the Changing of the Guard and wreathlaying ceremonies, over and over again. But on the inside every day is different, as the relief performs its mission while managing contingencies from weather to animals to visitors. The daily schedule may not change and the ceremonies may appear identical, but there is a lot going on behind the scenes.

The day begins between 0400 and 0500, when the relief reports to set up their uniforms and exercise, often a run just outside the cemetery. They finish by 0600 so they can start "gigging Quarters," or inspecting its cleanliness before accepting charge of Quarters by 0630. The next ninety minutes are a busy period to prepare for the day. The first task is to raise the flag, at 0630, the standard time for reveille in the Army. The platoon is responsible for the flagpole just south of the Amphitheater, one of two in Arlington (the other is at Arlington House). Arlington's flags fly at half-staff during funerals, so two guards return to lower the flag to half-staff at 0830, thirty minutes before the first funeral.

In between, the Sentinels complete other morning tasks. They close out the previous day's log book and start their own, as they have for sixty years. They also draft the day's guard roster; they pick shifts by order of seniority, but they also try to accommodate each other's preferences. "We'll shift around if another Sentinel needs to walk at a specific time, like if he has family or friends here to watch him," Cpl. Koeppel said. "We square each other away. It's close-knit here, so we look out for each other." Meanwhile, the new men are preparing their uniforms for the daily inspection at 0715.

The Tomb Platoon's daily log book dates back to 1959; here, two days from February 2019 are displayed.

In between tasks, the guards will scarf down some breakfast and fuel up on coffee or energy drinks. Here, too, the platoon has an intimate, family-like feel. One morning I was there, Ssg. Vincent called into the Quarters to ask if anyone wanted a sandwich from Subway. Ssg. Calderon and a couple of others relayed their orders. Ssg. Vincent returned and passed out the breakfast sandwiches, but did not ask to be paid. Ssg. Calderon noted, "That's a difference between here and the big Army. Next time we'll do a food run and pick up Vincent, so we don't pay every time. That didn't happen in my last post. You paid back each time." Even in something as mundane as buying breakfast, the sense of brotherhood within the platoon comes through.

As 0800 approaches and the morning BOLO concludes, the

day's first walker and changer get ready to go out the door. The last-minute uniform preparation is a team effort. Just like in the cemetery, the guards help each other "blouse up" by holding the blouse's pleats in place while the changer and walker buckle their ceremonial belts. But with tools and mirrors available, Sentinels can go further. They burn off loose threads with a cigarette lighter. They "tape off" the uniform with masking tape to remove lint. They wipe off smudges on the cap's bill and straps with a microfiber. They tuck away a loose shoestring into the shoe. Meanwhile, the changer and the walker use a spray bottle to douse their gloves with water to get a better grip on the rifle. Small things, to be sure, but all done as a way to honor the nation's war dead.

In the final moments before the changer exits the Quarters, he and the walker share a moment to focus on the coming ceremony. Some Sentinels have handshake and fist-bump routines. They all exchange the same ritual words on the way out the door, which I first heard between Ssg. Calderon and Garcia:

"I'm out the door, Sentinel Garcia."

"I'm right behind you, Sergeant."

"Have a good walk."

"Have a good change."

"I'll see you in the inspection block."

"I'll be there, Sergeant."

The changer stops at the door, gains ceremonial composure, hits the unlock button on the wall with his right hand, and throws the door open. The walker repeats the sequence moments later. The Changing of the Guard has begun. The ceremony will conclude in eight to ten minutes, when the off-going walker and the changer descend the steps to the Quarters and walk through the door held open by another guard.

———

Immediately following the Changing of the Guard is the window for a wreath-laying ceremony. The laying of wreaths at the Tomb reflects the timeless custom across cultures of placing flowers on the grave of a loved one, and thus expresses our love of the Unknowns and all those they represent. The relief can lay two wreaths after a change. (In the summer months, when the change occurs every thirty minutes, wreaths are laid only at the top of the hour.) Wreath ceremonies can occur every hour with some exceptions, and a relief can conduct up to fourteen wreath ceremonies per day in the winter months and sixteen per day in the summer. The heaviest periods are during spring break and the middle of summer.

Public wreath-laying ceremonies are open to any person or organization; the most common groups are schools and veteran organizations. Wreath-laying ceremonies are requested through the cemetery and groups obtain wreaths from local florists, who deliver them to the Quarters a day or two before the ceremony. When a wreath arrives, a guard accepts delivery, logs it on a roster, and hangs it on the wall. Wreaths accumulate quickly during high-volume days or after a day of inclement weather, when many groups postpone or cancel their ceremony. After a heavy snow day, for instance, I once saw more than thirty wreaths hanging on or leaning against the wall. On the day of a group's ceremony, a guard checks their attire and briefs them at the Quarters door fifteen minutes before the change preceding their ceremony.

Joining the changer and the off-going walker is a bugler from The U.S. Army Band. Two buglers work daily at the Tomb, one each for the morning and afternoon, and are affectionately called "Sergeant B," regardless of their names. I discussed the bugler's role with Staff Sergeant Jeffrey Northman. He said that the band's ceremonial section has twenty buglers who rotate between funerals and the Tomb, estimating that most buglers will complete five or six Tomb shifts each month. "The Tomb is the most work of all our missions," he explained, "because we play so much here and we also have to play weekends." Nevertheless, Ssg. Northman added that "we all love playing at the Tomb. It's a very special place and a special mission. We have a weird job, playing Taps all day long. Here, we have a chance to play for people who aren't actively grieving the loss of a loved one, so that's a nice change." "Sergeant B" and the Sentinels get to know each other well and many become friends and mentors, since the buglers tend to be older than the young guards.

After the bugler links up with the changer and the off-going walker in the Quarters, they verify that the correct wreath is staged and then return to the Plaza. As they approach, the walker on the mat steps into the box. All three salute the Unknowns as they pass the Tomb and the changer, the host for the ceremony, walks up the stairs to meet the group. The greeting between the host and the group, especially schoolchildren, is an endearing scene. Tomb guards by their nature are intimidating, and one can imagine what the kids feel as the tall, stone-faced soldier with mirrored sunglasses marches toward them. But at the top of the steps, the host relaxes, clasps his hands at his belt, and softens his demeanor. Ssg. Calderon said his goal is to "put them at ease. They look pretty scared, so I want them to know I'm a human being." He introduces himself, asks about the group, and thanks them for honoring the Unknowns. He then briefs them on the ceremonial sequence and answers any questions.

Meanwhile, the wreath-bearer and bugler prepare the Plaza for the ceremony. The bearer removes the previous wreath from the stand and places it on the east side of the Tomb. He then briefs the public, recognizing the group laying the wreath and asking visitors to stand and remain silent. The bearer returns to the bugler's side and the host leads the group down the stairs, while the wreath-bearer and the bugler converge on them. The bugler stops halfway and faces the Tomb, while the bearer continues and stops in front of the group. He steps forward and asks the front two members of the group to lay their hands on the wreath, and then leads them backward to the stand while the host calls "present arms" for everyone to salute. Once the wreath is laid, the bugler plays Taps and then salutes, after which the host calls "order arms" for everyone to drop their salute. Finally, the host leads the group up the stairs, where he shakes hands and thanks them again for honoring the Unknowns. If there is a second ceremony, the next group and its wreath is waiting, and the ceremony repeats itself.

Despite the thorough preparation, the presence of civilians on the Plaza can create unpredictable moments for the guards. Ssg. Calderon shared one memorable story with me. During a wreath ceremony for a middle school, as he saluted during Taps he saw out of the corner of his eye what he thought was water hit the Plaza. "I moved my salute hand an inch away from my face," he recalled, "just in time to see the kid in the back projectile-vomit all over the kid in the front." It got all over Ssg. Calderon's sleeve and trouser leg as well. But he held ceremonial composure. More amazing, he said, "I couldn't believe the kid getting puked on just stood there with his hand on his heart! I told him after the ceremony that was some of the best composure I've ever seen, so he should come be a Tomb guard when he's older." When I asked him what happened to the vomit on the Plaza, he said, "Nothing at first. I mean, the guard has to go on. So the new walker just walked right through it. After a few minutes, we decided we had to clean it up, but a mop would look undignified, so we sent a couple new men up in Class Bs with a bucket of water and some rags."

Wreaths collect throughout the day on the east side of the Tomb and remain there until after midnight, so each wreath honors the Unknowns for the full day. One of the relief's overnight duties is to collect the wreaths and move them off the Plaza, where the cemetery's grounds crew can remove them in the morning. The guards sometimes take roses or other pretty flowers from the wreaths to give to their wives. And they save meaningful banners from wreaths, for instance, one from their first wreath ceremony or from a unit with which they had served.

Between their walks and changes, guards must conduct hasty uniform maintenance, especially in the summer months when they have twenty minutes or less between changes. Sentinels usu-

Sergeant Tre Banda of the Tomb Platoon shines his uniform insignia with his full tacklebox of equipment next to him.

ally work outside for a few hours at a time, during which they
stay in uniform between outside shifts. Other guards therefore
help tape off the blouse again, polish smudges, and wipe down
the shoes. For a guard who sweats a lot, they may even steam out
his sleeves while he is wearing the blouse. After the hours-long
shifts, when the Sentinels change out of uniform, they use the
steamer to remove wrinkles from the sleeves and the belt line.
Some might even re-press the sleeves between walks or change
into an alternate blouse on muggy days.

The weather is a constant adversary to uniform maintenance.
Like the rest of The Old Guard, the Tomb Platoon has three
basic uniforms—blouse, overcoat, and raincoat—and follows the
same basic rule of blouse above forty-five degrees and overcoat
below it. But the Sentinels cannot move a ceremony inside because of inclement weather. They also wait to don raincoats until the rain actually arrives because they do not perform the rifle
inspection during the Changing of the Guard when wearing
raincoats, given the risk of mishandling the rifle. By contrast,
we wore raincoats at Charlie Company for funerals if rain was
merely forecast. Thus, most Tomb guards get drenched in their
blouses at least once and usually many times, something that
thankfully never happened to me, because a soaked blouse is a
ruined blouse. The guard must re-press it from scratch and start
over on most of the insignia, too.

But a guard cannot do much once he is caught in the rain. I arrived at the Tomb one night after a brief but monsoon-like storm.
A young new man in his blouse had waited in the box during
the day's final shift, but got soaked during the scheduled change.
When I asked why not stay in the box until the rain stopped, the
young guard responded without hesitation, "Sir, we never miss
a change." His unequivocal answer demonstrated how even the

newest guards quickly internalize the Tomb guards' dedication to duty and the Unknowns. They could have cut corners with no visitors present, but that was never even considered. We all laughed at his expense, but it was a laugh of brotherhood and shared sacrifice in service of a noble mission.

Moreover, even if a guard can get into a raincoat before a storm arrives, it will still degrade the shoes and scabbard, which both require hours of repair. That is why the Sentinels hate rain above all else. When I asked about inclement weather, Garcia answered for everyone: "Anything but rain." Ssg. Golden chimed in, "Oh yeah, a heat wave or a blizzard is better than a little rain." On a muggy summer day, the worst that can happen is a sweaty, wrinkled uniform, which dries out and gets a new press that night. Heavy snow requires even less work, because the guards wear the overcoat, which is easier to maintain, and they sometimes post in the box during snowstorms to avoid slipping. But nothing can protect against the rain, which makes a good soaking something of a rite of passage. McCutchen enthused, "Getting absolutely poured on when you're on the mat—that's the shot you want! Those are the best pictures and videos. They really show how serious we take the job."

Weather is not the only adversary that the Tomb guards must confront occasionally. Mother Nature also deploys bugs and animals. Sentinels are expected to maintain ceremonial composure at all times on the Plaza. While they train to swallow sneezes and ignore itches, critters are not so easy to train for.

Some guards face only a few gnats or maybe a mosquito. For others, the bugs aggressively attack. Garcia recalled a bug crawling into his ear during a wreath ceremony. "I was standing at present arms during Taps and all of a sudden I could hear this buzzing and then I felt a tickle. I thought, 'Holy cow, this bug is crawling up my ear.' He stayed in there the whole salute." When I asked what he did, Garcia shrugged and said, "I guess the movement from facing about and walking up the stairs got him out, because I didn't feel it after that."

But no one could top Ssg. Golden's experience, which he recounted with pride. "I had a big bug go up my nose, crawl up my nasal cavity, and down in my mouth. I chewed him up and swallowed him because I didn't want to open my mouth and break composure. I just had a little snack." When I asked why he did not blow the bug out of his mouth, the irrepressible sergeant said, "This is the Army, man! This is the Tomb! You don't just ignore the standard and do what you want." We all had a good laugh at his story. But Ssg. Golden also used the story as a lesson for his soldiers: the nation has entrusted them to guard and honor the Unknowns and, while they should not take themselves too seriously, they should take the job seriously.

The Tomb Platoon has one nemesis in the wild above all: squirrels. Trees surround the Plaza, with branches hanging over the marble banisters. Squirrels are a regular presence and are accustomed to people because of the large daily crowds. The squirrels often run onto the Plaza. Ssg. Calderon said of one squirrel, "He just kind of stood there looking at me, like 'what are you doing on my Plaza?' " They also scavenge from the wreaths on the ground, picking away tasty flower petals. A common fear is that a squirrel will scratch or chew the walker's shoes, or even go up his leg. Most guards told me stories about a squirrel running up a guard's trouser leg, though they admitted to not knowing the guard. While the story may be apocryphal, it reveals a deeper truth: no matter how audacious the squirrels are, the Tomb guards ignore them and keep walking the mat.

Human beings, regrettably, can also disturb the serenity at the

Tomb. Visitors who breach the rules of conduct usually mean no harm, but in these moments the crowd is reminded that the Tomb guard is a genuine guard. He brandishes the rifle across his chest, steps off the mat, and addresses the violator. The most common situations are excessive noise, a small child escaping his parent's grasp, or an adult trying to retrieve something that has fallen onto the Plaza. While most visitors never witness this scene firsthand, those who have seem surprised, even startled.

The guard on duty has discretion on how and when to engage a violator—to "break 'em off," in the platoon's lingo. For instance, most guards treat a hard-of-hearing elderly veteran or a special-needs child more gently than an unruly teenager. In those cases, the guard may not engage at all, but rather go into the box and call the Quarters to ask another guard to come handle the matter discreetly. When they do engage, some guards will speak politely but firmly: "It is requested that all visitors maintain an atmosphere of silence and respect at all times. Thank you." Other guards are more direct, with neither requests nor gratitude: "All visitors must maintain an atmosphere of silence and respect!" Many guards are parents, so they tend to be sympathetic to the parents of toddlers: "Visitors must keep their children behind the chains and rails. Thank you." But few guards tolerate adults who cross the rails for any reason: "Please stay on the other side of the chains and rails at all times!" These varied responses are good examples of the discretion and judgment entrusted to the Tomb guards, which is rarely apparent to a casual observer.

Most visitors, however, uphold the solemn atmosphere at the Tomb, even if some garner more attention than others. After laying a wreath on Memorial Day 2018, President Donald Trump visited the Quarters to meet the Tomb guards, get a brief, and sign the log book for posterity. Likewise, foreign heads of state, ministers, and defense chiefs visit regularly after wreath-laying ceremonies. Movie stars, musicians, and professional athletes also show up. What stands out about these occasions is the Sentinels' self-possession, which their intensive training instills. Ssg. Vincent commented, "They don't earn the badge till I'm confident they can solo-brief a foreign dignitary." These moments are just another instance in which The Old Guard represents the whole Army to the larger world.

But the guards agree that no visitors are more memorable than Honor Flight veterans. The Honor Flight Network brings veterans of World War II, Korea, and Vietnam to the capital region to visit their war memorials and other popular sites. Aside from their war memorials, the Tomb is a favorite site for them. Ssg. Golden expressed the guards' respect for these old warriors: "The best thing about the job? That's easy to answer. The Honor Flights." Cpl. Koeppel explained that his perspective matured as he progressed through training. At first, celebrities like Jon Bon Jovi and George Strait impressed him. Then he met one of the last living survivors of World War I and several Medal of Honor recipients. Now, he most appreciates the Honor Flights: "As you're laying a wreath, you hear Taps go off, you turn around, and they're all standing there, people who can't stand at any other time because of their age or disability. You know, it hits you." Ssg. Kempo reflected on the poignancy of these visits after noting that two Unknowns fought in World War II and the Korean War. He asked, "What if one of their battle buddies died and they didn't know what happened to him? What if he's the Unknown from that war?" Good questions, and a good reminder of the Tomb's special meaning across the ages.

Of all the visitors to the Tomb, though, none are more heartwarming than families. The Tomb places unusual strain not only on soldiers, but also their families. On one hand, Tomb guards are on duty "only" three days out of nine. On the other hand, those days last twenty-six hours and include weekends and holidays, while the guards use "off" days for uniform maintenance and other tasks. Ssg. Calderon, whose wife, Lisa, had their second and third children during his tour at the Tomb, said that the absences from his family are the hardest part of the job, though "it's definitely even tougher on my wife." Yet family support is essential. He attributed his success, especially in training, to her encouragement and assistance. Similarly, Garcia joined the Tomb platoon with the full support of his wife, Janai, and he earned his badge so quickly, he said, because he worked every day at the Quarters while his wife also worked. Like many working families, they spent time with the kids for dinner, baths, and bedtime, then he would work on his uniform, sometimes with Janai testing his knowledge. Without her, he said, "it would have been a struggle." Now "she's proud, and she enjoys this place as much as I do."

One reward for this strain on families is their visits to the Tomb and the Quarters. Garcia's wife and two kids come at least monthly. Like many young kids, his son Carter imitates him on the Plaza. I once saw Ssg. Courtney's wife, Elizabeth, bring their two girls, Belle and Holly, and her parents to the Quarters. When he returned from changing the guard, the girls asked for a hug. He said, "Yes, just don't touch the shoes," and leaned over at the waist while spreading his legs as wide as he could. And guards often bring family visiting the capital to the Quarters for a tour and brief.

After witnessing many such visits, I sensed that the pride these families feel for their Sentinels symbolizes how most Americans revere the Tomb and the Sentinels who guard it. Ssg. Golden's mother cried the first time she watched him walking the mat, mouthing the words "I love you, I'm so proud of you" whenever he faced her. He said, "It was a proud moment," if a bit embarrassing. I hear that same sense of pride and awe whenever people ask me about The Old Guard. These feelings are not lost on the Sentinels, as Ssg. Golden reflected. "When I die, I want my children to look at my life," he said, "and I want them to be proud of me. I can honestly say that being a Sentinel, I've achieved that. No matter anything I do for the rest of my life, I can always say I served as a Sentinel at the Tomb of the Unknown Soldier."

As the sun falls behind the Amphitheater, the relief prepares for the cemetery to close. The guards raise the flag to full-staff at 1630, once all funerals are complete. At 1715, the changer and off-going walker march to the flagpole to perform the Retreat ceremony. A small crowd often builds in the summer as visitors hear the distinctive click of the guard's steel-plated shoes on the stone path leading to the flagpole. The visitors probably do not notice that the two guards are not wearing gloves, which enables them to retrieve and fold the flag in a dignified fashion. Retreat is the only time Tomb guards leave the Quarters in ceremonial blues but without gloves.

The final changer of the day, whether at 1700 in the winter or 1900 in the summer, closes down the Plaza. After the fallout sequence, the changer returns to the middle of the Plaza and informs the crowd that the cemetery is closed and now "the Tomb of the Unknown Soldier becomes a restricted military post." He marches off for the last time, as a civilian security guard clears the Plaza of the remaining visitors.

The cemetery may be closed, but the relief's day is only half

over. That last change posted the evening BOLO, which begins
the overnight duty roster. If a Tomb Guard Qualification Course
is under way, the training relief arrives at 1900 and takes over
responsibility for the Plaza at 2200. If not, the relief's new men
are primarily responsible for guarding the Tomb. The overnight
guard shifts tend to last longer than an hour, giving the new men
more time to train.

On occasion, though, a Sentinel will conduct an overnight vigil,
also known as a "superman," as a way to test himself and honor
the Unknowns. On one rainy night, for instance, Ssg. Kempo

*A Tomb guard "walks the mat" during a snowy day. The Tomb Platoon
guards the Tomb round the clock, no matter the weather or conditions.*

posted at 1800 in raincoat and did not change out until 0700, maintaining ceremonial bearing for thirteen hours. When I asked him about the superman, he cited the sacrifice of the Unknowns: "They gave everything for us—not just their lives, but their whole identities. What is it to walk in the rain for thirteen hours in comparison?" Similarly, Ssg. Calderon conducted his last walk in ceremonial attire from 2100 to 0700 the next morning. And when a snowstorm shut down the cemetery, Ssg. Vincent took the opportunity to conduct a twenty-four-hour shift in combat fatigues, joking that "I knew the storm was coming, so I was really careful about how much I ate and drank."

Aside from these unusual but special vigils, the night largely belongs to the Sentinels. They follow "big boy rules," the colloquial Army term for soldiers who are expected to care for themselves and their equipment without supervision or external motivation. Many Sentinels get in another workout, either a run along the Potomac or a lift at the Fort Myer gym. One or more Sentinels usually go on a food run for the others.

Their main task overnight is uniform maintenance for the next duty day. Most Sentinels prefer to "get the uniform up" before they change out the next morning. Thus, they spend three to six hours overnight on their uniform, depending on the day's weather. Just like in uniform preparation, shoes and scabbards take the most effort; the most common scene during my evenings at the Quarters was a Sentinel, listening to an iPod, polishing and buffing. Sentinels also strip their blouses clean, re-press them, and re-pin them. If needed, they build replacement items from scratch—medals racks and buff straps, for instance—though most wait for the four-day break if possible.

This nightly level of care contrasts with what we did at Charlie Company, where we could go for weeks without stripping and re-pressing a blouse, instead just touching up the hot spots on the sleeves and belt line. Our Corfam shoes took only minutes to maintain. And I used the same medals rack during my entire tour at The Old Guard, as did many of my soldiers. Some of this contrast results from the much heavier wear at the Tomb, but the Sentinels truly go to the greatest lengths to honor the Unknowns.

The best time of day at the Tomb, in my opinion, is 2300. After an hour of collective training, all the Tomb guards except the one in charge of Quarters line up on the Plaza a couple of minutes early. At 2300, they salute the Unknowns as Taps begins to play over the Amphitheater's speaker. In the dark of night, when the Tomb is lit and framed by the cemetery's mall, and the mournful notes of Taps echo across the Plaza, the sense of gratitude for the fallen heroes in the cemetery is overwhelming. I spent many nights working at the Tomb simply to share this moment with the soldiers and the Unknowns.

After Taps, the relief commander may implement a "work-rest plan," the Army euphemism for sleeping. At least one Sentinel stays awake in charge of Quarters and to change out the guards. Other guards can get a short nap. At all hours, though, one can hear the distant whir of the rouger and the sander or the hiss of the press as Tomb guards continue their pursuit of perfection in honor of the Unknowns, whose sleep remains undisturbed a few feet away.

Last Walks

The Unknowns will rest for eternity and the Sentinels will never cease their vigil at the Tomb. But for each Sentinel, the day will finally arrive when he must conduct his Last Walk, a solemn yet celebratory occasion. By coincidence, on one of my first days observing the Tomb Platoon, I witnessed a Last Walk ceremony for a Sentinel I already knew. I first met Sgt. Dickerson at the Society of the Honor Guard reunion banquet on Veterans Day in 2016. The Society had asked me to speak at the dinner. Sgt. Dickerson and his girlfriend, Kylie, were seated next to me because he was then the newest badge-holder and thus responsible for leading the Sentinel's Creed.

Sixteen months later, I attended Sgt. Dickerson's Last Walk in March 2018. The Quarters were full of Tomb guards as he prepared to go out the door at 0800. Amidst the jokes and congratulatory wishes, an emotional intensity gripped his face as the bells began to sound. He later told me, "It was actually hard for me to get out the door," realizing it would be his last time on the Plaza. I followed him outside and watched a routine change ceremony, with one exception. Once Sgt. Dickerson had acknowledged the orders from the off-going walker, the changer said, "Sergeant Dickerson, for the last time, post." Since the cemetery had just opened, no public visitors were present—only the Tomb guards, Kylie, and his parents, Rick and Deann, who had flown in from California.

The Quarters rippled with energy and pride as Sgt. Dickerson conducted his last walk. The entire platoon attends a Last Walk ceremony, one of the few times they gather as a group. The whole chain of command was present, as were Sgt. Dickerson's friends from across The Old Guard. Kylie's parents arrived after taking a red-eye from California. They had to fight rush-hour traffic, and everyone was relieved when they made it on time.

For one person, though, this hour was bittersweet. I noticed on the closed-circuit television that Sgt. Dickerson stepped into the box for a few minutes. When we later discussed his Last Walk, he explained that "I was thinking about what I was going to say to everybody" in his speech, which he called "one

Staff Sergeant Kevin Calderon (right) conducts the last Changing of the Guard for Sergeant Jeff Dickerson (center) along with Specialist Antonio Garcia (left).

Sergeant Jeff Dickerson lays a rose at the Tomb during his Last Walk, while Specialist Antonio Garcia looks on from "the box."

of the most important things when a Last Walk happens." He revealed that "I thought about that a little bit, and I lost my composure on the mat. So I had to go in the box, straighten myself out."

No one seemed to notice that this stone-faced Sentinel choked up as he guarded the Unknowns for the last time. As the clock ticked toward 0900, the Plaza went from empty to filled with a couple hundred visitors. Last Walks are not announced in advance, but things were plainly different at this hour. Two dozen young men with extreme high-and-tight haircuts wearing black Tomb Guard shirts and jackets stood in formation on the Plaza. Officers and senior sergeants in dress uniforms lingered on the top of the stairs. As the bells tolled, a Sentinel in ceremonial uniform and five roses in hand walked a young woman in a black dress down the steps. After the usual change sequence, visitors got their first hint of what was happening in the fallout block when Ssg. Calderon directed, "Sergeant Dickerson, for the last time, fall out."

Ssg. Calderon then returned to the middle of the Plaza and informed the crowd that they were watching the Last Walk ceremony for Sgt. Dickerson and that "his fellow Sentinels would like to wish him good luck and Godspeed in his future endeavors." Meanwhile, Sgt. Dickerson had handed his rifle to a guard at the chains, rather than march to the Quarters as usual. He returned to the stairs, where he removed his sunglasses and gloves, symbolizing the end of his duty. He took the roses, gave one to Kylie, and kissed her cheek. He laid the remaining roses on the Tomb and the crypts for World War II, Korea, and Vietnam. A bugler played Taps as Sgt. Dickerson saluted the Unknowns one final time. When I asked him later what he was thinking while Taps played, he replied quietly, "I just hope they rest in peace." After the final note, he returned to Kylie's side, extended his arm, and they walked off the Plaza, together, for the last time.

We all reconvened a few minutes later in the chapel underneath the Amphitheater. The small space filled up quickly with family, friends, the Tomb Platoon, the chain of command, and even the CIF tailors who work closely with the platoon. Lieutenant Colonel Todd Burroughs, the 4th Battalion commander, became emotional as he started his speech, saying, "I choked up at my first Last Walk and I've choked up at every one since." He and Command Sergeant Major Lee Ward presented Sgt. Dickerson with an Army Commendation Medal for his service. Then his fellow Sentinels gave him a framed 4th Battalion guidon bearing his Tomb Badge number in Roman numerals—DCXLV—and a mounted M14 ceremonial stock. Finally, Sgt. Dickerson made the speech that had so occupied his mind on the mat. Addressing the Sentinels and the new men directly, he spoke of what the Tomb means for the nation, and especially for Gold Star Families:

> I joined because I wanted to make a difference. I thought it would be on a distant battlefield. Little did I know it would be here, for the Unknowns and the American people. My biggest motivation was knowing someone who had lost a loved one—a son or husband or dad—could come here and know how much we love them and how much we care. To my fellow Sentinels, I want you to remember how much you mean and how much this place means to them.

Tears, hugs, and pictures were all that was left.

A few days later, I sat down with Sgt. Dickerson. We talked

about his training and he observed that the Sentinels may guard the Unknowns, but by doing so they honor and remember all soldiers who have laid down their lives in defense of our nation. That is one reason why, he said, their knowledge includes so much information about other soldiers buried in the cemetery. In everything they do, Sgt. Dickerson added, the Sentinels try to embody a platoon motto carved into the M14 stock he had received after his Last Walk.

"Soldiers never die until they are forgotten. Tomb Guards never forget."

Among those soldiers never forgotten are three Sentinels who have fallen in defense of our nation. These Sentinels, who returned to regular infantry units after they left The Old Guard, are legendary within the Tomb's brotherhood. Their names and the dates of their deaths are among the first things a new man learns in training. And the Tomb Platoon continues to honor them in ways big and small.

Two Sentinels died in the Vietnam War: Staff Sergeant Bill Spates in 1965 and Sergeant Marvin Franklin in 1967. Sgt. Franklin is buried in his hometown of Oklahoma City, but his picture hangs in the Ready Room. Sgt. Spates had requested a burial near the Tomb should he die in combat; today, he rests just down the hill in Section 48. As I walked to his grave on Memorial Day 2018, I could see the Tomb despite the thick spring foliage. One could say Sgt. Spates now stands an eternal vigil with his unknown comrades in arms. Older Sentinels recall making similar walks down the hill to place flowers from the day's wreaths on the headstone. Many current Sentinels have his headstone rubbing, and his medals sit in the display case in the Foyer outside the Quarters.

For today's Sentinels, Staff Sergeant Adam Dickmyer hits closer to home. Ssg. Dickmyer served at the Tomb from 2004 to 2007. He continued with The Old Guard for another two years in Honor Guard Company, where he marched in President Barack Obama's inauguration and led the joint-service casket team at Senator Ted Kennedy's funeral. But having spent five years at The Old Guard during a time of war, Ssg. Dickmyer wanted to get in the fight. He transferred to my old division, the 101st Airborne. Within months, he deployed to Afghanistan at the peak of the surge into that country. Despite his lack of combat experience, or even substantial time with a tactical infantry unit, Ssg. Dickmyer excelled as a squad leader and was elevated in country to acting platoon sergeant. He was serving in that capacity when he was killed on October 28, 2010, by a buried improvised explosive device near Kandahar. The platoon's log book for the day notes his death in red ink and says simply, "We will not forget."

The Old Guard performed the dignified transfer for Ssg. Dickmyer the next day at Dover Air Force Base and then returned him to Arlington for eternity on November 17. After the memorial service on Fort Myer, they conducted a full-honor funeral for their fallen comrade. Sentinels marched in the long funeral procession from Fort Myer to Section 60 and watched as their fellow Old Guard soldiers laid him to rest. Later that day, the Sentinels hosted his widow, Mindy, at the Tomb for a wreath-laying ceremony in his honor.

Almost a decade later, even though no current Sentinel served with Ssg. Dickmyer, they hold him close to their hearts. His headstone rubbing is the only one hanging in the Ready Room. Ssg. Calderon explained that the platoon gets a fresh rubbing at least once a year, on the anniversary of his death. On that day, he added, the relief on duty visits his grave and leaves two dimes and a penny, in honor of the twenty-one-gun salute. The coins are shined, of course, to the Sentinel's standard of perfection. And most poignantly, the display case in the Foyer includes a mannequin wearing a replica of Ssg. Dickmyer's uniform. While few visitors recognize the uniform—it is not labeled—this reminder of their fallen comrade is the first thing the Tomb guards see as they exit the Quarters and the last thing they see as they return from guarding the Tomb.

Perhaps more than any ceremony or tradition at the Tomb, this silent tribute to Adam captures the meaning of the Tomb of the Unknown Soldier. The Unknowns represent every American who has worn our nation's uniform, especially those who died in combat. The Tomb is our national place of mourning. War widows and war mothers once visited the Tomb and held fast to the hope that the Unknown was their missing beloved. Those days have passed, yet during their walks today Sentinels still observe widows dressed in black, sobbing quietly at the edge of the Plaza. The heartbreaking scene is living witness to the unending power of the Unknowns and the guards who watch over them.

But the Tomb is also a place of memory and celebration. During my years in the Army, whether in Arlington or at memorial services overseas, chaplains often borrowed from General George Patton's old line that we should not merely mourn the soldiers who died, but also thank God that such men lived. I have always agreed with that—even more than mourning the death they endured, we ought to celebrate the lives they lived. Millions of people, untouched by war, visit the Tomb each year and leave with a sense of awe, inspiration, and love. Very few know the story of the Sentinel killed in Afghanistan who now rests down the hill in Section 60. Fewer still realize that his uniform is on display just around the corner. Yet the Tomb guards know, even if they do not advertise it. And if indeed soldiers never die until they are forgotten, the place of honor given to Adam's memory is testimony that Tomb guards never forget. Adam surely took comfort in that knowledge as he left the wire for the last time in Afghanistan, as no doubt did his eternal battle buddies in Section 60.

Epilogue:
"The Old Guard Never Stops"

The Old Guard labors every day to honor the memory of our nation's fallen heroes, so they indeed will never die in the hearts of their fellow citizens. Tomb Sentinels stand watch over the Unknowns. Caisson soldiers bathe their horses in the predawn darkness. Infantrymen scout grave sites to prepare for another day of perfect funerals. All dedicated to the selfless Americans who answered our nation's call in dangerous, trying times. The roll call of the dead grows by thousands every year in Arlington, and each soldier receives the very best that America's Regiment has to offer.

History lives inside Arlington's gates, but The Old Guard takes no breaks from history. No book, therefore, could capture all that The Old Guard does to honor America's heroes, because the regiment's work never ends. In the year during which I wrote this book, for instance, The Old Guard participated in historic events that underscore the simple message delivered every day inside Arlington: we will never forget and we will always honor.

The first historic occasion began in July 2018, when North Korea announced that it would return fifty-five sets of unidentified remains from the Korean War. General Vince Brooks, the commander of U.S. Forces Korea, knew the transfer would be complex. "This was going to be the biggest transfer of remains since the Korean War ended in 1953," he explained. "I wanted the pros, so we put in the call to The Old Guard." Gen. Brooks had a seasoned honor guard under his command—"it's modeled on The Old Guard," he noted—but the transfer "involved some new techniques for us, and would get international attention."

Back at Fort Myer, The Old Guard answered the call with two of its best soldiers: Captain Zach Kennedy, the regimental ceremonial and memorial-affairs expert, and Sergeant First Class Bryan Dospapas, the 75th Ranger Regiment veteran and former drill sergeant who now served as platoon sergeant for Charlie Company's Casket Platoon. "We were 100 percent surprised," Cpt. Kennedy recalled. "I bought a plane ticket before I knew what I was doing." Sfc. Dospapas jumped at the chance to participate in the historic mission, even though his wife was in the third trimester of her pregnancy. They departed for Korea "with no real guidance," Cpt. Kennedy said, "since there was really no precedent. 'Go be helpful' was the implied guidance."

They started helping immediately upon landing in Seoul. Though jet-lagged from the fourteen-hour flight on July 29, they had little time to spare with the transfer scheduled for August 1. They worked until after midnight with the honor guard, developing a plan and writing out sequences and key commands. Cpt. Kennedy and Sfc. Dospapas provided their subject-matter expertise but planned no role for themselves; the objective, according to Cpt. Kennedy, "was empowering the honor guard in Korea." After some needed rest, they spent two full days rehearsing the exact techniques and sequences with the honor guard. "They wanted to be there, and they knew what it meant to be there," Sfc. Dospapas said. "That mind-set made it very easy for Captain Kennedy and me to train them up."

A worldwide audience witnessed a flawless dignified transfer at Osan Air Base, but an incident after the cameras stopped rolling best illustrated our nation's commitment to our fallen heroes, and

Sergeant First Class Bryan Dospapas instructs a joint honor guard of American and Korean forces as they prepare for the transfer of fifty-five Korean War remains.

The Old Guard's responsibility in upholding that commitment. One of the two aircraft loaded with remains had a mechanical failure. Gen. Brooks called for a replacement aircraft and ordered another dignified transfer. "It was never even a question that we'd do the transfer with proper military honors," he explained, even though it might delay the arrival at Hickam Air Force Base in Hawaii. But the honor guard had not developed plans for or rehearsed an aircraft-to-aircraft transfer. "The Old Guard was on top of it," Gen. Brooks said. Cpt. Kennedy credited Sfc. Dospapas, who crafted a plan for the challenging sequence on the spot, then talked the honor guard through it and quickly rehearsed it with them. Gen. Brooks enthused, "The Old Guard squared us away and our team executed perfectly. I was so proud of them all." Cpt. Kennedy and Sfc. Dospapas watched as the aircraft took off to the east, with fifty-five sets of remains bound for American soil for the first time in sixty-five years.

A month later, The Old Guard honored two more unknown heroes from an older war as it dedicated the newest part of the cemetery. Arlington has expanded periodically throughout its history to address space constraints. The latest was the Millennium Project, which added twenty-seven acres to Arlington's northwest corner. The dedication connected Arlington's past with its future by interring two unknown Civil War soldiers from the Second Battle of Bull Run, whose remains were discovered three years earlier. Researchers with the National Park Service believe the two soldiers may have died from wounds suffered during the Union's failed assault on the third and final day of the battle—an assault in which The Old Guard participated. Now, 156 years later, they laid to rest their unknown comrades in arms.

"It was an incredible honor to be able to lead my soldiers in giving these two unknown soldiers the honors they deserved after all these years," observed Lieutenant Colonel Allen Kehoe, the 1st Battalion commander. He and his senior enlisted advisor, Command Sergeant Major Robert Carter, presided over the funeral, which included two caisson sections bearing the remains in Civil War–era "toe pincher" caskets made out of a fallen tree from the battlefield park. Lt. Col. Kehoe's troops rehearsed the mission six times, including full-force rehearsals two days out, one day out, and the morning of the funeral. Though the funeral followed the normal full-honor sequence, "the dual caskets and caissons added a wrinkle," he explained, "and it was obviously a new cemetery section for us. We just wanted to be sure to get everything right." From my vantage point, sheltered under a tent from the blazing summer sun, they did just that. The Old Guard executed a unique mission with unusual caskets, brutal heat, and intense media attention as if it were a routine, everyday mission. Lt. Col. Kehoe was proud of his troops, and he was right to be.

They also felt gratitude for the privilege of performing this unique mission. Arlington had not expanded in four decades, after all. "To be honest, I was a little overwhelmed and in awe in the moment," Lt. Col. Kehoe confessed. "I told them how fortunate we were that we were here and got to do the dedication and honor these unknown soldiers."

In the early morning darkness of December 1, 2018, a series of phone calls and text messages alerted The Old Guard that another historic occasion had arrived: the passing of President George H. W. Bush. As Americans awoke to the news, Old Guard troops had already begun reporting for duty that Saturday at Fort Myer. Along with the other military services' ceremonial units, The Old Guard forms a joint task force for state funerals. Though very rare—the last state funeral had occurred twelve years earlier for President Gerald Ford—these funerals have the highest stakes and the shortest timelines. Thus, the task force rehearses every quarter; during my tour at The Old Guard, for example, I led rehearsals at Washington National Cathedral as the officer-in-charge of a casket team. In 2018, the task force also had the benefit of performing funerals for former First Lady Barbara Bush and Senator John McCain, which, though not state funerals, allowed the troops an opportunity to operate together.

Because of its size and the Army's status as the oldest service, The Old Guard takes a leading role in the task force. 1st Battalion works in the capital region—Andrews Air Force Base, the Capitol, and the Cathedral—while 4th Battalion deploys "forward," in this case to Texas. The Fife and Drum Corps provides liaisons at each location; some had played the same role at President Ford's funeral. Old Guard officers and sergeants lead the color guards, casket teams, honor cordons, and guards of honor at each site. The Presidential Salute Battery fires the gun salutes in the capital.

The Old Guard had no advance notice of President Bush's deteriorating condition, so many soldiers scrambled to get back to Fort Myer. Lieutenant Colonel Todd Burroughs, the 4th Battalion commander, was in North Carolina with his family. He had just gone to bed when he got the call, but he got up and drove back overnight to fly with his troops to Texas. Hotel Company, which had the lead at Andrews, was on scheduled leave. According to Captain Chris Lucas, the company commander, "I had to start figuring out who was within a two-hundred-fifty-mile range so I could man all our details."

Beginning with that assembly of troops on Saturday morning, The Old Guard worked round-the-clock for the next six days to honor the forty-first president. On Sunday, Hotel Company rehearsed the arrival ceremony at Andrews and Delta Company did the same at the Capitol; in Texas, Honor Guard Company rehearsed in Houston and at Texas A&M. On Monday, Bravo Company walked through the Cathedral sequences, while Honor Guard soldiers performed the departure ceremony for President Bush at a windy Ellington Field outside Houston. "The wind was so bad that the color bearer had to modify his stance," Lt. Col. Burroughs recalled, "and one of the flagstaffs was bent."

As Cpt. Lucas's troops welcomed the president back to Andrews one last time, I greeted the Delta Company soldiers at the Capitol Rotunda before other senators gathered there. Soon the motorcade approached and what sounded like a distant explosion rattled the building. "What's that?" asked an alarmed senator. "That's the Presidential Salute Battery firing a twenty-one-gun salute," I answered. A few minutes later, the Bush family entered the Rotunda, followed by the joint casket team and its officer-in-charge, Captain Jason D'Elosua. They placed the casket on the Lincoln Catafalque. The assembled mourners then bowed their heads for a prayer, during which Cpt. D'Elosua's team silently departed and the Guard of Honor, led by Lieutenant Josh Paldino, entered and surrounded the casket. An hour later, the service ended and the dignitaries departed.

But the Guard of Honor remained, standing vigil, as it would until Wednesday morning. Each of the five services had one member on a vigil shift, and the officer role also rotated among the services. Yet Lt. Paldino remained in charge of the Guard of Honor, with operational command of several officers who out-ranked him, another sign of The Old Guard's central role. "It was pretty special," he said, "to see so many people come in the middle of the night to pay their respects." Among the late-night mourners were President Donald Trump and First Lady Melania Trump, as well as President George W. Bush. I visited the guards several times during their vigil, struck as always by their youth—many were born after President Bush had left office in 1993. But they carried out their duty like seasoned veterans.

On Wednesday morning, the vigil approached its end, and Cpt. D'Elosua's casket team gathered in the anteroom to prepare for the departure when Representative Nancy Pelosi arrived and thanked the team. "She said, 'I called him sweetheart, because that's what he was,'" Cpt. D'Elosua recalled. "President Bush 43 overheard her and chimed in, 'Nancy, why didn't you ever call me sweetheart?'" With that kidding aside, they took their positions and Cpt. D'Elosua's team carried the casket down the

Captain Chris Blanchard (facing away at left) salutes as the joint casket team transfers the remains of President George H. W. Bush at the Washington National Cathedral on December 5, 2018.

east steps of the Capitol and into the motorcade for the Cathedral, where thousands of people waited for the funeral service.

Among those waiting was Captain Chris Blanchard of Bravo Company, the officer-in-charge at the Cathedral. The casket team handled the arrival without a hitch and waited behind the scenes during the touching service. But they encountered trouble during the departure sequence. As I waited with other senators to leave, I noticed on the television screens that the casket team still had not exited the Cathedral. I later learned that the large number of clergy were delayed, leaving the team to hold the remains for several minutes in the narthex. "We totally improvised," Cpt. Blanchard noted, "but the American people never noticed," a reminder that no amount of planning and rehearsals can substitute for leadership, poise, and judgment.

After honors from Cpt. Lucas's team, President Bush and his family departed Andrews for Ellington Field, where Lt. Col. Burroughs and Honor Guard Company awaited his return. The services in Texas were smaller and less public than those in the capital region, but no less meaningful. President Bush lay in repose overnight at St. Martin's Episcopal Church in Houston. The church was too small for a full Guard of Honor, so a single soldier stood vigil over the president. Lt. Col. Burroughs and Captain Corey Morgan were among the officers who spent the night in silence and alone with the old Navy pilot.

But not every memorable moment was so poignant. While the joint casket team waited at the church, they heard a thick, German-accented voice yell, "You guys are awesome!" They turned around and saw former Governor Arnold Schwarzenegger, a close friend of President Bush. The young, burly casket-team members chatted with the old bodybuilder and snapped pictures together. "Those guys lift a lot of weights and Schwarzenegger is probably their hero," Lt. Col. Burroughs remarked, "but that day, they were his heroes."

Finally, after a ceremonial train to Texas A&M, President Bush was laid to rest—yet his was not the only funeral performed by The Old Guard that week. Far from the spotlight, Charlie Company had remained at Arlington to conduct the regularly scheduled funerals. According to First Sergeant Jonathan Lyons, who had recently taken charge of Charlie, "a lot of families expected their funerals to be cancelled, so they were very grateful we still carried out our mission." As always, funerals inside Arlington remained the priority mission for The Old Guard. Staff Sergeant Jeremiah Anderson-Kappa, the casket-team leader at the Capitol, spoke for everyone when he said, "Our standards remain the same, whether it's President Bush or a private first class." And I suspect President Bush would have agreed.

While these three missions were rare, every Old Guard soldier will contribute in his own way to the regiment's storied history. Colonel Jim Tuite took over command from Colonel Jason Garkey during my research for this book. On his first and only tour with The Old Guard, he brings the same sense of history and no-fail mind-set as did his predecessor. He and his senior enlisted advisor, Command Sergeant Major Ed Brooks, have only two years on the job and they both feel a sense of urgency about their responsibilities as the regiment's senior leaders.

"Excellence doesn't just happen," Col. Tuite said. "It's the product of habits and systems." The Old Guard's traditions alone can inspire those habits in its soldiers. "I was in Afghanistan when I learned I was taking command," he recalled, "and something just clicked. It was on my mind, I was PT-ing harder, I even felt my posture change." But strong leadership helps to uphold and perpetuate the regiment's heritage. During Thanksgiving Dinner with his soldiers, Col. Tuite shared with me one of his techniques. "I've started attending the morning call-out every once in a while," he said, referring to the primary funeral company's final huddle to review the day's funeral schedule. "When the soldiers realize I'm there, I tell them, 'I'm here because there's a very special funeral today.' Most of them start looking at the MA Final, searching for a VIP, but one of them usually gets it: 'I know which one it is, sir. All of them.' "

The pride and patriotism expressed by that soldier endure across the ages at The Old Guard, even as the soldiers come and go. Many soldiers featured in this book have already departed by now; within a few years, the entire regiment (aside from the Fife and Drum Corps) will have turned over. And that is as it should be, according to Col. Tuite. "The Old Guard is like a river," he reflected. "A strong and healthy river always has different water running through it, but its quality and character never changes." While the soldiers will come and go, said Sgt. Maj. Brooks, "The Old Guard never stops." Grizzled veterans like First Sergeant Jody Penrod and Sergeant First Class Chris Taffoya pass the torch to young soldiers like Antonio Garcia, who recently was promoted to sergeant and will in turn teach the next generation of Old Guard soldiers.

What remains is The Old Guard's sacred duty at Arlington. For the fallen and their families, The Old Guard honors their service and sacrifice. For us, the living, The Old Guard embodies our respect, our gratitude, our love for those who have borne the battles of a great nation—and those who will bear the burdens of tomorrow. No one summed up better what The Old Guard of Arlington means for our nation than did Sergeant Major of the Army Dan Dailey. He recalled a moment with a foreign military leader while driving through the cemetery to lay a wreath at the Tomb of the Unknown Soldier. "I was explaining what The Old Guard does and he was looking out the window at all those headstones. After a long pause, still looking at the headstones, he said, 'Now I know why your soldiers fight so hard. You take better care of your dead than we do our living.'"

Notes on Sources

This book was made possible by the support of The Old Guard and its soldiers. Over many months, they allowed me to observe their missions while patiently answering my questions and providing much of the source material for the book. I could not possibly name all the soldiers who contributed in one way or another, but I do want to identify those who sat for interviews or otherwise cooperated over many encounters. While some of these names might not appear in the book, they provided critical insights and assistance along the way.

My research started at the top, with The Old Guard's regimental leadership. Colonel Jason Garkey and Command Sergeant Major Scott Beeson jump-started the effort and their successors, Colonel Jim Tuite and Command Sergeant Major Ed Brooks, helped me finish up. Others in the regimental headquarters include Major Eric Alexander, Major Max Pappas, Major Stephen Von Jett, Captain Zach Kennedy, Sergeant First Class Dave Aranzamendi, Sergeant First Class Eric Cutchell, Staff Sergeant Thomas Dodson, Staff Sergeant Steven Wood, Staff Sergeant Mark Mehaffie, Sergeant Michael White, Sergeant George Huley, Corporal Ashton Blancher, and Specialist Matthew Gibbs.

The soldiers of "One Legion," or 1st Battalion, not only refreshed my recollection about the conduct of memorial affairs inside Arlington National Cemetery but also taught me what happens outside the line infantry companies. The battalion commander, Lieutenant Colonel Allen Kehoe, spent hours with me. I also interviewed his predecessor, Lieutenant Colonel Jody Shouse, whom I knew as Major Shouse during his previous tour with the regiment. Command Sergeant Major Robert Carter was a helpful presence at Old Guard events. Major Eric Hanth helped me understand the battalion's capabilities, and his memorial-affairs expert, Captain Greg Rhodes, answered my questions about even the smallest details. I also learned from the many soldiers who lead and perform funerals every day: Captain Jason D'Elosua, Captain Chris Blanchard, Captain Chris Lucas, Captain Dave Heikkila, Captain Mike Callender, Lieutenant Dave Marthy, Lieutenant Josh Paldino, Sergeant First Class Chris Taffoya, Sergeant First Class Josh Wood, Sergeant First Class Isaac LaBelle, Staff Sergeant Jeremiah Anderson-Kappa, Staff Sergeant Patrick McAllister, and Sergeant Brian Harrison.

I particularly want to note the contribution of Charlie Company, my old unit. They permitted an immersive look at their operations over many weeks. Captain Larry Harris, Captain Lukas Findley, Lieutenant Tom Grages, First Sergeant Raymond Wrensch, First Sergeant Jonathan Lyons, Sergeant First Class Bryan Dospapas, Sergeant First Class David Taylor, Staff Sergeant Joshua Bartlett, Staff Sergeant Jared Dillon, Specialist Andrew Hager, Specialist Michael Mueller, and Specialist Olivia Scott all gave generously of their time and knowledge.

The "Warriors" of 4th Battalion educated me about the ceremonial units to whom I had less personal exposure during my Old Guard tour. Lieutenant Colonel Todd Burroughs and Command Sergeant Major Lee Ward were constant sources of useful information. Captain Corey Morgan, the ceremonies expert on the battalion staff, spent hours answering my rudimentary questions and tracking down information. I enjoyed learning about the battalion's exotic units and special events from Captain Rob

Schaar, Captain Kevin Doherty, Captain Dick Tallman, Captain Travis Roland, Captain Zach Watts, Captain Travis Womack, Lieutenant Adam Scheenstra, Lieutenant Steve Webster, Sergeant Major Billy White, First Sergeant Matt Craig, Sergeant First Class James McFatridge, Sergeant First Class Jonathan Gibson, Staff Sergeant Logan Lewis, Sergeant Iwona Kosmaczewska, Corporal Chandler Kelley, Specialist Mario Arias, Specialist Manuel Salazar, Specialist Alex Ward, Private First Class Logan Stack, and Private Khalif Kroma. One of those events was the retirement ceremony for Lieutenant General (Ret.) H. R. McMaster, and I benefited from hearing H.R.'s perspective as an honoree at an Old Guard ceremony.

As evidenced in chapter 6, I spent a lot of late nights, weekends, and holidays at the Tomb of the Unknown Soldier. I could not have written that chapter without the support of the Sentinels. I leaned especially on Captain Vic Farrar, Staff Sergeant Kevin Calderon, Staff Sergeant Garrett Golden, Staff Sergeant Shane Vincent, Staff Sergeant Craig Hudson, Staff Sergeant Justin Courtney, Staff Sergeant Dallas Kempo, Sergeant Jeff Dickerson, Sergeant Antonio Garcia, Corporal Matthew Koeppel, Specialist Mike McCutchen, Specialist Nathan Voell, Specialist Chris Johnson, and Private First Class Trevor Drahem.

Aside from The Old Guard, many other soldiers contributed to this book. General Mark Milley, the Army Chief of Staff, lives down the street from the regimental headquarters and participates regularly in its ceremonies. We discussed The Old Guard's role in our Army and our nation, as well as his experiences downrange as a wartime commander. General Jim McConville, the Army Vice Chief of Staff, shared his thoughts about Dover missions and The Old Guard, as did Sergeant Major of the Army Dan Dailey. General (Ret.) Vince Brooks, the former commander of U.S. Forces Korea, provided the inside story of the historic transfer of fifty-five unidentified remains from the Korean War.

The Military District of Washington is the higher headquarters of The Old Guard and the unseen master of ceremonies, so to speak, for world-famous events such as presidential inaugurations and state funerals. Major General Michael Howard, the commanding general, was a fixture at Old Guard events over the last year, from the state funeral for President George H. W. Bush to the change-of-command ceremony between Col. Garkey and Col. Tuite. Gen. Howard provided insights in both his private comments and his public remarks. Colonel (Ret.) Jim Laufenburg is now a top official at the District, but he previously served as The Old Guard commander during 9/11 and as the Commander of the Guard at the Tomb of the Unknown Soldier. Over many conversations, Jim offered context, information, and wisdom about The Old Guard and Arlington. Mike Wagner, the District's chief planner for national events, supplied a wealth of information about state funerals. Major General (Ret.) James Jackson, the commanding general on 9/11, shared his experiences on that unforgettable day.

I also benefited from the generosity of many other soldiers, past and present, who consulted with me over the last year. Major General Brian Mennes explained the role of Army generals in the official party during Dover missions. Chaplain (Colonel) Scott Jones and Chaplain (Major) Eric Bryan reflected on their essential roles at Fort Myer and Arlington National Cemetery. Staff Sergeant Jeffrey Northman discussed the role of The U.S. Army Band's buglers during funerals in the cemetery and wreath-laying ceremonies at the Tomb. Lieutenant Colonel (Ret.) Steve Smith shared the Army's thinking that led to The Old Guard's three deployments during the war on terror. Joe Mercer, first an Old

Guard veteran and ever since an Arlington representative, supplied insights into the cemetery's operations. Christie Kehoe was never a soldier, but she held down the even tougher job of a soldier's wife; with her husband in charge of 1st Battalion, she now works as an Arlington Lady and she shared her experiences with that special organization.

Though this book tells the stories of soldiers, I could not have completed chapter 1 without the support of airmen and others at Dover Air Force Base, where I returned in July 2018 for the first time in a decade. Colonel Joel Safranek, commander of the 436th Airlift Wing, and his vice commander, Colonel Corey Simmons, as well as his senior enlisted advisor Chief Master Sergeant Anthony Green, welcomed me back and explained how the base has changed since my days. Colonel Dawn Lancaster, commander of the Air Force Mortuary Affairs Operations, led the day of briefings and tours, providing invaluable information about how the dignified transfer of remains has evolved for The Old Guard with the introduction of families and the media. She also gave me a behind-the-scenes look at what happens at Dover, where her team treats our fallen heroes with the highest honors and utmost care. I benefited from my conversations with Captain Jesse Gilbert, Technical Sergeant Dorothy Whitfield, Technical Sergeant James Hunter, Staff Sergeant Luis Diaz, Staff Sergeant Fred Heston, Staff Sergeant Ron Holmes, Staff Sergeant Michelle Johnson, and Chris Schulz. Colonel Lou Finelli, Director of the Armed Forces Medical Examiner System, which shares a roof with Mortuary Affairs, explained how the military identifies our fallen and learns lessons from their deaths to save the lives of their comrades in arms. Next door to Mortuary Affairs is the Joint Personal Effects Depot. Lieutenant Colonel Laura Wood and Nelson Delgado demonstrated how their team ensures that the family receives their fallen hero's personal effects.

My contemporaries in the Army contributed beyond measure to this book, both with their own experiences and by refreshing my recollection. Colonel (Ret.) Joe Buche was the best regimental commander a platoon leader could hope to have. Gary Kaldahl was a critical link between our time at Arlington and today's Old Guard—and a strict grader of all my uniform and marching tests, for the record. Dave Beard was the best company commander I had in the Army. Doug Coutts was and remains a close friend who provided regular azimuth checks as I wrote this book. No platoon leader could hope to have better platoon sergeants than Jody Penrod and Stan Villiers. The same goes for Javy Montanez as a first sergeant, with whom I shared good laughs and reminiscences during my research and writing. Stephen Anthony was among the best soldiers I ever had, and a constant source of support during the research for this book. Although I did not know Dave Carnahan during our time in the Army, I revere his heroic efforts to save the crew and passengers of Easy Four-Zero. Major Josh Headley and Major Wes Pierce, both still carrying the rucksack of responsibility for our nation, shared their poignant perspectives about the hours following the death of Corporal Ryan Buckley. Josh and Wes were very good peer-mentors to me in Iraq, and I am grateful for their service then and today.

Finally, I want to thank the families of the fallen. They have sacrificed more than we can imagine. The family of Colonel Leo Thorsness worked with my office in advance of his funeral and welcomed me on that memorable day. Robert Stokely shared his poignant story about his son's burial at Arlington. I learned a lot from hearing their perspective.

Though the core of this book is today's soldiers, I depended on the written record for the historical account of The Old Guard and Arlington National Cemetery. In chapter 2, I drew the history of The Old Guard from several books, essays, pamphlets, and other written materials. Not surprisingly, these materials are somewhat limited for the regiment's early days. Two good sources for the early organization and operations of the Army and hence The Old Guard are *Infantry Regiments of the U.S. Army* by James A. Sawicki and *Infantry, Part 1: Regular Army* by John K. Mahon and Romana Danysh.

One indispensable resource is James H. McRae's "Third Regiment of Infantry" in *The Army of the U.S., Historical Sketches of Staff and Line with Portraits of Generals-in-Chief*, which documents the regiment's first century of service to our nation. McRae contributed to this Army publication in 1896 when he was a lieutenant in The Old Guard, shortly before he earned the Silver Star as I mention in chapter 2. He later reached the rank of major general, commanding a division under General John Pershing in the American Expeditionary Forces during World War I. Today, McRae rests in Section 3 of Arlington.

Speaking of "Black Jack" Pershing, his memoir *My Life Before the World War, 1860–1917* provided good context for The Old Guard's deployments to the Philippines and to the Mexican border during World War I. I often used this technique—tracking The Old Guard's movements with McRae and then using other source material to flesh out the details—for their eighteenth- and nineteenth-century operations. For instance, U.S. Grant's *Personal Memoirs* brought to life The Old Guard's many battles in the Mexican War, as did Douglas Southall Freeman's *R. E. Lee*. Likewise, a short manuscript, *The 3rd U.S. Infantry During the Civil War*, by Ryan Quint, built upon McRae's work for the Civil War.

Along with McRae, perhaps the most helpful resource for chapter 2 was the Army's Center of Military History (https:// history.army.mil). The Center's many books and pamphlets aided my understanding of the regiment's first century—except for when they distracted me with fascinating detours into our nation's military history. In particular, I recommend *American Military History, Volume I: The United States Army and the Forging of a Nation, 1775–1917,* edited by Richard W. Stewart, as an outstanding reference book. For the oft-forgotten War of 1812, Richard V. Barbuto's *The Canadian Theater, 1814,* offered useful details. Stephen A. Carney has an outstanding trilogy on the Mexican War: *Guns Along the Rio Grande: Palo Alto and Resaca de la Palma*; *Gateway South: The Campaign for Monterrey*; and *The Occupation of Mexico, May 1846–1848.* I benefited from the Center's rich vein of Civil War history: *The Regular Army Before the Civil War, 1845–1860,* by Clayton R. Newell; *The Civil War Begins: Opening Clashes, 1861,* by Jennifer M. Murray; *The Virginia Campaigns, March–August 1862,* by Christopher L. Kolakowski; *The Maryland and Fredericksburg Campaign, 1862–1863,* by Perry D. Jamieson and Bradford A. Wineman; *The Chancellorsville Campaign, January–May 1863,* by Bradford A. Wineman; and *The Gettysburg Campaign, June–July 1863,* by Carol Reardon and Tom Vossler. Stephen Everett graciously searched the Center's archives for source material.

Two books—*The Old Guard in 1898,* by Richard M. Lytle, and *The Old Guard in the Philippine War,* by Greg Eanes—touch upon The Old Guard's role in the Philippine Insurrection, while also recounting some of its subsequent history. Army records improved in this period as well, making original documents from the National Archives and the Library of Congress—with the help of their outstanding staff—a common source for The Old Guard's years at Fort Snelling, its World War II activities, and its reactivation in 1948 as the Army's official ceremonial unit. I also benefited from the historical materials at the U.S. Army

Heritage and Education Center at the Army War College, with the assistance of Richard Baker and Adria Olmi. Jacqueline Hack at the Army Institute of Heraldry helped locate old regimental documents.

With The Old Guard's prominent role in the nation's capital, media coverage also becomes more common and useful in the mid–twentieth century. The *Washington Post* especially has covered its hometown regiment for the last seven decades, from the reactivation to the MLK riots to 9/11 and subsequent deployments. The U.S. Army News Service is also a good source for Old Guard news in recent decades, as well as historical reflections. Finally, I drew the quotes about 9/11 by Old Guard soldiers from *Then Came the Fire: Personal Accounts from the Pentagon, 11 September 2001*, a remarkable collection of firsthand stories from that day edited by Stephen Lofgren.

Unlike The Old Guard, a rich historical literature exists for Arlington National Cemetery. I touch on only the high points in chapters 2 and 6. Two recent standard works are *On Hallowed Ground: The Story of Arlington National Cemetery*, by Robert M. Poole and *Where Valor Rests: Arlington National Cemetery*, a coffee-table book with essays and beautiful photographs. Both books provided valuable historical context, and for those interested in learning more about "our most sacred shrine," I strongly recommend both. An older, more obscure, but fascinating work is *Arlington House: The Story of the Robert E. Lee Memorial*, by Murray H. Nelligan, a former National Park Service historian at Arlington House. Matthew Penrod, another Arlington House historian, recommended Nelligan and reviewed the history chapter. *Arlington House* deepened my understanding of not only Robert E. Lee's connection to this sacred ground, but also George Washington's. His correspondence—including that from Valley

Forge—collected at *Founders Online* (https://founders.archives
.gov) demonstrates his keen interest in the land that became Arlington. For a much deeper history of that land, see *Four Mile Run
Land Grants*, by Charles W. Stetson.

The original source material for Arlington National Cemetery
is also extensive. Arlington's own archive includes official documents from its creation, the construction of the Tomb and the
interment of the Unknowns, and other notable moments. Tim
Frank, an Arlington historian, was especially helpful in providing the most valuable information. And while anyone can read
the Supreme Court's opinion in *United States v. Lee*, the colorful
backstory is available in Enoch A. Chase's 1929 essay, "The Arlington Case," in the *Virginia Law Review*.

Finally, I highly commend the websites and social-media sites
for The Old Guard. These sites contain useful historical material, as well as timely information and beautiful photographs and
videos from today. Readers can learn more about America's Regiment at its website (https://www.oldguard.mdw.army.mil/reg
iment) and follow it on Facebook (https://www.facebook.com/
usarmyoldguard), YouTube (https://www.youtube.com/user/Old
GuardVideo/videos), and Twitter (https://twitter.com/usarmy
oldguard). I also highly recommend The Old Guard's Flickr account (https://www.flickr.com/photos/theoldguard), from which
I drew several photographs used in this book. And for more information about the Tomb of the Unknown Soldier and its Sentinels, the Society of the Honor Guard, Tomb of the Unknown
Soldier (https://tombguard.org) has a wealth of information.

Readers can also learn about and follow Arlington National
Cemetery on the internet. The cemetery's website (https://www
.arlingtoncemetery.mil/) includes historical material, standards
for burial eligibility, a guide for the conduct of funerals, a daily
list of funerals, photographs, videos, and more. For the historical

connections of George Washington and Robert E. Lee to Arlington, I recommend the websites for Mount Vernon (https://www.mountvernon.org/) and Arlington House (https://www.nps.gov/arho/index.htm). Arlington's history also lives every day on Facebook (https://www.facebook.com/ArlingtonNatl/) and Twitter (https://www.twitter.com/@arlingtonnatl).

Acknowledgments

I must first thank The Old Guard and its leaders and soldiers. They not only served as sources and subjects, but were also a wellspring of inspiration and encouragement. It was very good to be back among soldiers so much during this past year. I especially want to thank the regiment's senior leadership for their support. First Colonel Jason Garkey and Command Sergeant Major Scott Beeson, then Colonel Jim Tuite and Command Sergeant Major Ed Brooks welcomed me back to Fort Myer with open arms and ensured that I had command support at every step. I also want to thank Captains Zach Kennedy, Greg Rhodes, and Corey Morgan. "Iron major" is an Army term for the mid-career officers who get things done behind the scenes for colonels and generals. But The Old Guard expects more from younger soldiers and these three were "iron captains" who took my calls, answered my texts, tracked down documents, and arranged for soldier interviews.

The Army Chief of Staff, General Mark Milley, appears as a "character" in the book, but he also supported the book from start to finish. I appreciate his enthusiasm for the project. Likewise, Colonel (Ret.) Jim Laufenburg appears multiple times in the book, yet helped even more behind the scenes. Jim is an Old Guard institution.

Arlington National Cemetery officials also supported my research over dozens of visits. I thank Karen Durham-Aguilera, Katharine Kelley, and Micheal Migliara. I want to express special gratitude to Tim Frank, an Arlington historian who works near the Tomb of the Unknown Soldier.

A crack team of advisors and assistants supported me over the last year. John Noonan provided excellent research assistance and help with the manuscript. Stephen Anthony—one of my old soldiers from Charlie Company—managed logistics and schedules at Fort Myer and Arlington. Joni Deoudes kept everything running smoothly. My deputy chief of staff and counsel, Brian Colas, managed the Senate's contract-review process.

My literary agent was Javelin. I thank Keith Urbahn and Matt Latimer for the help with the book proposal, auction, and marketing. They offered sound counsel to a first-time author. I also thank David Thompson, my old friend who served as my lawyer for this book.

Peter Hubbard was my editor at William Morrow. Peter provided just the right amount of editorial feedback, and his suggestions uniformly improved the book. I am grateful to Peter for helping me tell The Old Guard's story. I also appreciate the contributions of the larger HarperCollins team, including Liate Stehlik, Nick Amphlett, Andrea Molitor, Kelly Rudolph, Rich Aquan, Benjamin Steinberg, and Tavia Kowalchuk.

I want to thank the friends who acted as sounding boards, contributed ideas, and helped with the manuscript, particularly Larry Arnn, Hugh Hewitt, Brett O'Donnell, Brad Todd, and Dan Senor. Walter Russell Mead gave me pointers about how to write history, which is akin to Nolan Ryan trying to teach me how to throw a fastball. Jamie Gangel and Daniel Silva advised me at every step. And I owe special thanks to Doug Coutts—not just my executive officer at Charlie Company, but also my campaign manager and Senate chief of staff for all these years.

I am blessed to be surrounded by a large and wonderful family. My in-laws, Mark and Susan Peckham, encouraged me from the outset and asked helpful questions from a reader's perspective along the way. Susan also turned her genius for design and marketing to the book's title and cover.

My sister and her husband, Sarah and Jay Patterson, brought their children to Arlington last summer and allowed me to test out some themes and stories on them. Sarah also has supplied a lifetime of big sisterly love and advice.

My parents, Len and Avis, taught me from my earliest days to love our country and honor those who serve—like my dad in Vietnam. They were understandably fearful when I enlisted in a time of war, but I did so in no small part because of what I learned from them. I am grateful for their love and encouragement over the years.

Finally, I owe more gratitude to my own family than I could ever describe. Cowboy was my writing companion for the last year. He kept me good company. Gabriel and Daniel tolerated daddy's absence more often than he would have wished. They also stayed on their best behavior during our visits to Arlington. Seeing our young sons walk among the heroes underscored how much that sacred ground means to our country across the generations.

Anna made this book possible, as she makes all things possible for me. I can now add eagle-eyed editor to her many other titles—wife, mother, partner, friend. Anna is a patriot who has nobly served our country and also sacrificed for me and our family. If you enjoyed this book, you owe her a big thank-you, as I do every day. Anna, I love you very much.